REFERENCE GUIDES TO RHETORIC AND COMPOSITION

Series Editor, Charles Bazerman

REFERENCE GUIDES TO RHETORIC AND COMPOSITION
Series Editor, Charles Bazerman

The Series provides compact, comprehensive and convenient surveys of what has been learned through research and practice as composition has emerged as an academic discipline over the last half century. Each volume is devoted to a single topic that has been of interest in rhetoric and composition in recent years, to synthesize and make available the sum and parts of what has been learned on that topic. These reference guides are designed to help deepen classroom practice by making available the collective wisdom of the field and will provide the basis for new research. The Series is intended to be of use to teachers at all levels of education, researchers and scholars of writing, graduate students learning about the field, and all who have interest in or responsibility for writing programs and the teaching of writing.

Parlor Press and The WAC Clearinghouse are collaborating so that these books will be widely available through low-cost print editions and free digital distribution. The publishers and the Series editor are teachers and researchers of writing, committed to the principle that knowledge should freely circulate. We see the opportunities that new technologies have for further democratizing knowledge. And we see that to share the power of writing is to share the means for all to articulate their needs, interest, and learning into the great experiment of literacy.

Invention in Rhetoric and Composition

Invention in Rhetoric and Composition

Janice M. Lauer

Parlor Press
West Lafayette, Indiana
www.parlorpress.com

The WAC Clearinghouse
http://wac.colostate.edu/

Parlor Press LLC, West Lafayette, Indiana 47906

S A N: 2 5 4 - 8 8 7 9

Library of Congress Control Number: 2003115230

Lauer, Janice. M.

Invention in rhetoric and composition / Janice M. Lauer

   p. cm. — (Reference guides to rhetoric and composition)

Includes bibliographical references, glossary, and index.

   ISBN: 1-932559-06-X (paper)
   1. Invention (Rhetoric) 2. English language—Rhetoric—Study and
   teaching 3. English language—Writing. I. Title. II. Series.

ISBN 1-932559-06-X (Paper)
ISBN 1-932559-07-8 (Cloth)
ISBN 1-932559-08-6 (Adobe eBook)
ISBN 1-932559-09-4 (TK3)

Series logo designed by Karl Stolley.
This book is printed on acid-free paper.

Parlor Press, LLC is an independent publisher of scholarly and trade titles in print and multimedia formats. This book is also available in cloth, as well as in Adobe eBook and Night Kitchen (TK3) formats, from Parlor Press on the World Wide Web at http://www.parlorpress.com. For submission information or to find out about Parlor Press publications, write to Parlor Press, 816 Robinson St., West Lafayette, Indiana, 47906, or e-mail editor@parlorpress.com.

The WAC Clearinghouse supports teachers of writing across the disciplines. Hosted by Colorado State University's Composition Program, it brings together four journals, three book series, and resources for teachers who use writing in their courses. This book will also be available free on the Internet at The WAC Clearinghouse (http://wac.colostate.edu/) one year from the date of print publication.

In memory of my husband,
David Hutton (1928-1999)

Contents

Foreword

This volume, *Invention in Rhetoric and Composition* by Janice M. Lauer, launches the Reference Guides to Rhetoric and Composition series. Invention is a fitting topic for the initial volume in this undertaking, for it addresses some of the most basic questions a writer asks: what should I write about? To whom? And why? What materials can I use? Where can I find them? What will move and persuade my readers? How can I even begin to think about what I might write?

These writers' questions rest on even more fundamental philosophic questions about the nature of writing: What can we as individuals and communities know and claim? How do we know things and how might we share that knowledge with others? How can we represent what we know and believe and how does representation realize or transform our beliefs and knowledge?

Invention also raises the most practical classroom questions: How can we help our students find subjects they want to write about, topics on which they will have much to say, and that will lead others in the classroom to think more deeply? How can we help our students locate the fundamental impulses to communicate important messages to others through writing?

Because invention raises such fundamental problems of theory and practice, its history extends back to the earliest reflections on effective communication in classical rhetoric. Thus this volume ties together some of the most ancient rhetorical wisdom with some of the most contemporary thinking about what it is to compose a text. Because *Invention in Rhetoric and Composition* ties together some of our most ancient and modern thinking, it is especially fitting that this book initiates the Reference Guides to Rhetoric and Composition series, which will attempt to bring together the wide range of learning applicable to learning to write at all levels of education and in all settings.

Charles Bazerman
Series Editor

Acknowledgments

The roots of this book go back decades to when I was fortunate to learn of rhetorical invention during my MA study at St. Louis University with Fr. Walter Ong, whose writings about Peter Ramus stimulated my interest. Then at the University of Michigan, when I was beginning my dissertation on invention in composition, I met my good friend Richard Young coincidentally at a CCCC, and we began a series of dialogues on invention that have continued to this day. I owe thanks to my fine students in Detroit and West Lafayette who have collaborated with me in developing and teaching inventional heuristics to guide students' writing. Through my years teaching at Purdue, I have had the good fortune of working with excellent graduate students, who have contributed to my investigations into the history and theory of invention. Their narratives about inventional issues form a part of the intertext of this book. I am grateful to members of our women's reading group at Purdue, Shirley Rose, Janet Alsup, Mickey Harris, and Linda Bergmann, who have been critical readers of this text, offering good advice. As an editor for this series, Charles Bazerman has also offered excellent suggestions, as has David Blakesley at Parlor Press. I owe a debt to friends like Jim Berlin, Ulla Connor, Ed Corbett, Janet Emig, Richard Enos, Sharon Hamilton, Patty Harkin, Regina Hoover, Jim Kinneavy, Andrea Lunsford, Gene Montague, Louise Phelps, Jim Porter, Pat Sullivan, Irwin Weiser, and Ross Winterowd for our conversations about rhetoric and teaching over the years. Special thanks go to Janet Atwill for her invaluable assistance with the manuscript, to Kelly Pender for her fine chapters, and to Julia Romberger for her careful editorial work on this text.

My family has kept me going during the long gestation of this work: my mother and father, my sister Carolann, niece Erica, nephews John and Bradley, and my step-sons David, Cameron, and Daniel and their families. Most of all, I dedicate this book to the memory of my husband, David, whose love sustained me through the many years leading to this book's development.

Janice M. Lauer

1

Introduction and Overview

Invention has always been central to rhetorical theory and practice. As Richard Young and Alton Becker put it in "Toward a Modern Theory of Rhetoric," "The strength and worth of rhetoric seem [. . .] to be tied to the art of invention; rhetoric tends to become a superficial and marginal concern when it is separated from systematic methods of inquiry and problems of content" (127). Yet by the mid-twentieth century, invention and rhetoric itself had disappeared from English Studies, including composition. In the 1960s, however, as Rhetoric and Composition was forming as a disciplinary field, one of its first focuses was on invention. Some scholars examined the loss of invention during the Renaissance and its vestiges in early nineteenth-century instruction. Others developed new inventional theories and practices, including conceptions of rhetoric as epistemic. This volume offers readers an account of some major discussions of this core rhetorical component, including an overview of the history of invention that stretches back to the Sophists and a narrative of developments in inventional theory since the mid-twentieth century. It will also examine the intimate connections between inventional theory and composition pedagogy.

All writers face the problem of finding subjects to write about and of developing these subjects. Invention provides guidance in how to begin writing, to explore for ideas and arguments, to frame insights, and to examine the writing situation. Although rhetorical invention is a broad and complex term that will require this entire volume to clarify, at the outset it may be helpful to identify some of its features. Of all the five canons—or major parts—of classical rhetoric, invention is the only one that directly addresses the content of communication as well as the process of creation, thus dealing with one of the most visible parts of published rhetorical performance, the content, and one of the most often invisible—the process by which a writer produced that content. The term *invention* has historically encompassed strategic acts that provide the discourser with direction, multiple ideas, subject matter, arguments, insights or probable judgments, and understanding of the rhetorical situation. Such acts include initiating discourse, exploring alternatives, framing and testing judgments, interpreting texts, and analyzing audiences. As this book will illustrate, various theories of invention include some or all of these acts and differ in their conceptions of the purposes of invention and its underlying epistemology. Because invention has both theoretical and practical importance for writing theory and the teaching of writing, this text will offer an historical review of issues in invention theory and pedagogy. The text will also offer two chapters dealing with contemporary work on invention: one on theoretical issues and one on issues in inventional pedagogy. Although invention is only one part of rhetoric, it keeps raising questions that implicate the whole of composition and other fields, as this text will demonstrate.

Issues in Rhetorical Invention

In order to highlight the contentious nature of the narrative of invention and its pedagogical impacts, Chapter 3 will demonstrate that theories and pedagogies of invention have been embedded in spirited historical debates over both the primary texts and their secondary interpretations. Chapter 4 will present modern and contemporary theories of invention since the 1960s, examining issues over the nature, purposes, and epistemology of invention. Chapter 5 will focus on disagreements over inventional pedagogies since the 1960s. My purpose in these chapters is to represent the debates clustered around these issues, noting the points of conflict and agreement. I do so to narrate an account of rhetorical invention that pays attention to how power has circulated in this saga. The major issues that will be examined are discussed below.

Differences over the Nature, Purpose, and Epistemology of Rhetorical Invention

The Nature of Invention. Theorists differ over what rhetorical invention encompasses. In some theories, invention is restricted to exploratory activity: constructing or finding lines of argument, examining subjects, searching for material to develop texts, articulating goals, and/or researching for intertextual support for a discourse. In other theories, invention is also conceived to include the initiation of discourse, e.g., posing questions or selecting subjects; the formation of probable judgments, focuses, insights, or theses; and the rhetorical situation: contexts, readers, and discourse communities. Scholars also discuss whether inventional practices are non-discursive acts or are symbolic, particularly written, acts and whether invention is tacit or explicit. They also argue over whether invention is individual or social and over the extent to which invention engages writers in examinations of political, social, and economic conditions. Finally, scholars differ over whether writers exercise agency in inventional activity or whether they are written by these acts.

The Purpose of Invention. Theorists also posit different purposes for invention (e.g., to lead to judgments, reach new insights, locate arguments to support existing theses, solve problems, achieve identification, reach self-actualization, or locate subject matter for texts). These purposes entail different epistemologies and inventional strategies. They also imply somewhat different conceptions of the composing process and of its originating acts. For example, if invention's purpose is to locate arguments to support a thesis, the composing process would likely begin with an existing thesis. If invention's purpose is to reach new insights, the process would likely begin with questions. Theorists also disagree over whether invention is hermeneutic or heuristic or both (i.e., whether invention's purpose is to interpret and critique existing texts, produce new texts, or both).

Invention's Epistemology. The third disputed aspect centers on the epistemology underlying inventional processes. Historical scholars continue to debate whether rhetorical invention helps writers to construct new knowledge or only to find arguments or material to support and convey judgments reached elsewhere (e.g., through philosophy or science). Finally, rhetoricians (theorists of rhetoric) also argue over whether rhetorical invention can function only in certain subject areas or in all kinds of arenas.

These issues, which began with the Sophists, as Chapter 3 illustrates, extend to current disputes about rhetoric as epistemic and postmodern views of epistemology as rhetorical. An era's position on these questions has had important consequences. It has determined how central a role rhetoric played in both the academy and the professions and how much respect was accorded rhetorical research and teaching.

Arguments over Inventional Pedagogy

The second broad issue this text addresses centers on differences over inventional pedagogy. Here, too, the arguments extend back to the Sophists. A major disagreement festers over whether rhetorical invention is an art that can be taught or a natural ability that can only be nurtured; another discussion and debates continue over the relative importance of natural talent, practice, imitation, or art in educating a writer or speaker. Over the centuries, advocates of one or the other of these pedagogies or of their integration have expressed their views vigorously, and today these debates are as heated as ever. Since the 1960s, new questions have arisen over heuristic procedures (see Chapter 2). Can they aid rhetorical invention? Which heuristics best guide invention for different writers and situations? Should student writers use strategies to prompt and shape the direction of their writing process? How can writers best learn to select and deploy different arguments? Which heuristics are more effective—general or discipline-specific ones?

Organization and Scope of the Text

Following the format for this series, Reference Guides to Rhetoric and Composition, Chapter 2 offers some definitions of pervasive terms. Chapter 3 examines the history of the above issues, demonstrating that many of the questions debated today have been argued since the time of the Sophists. It is important to note that these historical disagreements occurred not only among the primary texts themselves (e.g., Plato's *Phaedrus* and Cicero's *De Oratore*) but also among scholarly interpretations of each primary text. My presentation of this historical scholarship will only be illustrative because of the constraints of a reference volume and the massive body of historical interpretation. Although the two broad sets of issues (over theory and pedagogy) introduced above are inextricably bound, they will be treated separately here. Chapter 4 examines issues regarding the nature, purposes, and epistemology of invention in modern and contemporary theories of invention. Chapter 5 investigates issues of inventional pedagogy. These two chapters present work by scholars in the disciplines of Rhetoric and Composition, Communication, and other fields like Classics. Although the focus of this text is on invention in the discipline of Rhetoric and Composition, the scholarship on invention in other fields forms an essential part of the intertext of those studying and teaching written discourse. The text does not treat invention's relationship to audience, readers, or discourse communities because these subjects are handled in another volume in this series. Chapter 6 provides a glossary of terms. Chapter 7 offers an annotated bibliography of selected texts on theories of rhetorical invention and pedagogy.

2

Definitions

For those new to the study of invention, this brief introduction of some key terms will set the stage for a fuller elaboration of these terms in the later chapters. Definitions are also to be found in the Glossary in Chapter 6.

Classical Terms

Many of our rhetorical terms come from the Greek and Roman rhetoricians. Aristotle defined rhetoric as a techne (art), characterizing an art as the knowledge of principles and strategies to guide a complex activity like rhetoric. He thought of invention as a faculty of the rhetor (speaker or writer), who used it to guide his discoursing and a practice that could be studied and taught. Because this knowledge was used to produce something that affected others, it differed from that learned in science or philosophy. Aristotle argued that those who learned and practiced an art were better off than those who only engaged in the activity unguided because the former knew why they were doing something and could teach the art to others.

Invention was one of five terms used by Aristotle to characterize the parts of the rhetorical process. The other terms were *arrangement, style, memory,* and *delivery.* Inherent in the notion of invention is the concept of a process that engages a *rhetor* (speaker or writer) in examining alternatives: different ways to begin writing and to explore writing situations; diverse ideas, arguments, appeals, and subject matters for reaching new understandings and/or for developing and supporting judgments, theses and insights; and different ways of framing and verifying these judgments. The acts of invention often occur intensely in the early phases of writing but can continue throughout the composing process. As this volume will demonstrate, throughout rhetorical history as well as in the twentieth century rhetoricians have held different views of what constitutes invention.

One of the earliest terms deployed by the Sophists (fifth century BCE theorists and teachers of rhetoric) was *kairos*, a term never subsequently translated into Latin or other languages. The term, meaning "the right moment; the right place," characterized an appropriate situation in which rhetoric could occur. Because rhetorical discourse was always tied to a specific time and place in contrast to philosophical or scientific discourse, which were thought to transcend concrete circumstances, it was important that the very initiation of discourse be "right." As Chapter 3 illustrates, scholars have differed over what "rightness" meant for the Sophists and other rhetors, as well as whether the rhetor could interact with or control *kairos*. In the later Greek period and especially the Roman period, the terms *stasis* (Greek) and *status* (Latin), also never translated into English, named a strategy to determine the starting point of discourse. Assuming that discourse began with an issue, rhetors used this strategy to determine the point at issue, deciding whether it was a question of fact, definition, or value and then pursuing one of these. Notice that this strategy initiated the discursive process with a question to answer or a conflict to resolve, not with a judgment or thesis already at hand. *Status* has been deployed not only in rhetorical history but also in current writing and speaking.

Another important term, *dissoi logoi,* represented the Sophists' epistemology of probability—that there were two contradictory propositions on every matter. They argued these two sides of a matter, relying on the situation to determine the just or unjust, the truth or falsehood, and making decisions on the basis of *kairos*.

Aristotle also identified topics (*topoi*), lines of argument and categories of information that were effective for persuasion, listing and grouping these topics so that they could be taught to others. Aristotle listed two broad types: 1) twenty-eight common topics (lines of reasoning) that could be used for any types of discourse; and 2) special topics, categories of subject matter that provided content for specific types of discourse, such as political (deliberative), judicial, or ceremonial (epideictic). Rhetors thereafter could peruse these lists of possibilities, selecting some to help them investigate their own subjects. The difference between the topics and *status* is that writers can choose many topics from these lists, while they have to select only one of the alternatives in *status* to follow. Aristotle not only created lists of topics but also analyzed the structures of rhetorical reasoning. In contrast to philosophers and scientists, who used deduction or induction as strict ways of reasoning, rhetors had their own yet parallel ways of reasoning: the enthymeme and the example. Using the enthymeme, the rhetor started with a premise that came from the audience and then reasoned to a probable conclusion. The example, an extended narrative or elaborated case, also yielded probable conclusions.

Modern Terms

Since the 1960s, a number of new terms have emerged. Some of the most common will now be defined. The term *epistemic* when connected to rhetoric means the construction of knowledge through discourse. In the 1960s, scholars like Robert Scott argued that rhetoric creates knowledge, not just transmits it and gives it effectiveness. Related concepts are the situatedness of knowledge (limited to a particular context) and the probability of knowledge so generated. Probable knowledge, which falls between certainty and mere opinion, is supported with good reasons and evidence. Since Greek times, rhetoric has always functioned in the realm of probability. In the process of establishing a discourse's probability, the rhetor uses warrants, lines of argument that connect a starting premise to a conclusion, often implicitly. In *Uses of Argument*, Stephen Toulmin referred to warrants as rules, principles, inference licenses, or practical standards that show how data bear on a claim.

Another term that emerged in the 1960s was *heuristics*, the study of the processes of discovery. Psychologists characterized heuristic thinking as a more flexible way of proceeding in creative activities than formal deduction or formulaic steps and a more efficient way than trial and error. They posited that heuristic strategies work in tandem with intuition, prompt conscious activity, and guide the creative act but never determine the outcome. Heuristic procedures are series of questions, operations, and perspectives used to guide inquiry. Neither algorithmic (rule governed) nor completely aleatory (random), they prompt investigators to take multiple perspectives on the questions they are pursuing, to break out of conceptual ruts, and to forge new associations in order to trigger possible new understanding. Heuristic procedures are thought to engage memory and imagination and are able to be taught and transferred from one situation to another. While students typically use heuristics deliberately while learning them, more experienced creators often use them tacitly, shaping them to their own styles. Richard Young, in "Toward a Modern Theory of Rhetoric," posited: "There are two different (though related) kinds of heuristic: a taxonomy of the sorts of solutions that have been found in the past; and an epistemological heuristic, a method of inquiry based on assumptions about how we come to know something" (131). Young has defined the process of inquiry as beginning with an awareness and formulation of a felt difficulty followed by an exploration of that unknown, then proceeding through a period of subconscious incubation to illumination and verification (*Rhetoric: Discovery and Change* 73-76). Others have referred to illumination as insight, which Bernard Lonergan defined as finding a point of significance, reaching new understanding. He explained that insight comes as a release to the tension of inquiry and is a function of one's inner condition or preparation.

Two of the prominent sets of early heuristic procedures were the tagmemic guide and the pentad. Richard Young and Alton Becker developed the "Tagmemic Guide," drawing on the tagmemic linguistics of Kenneth Pike. Young suggested that writers explore their problems for inquiry guided by nine directives based on viewing their issue from three perspectives: as a particle, a wave, and a field and noting their subject's distinctive features, range of variation, and distribution in a network. Kenneth Burke developed the pentad originally as a guide for the interpretation of texts within his theory of dramatism, which views language as symbolic action. Compositionists, however, began using the pentad to explore their subjects to produce texts. The pentad helps the writer to seek five motives of any act: scene, act, purpose, agent, and agency and to generate their ratios, the interaction between two terms. Later Burke added a sixth term, *attitude*, and argued for the importance of circumference, the surrounding situational context. In addition, Burke introduced the notion of terministic screen, the discursive medium through which we know things but which blinds us from knowing other things.

The use of *hermeneutic practices*, methods of interpretation, as invention goes back to St. Augustine's rhetorical analyses of biblical texts. As a counterpoint to heuristics, hermeneutic practices of various kinds have been advocated for rhetoric: 1) using topics, tropes, ideologies to interpret texts, convincing others of the truth of their explications (Mailloux); 2) engaging in invention as questioning not *what* but *why,* following clues and hints as to where meaning is localized, and participating in Heidegger's understanding of "truth as a happening in human existence" (Worsham 219); and 3) performing dialogic, open-ended, and non-systematic acts in a paralogical rhetoric (Kent 1989).

Terms from Poststructuralism, Postmodernism, and Cultural Studies

The rise of poststructuralism, postmodernism, and cultural studies (see the Glossary, Chapter 6, for discussion of these three movements) has introduced new terms that bear on invention. The term *intertextuality* signifies the interdependence of texts as sources of their meaning. James Porter identified two kinds of intertextuality: iterability (the inclusion of parts of one text in another, e.g, quotations) and presupposition (the assumptions a text holds about its readers, subject matter, and situational and cultural context) ("Intertextuality"). Another phrase, *signifying practices*, describes the characteristic means by which a community produces and analyzes meaning. Such practices are influenced by the dominant ideology. As applied to invention, *signifying practices* refers to those inventional strategies that are typical of particular peoples and communities. Another important term for invention is *subjectivity*, used by postmodernists to characterize not only the means of self-knowledge but particularly the amount of agency or control writers have over their writer positions. They replace the term *self* with *subject*, which they consider fragmented and not unified, changing, and constructed by dominant ideologies (systems of power that govern beliefs in what is real, what is good, what is desirable, and how power should be distributed). A related phrase is *cultural codes*, signifying practices that govern the ways people fashion their subjectivities and interpret experiences.

3

Historical Review: Issues in Rhetorical Invention

The inventional issues discussed in Chapter 1 extend back through rhetorical history to the Sophists. Many of the oppositional positions seen in contemporary work on invention can be found in previous eras. Major rhetoricians and their subsequent interpreters have disagreed over the nature, purpose, and epistemology of invention. Contemporary scholars also point out that in earlier periods rhetoricians held narrow views of who could hold the subject position of rhetor (i.e., who could engage in rhetoric and hence in invention). This text offers a sample of these divergent points of view on invention, as the following quotations and the remainder of the chapter illustrate:

> As things are now, those who have composed *Arts of Speech* have worked on a small part of the subject; for only *pisteis* [proofs] are artistic (other things are supplementary), and these writers say nothing about enthymemes, which is the "body" of persuasion, while they give most of their attention to matters external to the subject. (Aristotle, *On Rhetoric* 30)

> There are two parts of rhetoric: Style (*elocutio*) and Delivery (*prenuntiatio*); these are of course the only parts, the ones proper to the art. [. . .] Rhetoric therefore will keep this particular task, that it takes the matter found and related by Dialectic, and laid out in clear and correct speech by Grammar, and then it

embellishes it with the splendor of the ornaments of style, and renders it acceptable with the grace of vocal tone and gesture. (Peter Ramus, *Arguments against Quintilian*, 27-28)

The invention of speech or argument is not properly an invention: for to invent is to discover that we know not, and not to recover or resummon that which we already know: and the use of this invention is no other but, out of the knowledge whereof our mind is already possessed, to draw forth or call before us that which may be pertinent to the purpose which we take into our consideration. So as to speak truly it is no invention, but a remembrance or suggestion, with an application; which is the cause why the schools do place it after judgment, as subsequent and not precedent. Nevertheless, because we do account it a chase as well of deer in an enclosed park as in a forest at large, and that it hath already obtained the name, let it be called invention: so as it be perceived and discerned, that the scope and the end of this invention is readiness and present use of our knowledge, and not addition or amplification thereof. (Francis Bacon, *Advancement of Learning*, 58)

Knowledge and science must furnish the materials that form the body and substance of any valuable composition. Rhetoric serves to add the polish. (Hugh Blair, *Lectures on Rhetoric and Belles Letters,* 32)

The finding of arguments with a view to the proof of truth—technically termed invention—belongs to the rhetorical process. (M. B. Hope, *The Princeton Textbook in Rhetoric*, 17)

Part 1: Theoretical Issues

As the above quotes illustrate, invention has been positioned different-ly in rhetorical history. In the sections that follow I will examine the three issues discussed in Chapter 1: differences over what constitutes invention, over its purpose, and over its underlying epistemology.*

Greek Views

There were three dominant Greek conceptions of invention, empha-sizing different features and emanating from different epistemologies. The Sophists concentrated on the earliest moment of discourse, *kairos*, and subscribed to a *dissoi logoi* epistemology. Plato emphasized the in-ventional role of dialogue, but his commentators have argued over his purposes for invention and its epistemology. Aristotle developed the most explicit theory of invention, providing a conception of its nature, articulating his view of its purpose (which interpreters have contested), and explicating its probable epistemology.

Interpretations of Sophistic Invention

To the extent that one can speak of the Sophists as a group (Schiappa, 1992), scholars have discussed the Sophists' interest in the earliest act of discourse, its initiation, foregrounding the term *kairos*. Most agree that for the Sophists conflict or dissonance triggered the start of dis-course; modern commentators, however, have disagreed over whether *kairos* controlled the discourser or the discourser controlled *kairos*. Scholars have also argued over the character and implications of the *dissoi logoi* and have differed over whether Gorgias and other Sophists were skeptics, relativists, tragic philosophers, or social constructors of knowledge.

In the *Dissoi Logoi*, an unknown author demonstrated that it is possible to argue on two sides of a matter, making a case for the dif-ference and sameness of good and bad, the seemly and disgraceful, the just and unjust, truth and falsehood, and so on. The author in one case stated that ""To sum up, everything done at the right time is seem-

---

* The scholarship cited in the discussion of these issues is intended to be il-lustrative, not exhaustive—an impossibility in this kind of text.

ly and everything done at the wrong time is disgraceful" (283). The statement contains an apparently contradictory way of knowing and a theory of *kairos*, "the right time." Mario Untersteiner described *kairos* as the right moment, an instant in which the intimate connection between things is realized (111). *Kairos* implied contrast and conflict as the starting point of the treatment of *logos*. Untersteiner pointed out that Gorgias's *Helen* and *Palamedes* started with contraries, both of which could be true, while Gorgias's *On Being* started with contraries and argued for one side and disproved the other. Untersteiner went on to explain that justice and right decisions could be achieved if the judgment is made at the right moment. *Kairos* entailed the decision to accept one of the alternative *logoi*, breaking up the cycle of antithesis and creating something new (161). John Poulakas associated a sense of urgency and risk with *kairos* because the rhetor confronted contingent elements of the situation. *Kairos* dictated what must be said. He called *kairos* the radical principle of occasionality ("Toward a Definition of Sophistic Rhetoric"). Bernard Miller related the sophistic notion of *kairos* to Heidegger's idea of an ontological dimension of language that possesses humankind: *kairos* is the *augenblick* in which Being is nearest to humans. Miller described *kairos* as qualitative time, based on competing *logoi,* the moment of decision. James Kinneavy maintained that *kairos* "brings timeless ideas down into the human situations of historical time. It thus imposes value on the ideas and forces humans to make free decisions about these values" ("*Kairos*" 88). Michael Carter argued that for the Pythagoreans, including Empedocles, the universe is a collection of agonistic relationships originating in the opposition of monad and dyad, which are bound together in harmony though the principle of *kairos*, thus creating the universe. He maintained that for Gorgias, *kairos* was the principle of conflict and resolution and for Protagoras, the rhetor could discriminate between the greater and lesser probability of truth within a community (*Stasis* and *Kairos* 103). He also noted that the concept of right in *kairos* contained an ethical dimension—what at the crucial time seemed to be the truest *logos*. Carter maintained that later, especially in the Roman period, the development of *status,* identifying the point at issue, offered a way for the rhetor to gain some control over the moment. Thus, most of these interpreters described this initiating moment of discourse as entailing contrasts, conflicts, competing *logoi*, opposites, or contradictions. They differed, however, in the extent to which the rhetor could control *kairos* or be overwhelmed by it, propelled to discourse as Miller's Heideggerian interpretation posited.

Another aspect of invention that has received considerable scholarly attention has been sophistic epistemology. Kathleen Freeman explained that in Protagoras's theory of knowledge "each individual's perceptions are immediately true for him at any given moment, and that there is no means of deciding which of several opinions about the same thing is the true one; there is no such thing as 'truer' though there is such a thing as 'better'" (*The Pre-Socratic Philosophers* 348). Freeman pointed out that this precept led Protagoras "to deny the Law of Contradictories, which rules that the same attribute cannot at the same time both belong and not belong to the same subject in the same respect" (349). He asserted instead that "there were two contradictory propositions on every matter" (349). According to Freeman, Plato considered these precepts to reduce all knowledge to sensation, doing away with "any possibility of stable knowledge of any kind" (349). This view was also "taken to mean that objects do not exist except while someone is perceiving them" (349). She cited Protagoras' instruction as a study of opinions and their means, constituting the art of persuasion (*Pre-Socratic*). Janet Atwill claimed that "Protagoras's theory of knowledge *is* his theory of value; epistemology collapses into axiology" (*Rhetoric Reclaimed* 139). She further demonstrated that while his theory of knowledge is relativistic, it does not give way to skepticism or solipsism. Richard Enos posited that for Empedocles, the "juxtaposition of antithetical [opposing or contrasting] concepts was more a matter of correlative balancing of thesis and antithesis than it was of intellectual inconsistency" ("The Epistemology" 40). He explained that Gorgias's epistemology was "based on a system of investigation in which probable knowledge or opinion was revealed as a synthesis from dichotomous antithetical positions" ("The Epistemology" 50; see also *Greek Rhetoric before Aristotle*).

Untersteiner argued that Gorgias was neither a skeptic nor a relativist but "a tragic philosopher and an irrationalist. Knowledge of the power possessed by the irrational constituted the victory of the tragic" (159). Man could not escape antitheses. Untersteiner noted that for Gorgias, there were two kinds of knowledge: that of perpetually recurring doubt and that driven by the force generated by the tragic element. Knowing the irreconcilable conflicts, man yet acted (159). Decision was based on *kairos*, which "breaks up the cycle of antitheses and creates an irrational epistemological process of deception and persuasion" (161). In Untersteiner's interpretation of Gorgias, "truth" could not be incarnated in *logos*: the universal was split by the irrational concurrence of certain special circumstances. Antithesis opposed one philosophical system to another, canceling them out on the purely logical plane but rescuing them in the practical sphere by persuasion (141). For Gorgias, then, according to Untersteiner, persuasion was a force in the face of the ambivalence of *logos*, a position that *Helen* and *Palamedes* illustrated. The purpose of the *logos* in these works was to create happiness by creating a new situation in the human mind (114). In *Helen*, man did not rule the world with *logos* but the *logos* of the contradictory world ruled man. The world was not a creation of the mind, capable of endowing it with order and harmony. In *Palamedes*, it was impossible to prove the truth of what happened and what was willed. The problem lay in the hearers, leaving the final appeal for kindness and time (122). Untersteiner also pointed out that Gorgias considered persuasion to be "deception" because one convinced the audience of one meaning knowing that the opposite also had probability (111).

In *Rereading the Sophists: Classical Rhetoric Refigured*, Susan Jarratt argued against the dualistic view of *mythos/logos* during the fifth century BCE, demonstrating the evolutionary rather than revolutionary changes during this period. She challenged the idea of a "mythic" consciousness in Homer and analyzed the "mixed discourse" in Gorgias and Protagoras, positing that "Acknowledging an epistemological status for probability demands in discourse a flexible process of ordering or arranging, a feature of both *nomos* (a social construct involving ordering) and narrative" (47). She noted that Protagoras likely understood the *dissoi logoi* as a means of discovering *a* truth, a starting point for rhetorical work. He rejected any truth outside of human experience. For Gorgias, she argued the *logos* was a holistic process of verbal creation and reception different from the rational conception of Aristotle and Plato. Agreeing with Jacqueline de Romilly, she noted that Gorgias's power came from the rational control of *techne* (art), a self-conscious relation to discourse. For the Sophists, then, she maintained that *nomos* was a "middle term between *mythos* and *logos*," "a self-conscious arrangement of discourse to create politically and socially significant knowledge" (60).

Bruce McComiskey interpreted Gorgias's *On Non-Existence,* the *Encomium of Helen,* and the *Defense of Palamedes* as "a wholistic statement about communal and ethical issues of *logos* "(*Gorgias and the New Sophistic Rhetoric* 12). In these texts he found Gorgias articulating "a relativist epistemology within which his *kairos*-based methodology was perfectly consistent" (12), unlike its characterization in Plato's *Gorgias.* McComiskey argued that *On Non-Existence* "theorizes the impact external realities have on the human psyche, the *Helen* explores the unethical workings of persuasion on the human psyche, and the *Palamedes* illustrates *topoi* (places) for the invention of ethical arguments" (12). He demonstrated that for Gorgias "all human beliefs and communicative situations are relative to a particular *kairos* or "right moment" (22) and that this epistemology grounds his "belief in the distorting process of sensory perception." (23). McComiskey complicated this view of Gorgias's epistemology by saying that Gorgias did "believe in certain conceptions of 'knowledge' and 'truth' and in some circumstances 'opinion' was insufficient" (24). Further he commented that from the Greek terms it is clear that "Gorgias's word for knowledge (*eidô*) is different from Plato's word (*episteme)* for the same English concept of knowledge. Plato's word implies an understanding that exists prior to any given situation in which it might be applied" (25) Gorgias's term entails "an understanding that is derived empirically from a situation" (25). Speaking of the purpose of Gorgianic rhetoric, he argued that it was concerned with the greatest good of the community (27-28). (See also "Gorgias, *On Non-Existence*: Sextus Empiricus.)

Thus, scholars have differed over Sophists' views of the nature of the initiation of discourse, the role of persuasion in relation to logos, the power of *kairos*, and the epistemologies of various Sophists.

Interpretations of Plato's Views of Invention

Plato's mature view of invention can be found in the *Phaedrus.*, which illustrated rather than systematizes the topics. Again, the examples below illustrate but do not exhaust the discussion of these issues. He does, however, mention or exemplify four sources for the initiation of discourse: inspiration of the muses (13, 16, 17, 54), dissonance between the two speeches that prompts the third speech, adaptation to the situation (*kairos*) by knowing the souls of the audience (58, 67, 70), and love itself. The modern commentator, Martha Nussbaum, in

The Fragility of Goodness, argued that the entire *Phaedrus* was an apologia for *eros* as the motivator or initiator of philosophical discourse: to reach insight one needed personal love and passion, the ferment of the entire personality, even certain aspects of madness. She demonstrated that these ideas represented Plato's recantation of some of his former positions.

A number of interpreters have differed over Plato's view of the purpose and epistemology of invention. Some have maintained that Plato considered invention's goal to be locating support for judgments and truth found outside of rhetoric and then adapting these truths to various audiences. In a set of articles in *Rhetoric Society Quarterly,* several prominent rhetoricians held that for Plato, invention and rhetoric were not epistemic. Donald Bryant contended that for Plato the art of persuasion was needed to communicate truths mastered and understood elsewhere (10). Richard Enos took the same position, holding that for Plato dialectical knowledge was a precondition for rhetoric (17). Michael Leff said that Plato rendered the conception of genuine rhetoric paradoxical. Language remained incorrigible on the metaphysical level yet "performed a morally justifiable function by imparting a tendency toward truth in the soul of the auditor" (22). As Leff concluded, for Plato true rhetoric was possible only with "an intuitive grasp of the truths that extend beyond language" (23). In *Plato, Derrida, and Writing,* Jasper Neel contended that Plato defined what counted as thinking: Truth was separable from and superior to the knower and couldn't be found in writing; Plato refused to see writing as the originator of thinking.

In contrast, others have claimed that Plato viewed invention as a process of inquiry and reasoning. William Covino held that the *Phaedrus* is about the art of wondering and about rhetoric, writing, and reading as play within an expanding horizon (21). Jan Swearingen, in "The Rhetor as Eiron," argued that Plato considered dialogue the true rhetoric, a mode of philosophical reasoning, a midwifery that brings forth meaning, and an analysis that leads to synthesis or truth. She maintained that "the Platonic *episteme,* means of knowing, were [. . .] distinctly different from the instrumentalist rhetoric of the sophists" (295). For Plato, "'intent' was not only a determinant of semantic meaning, but also a criterion for epistemological and ethical evaluation" (308). In "Dialogue and Dialectic," Swearingen described Plato's dialogue as a "ritual of communal philosophizing and philosophy as a way of knowing that can only be conducted dialogically" (49). In an encyclopedic essay on Plato, she commented that in the *Phaedrus*, Plato sketched a true rhetoric—"a dialogical-dialectical method that strongly resembles modern paradigms for a 'rhetoric of inquiry'" (526). Swearingen commented on Plato's use of the feminine metaphors of midwifery and weaving to characterize knowledge construction ("Eiron"). Page duBois, on the other hand, critiqued Plato for appropriating the reproductive metaphors for male philosophers in order to authorize them, an argument that Swearingen subsequently rebutted. (See also Swearingen, *Rhetoric and Irony.*) Charles Griswold theorized that the *Phaedrus* was concerned primarily with self-knowledge realized through the dialectic of rhetoric—that *logos* itself was fundamentally rhetorical (161). Ronna Burger argued that for Plato writing was a necessary precondition for the development of thought, freeing human memory from preserving common opinions and creating a distance from the authority of tradition. Writing and rhetoric were processes of erotic dialectic.

Thus, scholars have differed over Plato's views of the purposes and epistemology of rhetoric; creating knowledge or only conveying it; dealing with truth outside of rhetoric or rhetorical dialogic.

Inventional Issues in Aristotle's Rhetoric

In the *Rhetoric*, Aristotle delineated several acts of invention and constructed arts (strategies or principles) for analyzing the discourse situation and categorizing its matter; arts for exploring using the 28 common topics (lines of argument that could be used across types of discourse, e.g., definition) and the special topics (categories that prompted the rhetor to find appropriate content); and arts for framing its probable rhetorical epistemology facilitated by the enthymeme and the example (informal versions of deduction and induction). As the following examples of scholarship reveal, these elements have been differently interpreted.

Scholars have disagreed over whether Aristotle's *Rhetoric* included a discussion of the initiation of discourse. Kinneavy, for example, originally maintained that Aristotle had no concept of *kairos*, but later he and Catherine Eskin discussed the crucial role of *kairos* in the *Rhetoric*, basing their interpretation on the fact that the text was built around the concept of "in each case." Yameng Liu argued that despite Aristotle's familiarity with *stasis*, he had serious reservations about its applicability to rhetoric because he saw it as only occasionally useful for local functions (55). Also, he argued that because Aristotle emphasized deliberative discourse, *stasis,* which was typically proposed for forensic discourse, was not helpful (56). William Grimaldi claimed that Aristotle's *Rhetoric* had a different initiating strategy, explaining that the possible/impossible, past fact/future fact, and size were not topics but common requisites or preconditions for rhetoric into one of which the subject had to fit before the rhetor could responsibly engage in discourse (*Studies in the Philosophy of Aristotle's Rhetoric*). Others interpreters like Otto Dieter, Wayne Thompson, and J. Backes concluded that Aristotle's *Rhetoric* had elements of *stasis.*

Scholars also have differed over Aristotle's conception of the purposes of the common topics. Several have taken the position that the topics engaged the rhetor in reasoning, constructing knowledge, or creating interpretations. Grimaldi characterized the 28 common topics as "natural ways the mind thinks" (*Studies* 130) in order to locate lines of reasoning and inferential patterns. He maintained that Aristotle viewed rhetoric as a general art of human discourse, a theory of language for serious communicators when they "seek to determine truth or fallacy in real situations" (*Studies* 18). He held that Aristotle considered rhetoric as enabling language to become a medium for apprehending reality (*Studies* 124-26). Also taking an epistemic view of the topics, Richard Enos and Janice Lauer described Aristotle's topics as socially shared instruments for creating probable knowledge (24, 37-44).

Other scholars have contended that the topics did not have an epistemic function but rather operated to communicate what was already known. E. M. Cope called the topics aids to memory, haunts, mines, and stores. Thomas Conley described them as a process of reasoning backward from "given" conclusions in order to find premises that would lead the hearer to a conclusion ("'Logical Hylomorphism' and Aristotle's *Konoi Topoi*" 94). Arguing that both the special and common topics could be viewed as warrants, James Murphy in *A Synoptic History of Classical Rhetoric* considered the topical search as finding rather than creating, conscious choice among a fixed stock of alternatives (57), while Donovan Ochs In "Aristotle's Concept of Formal Topics," deemed the topics ways of relating predicates to subjects. Other interpretations of Aristotle's purposes for invention include Michael Leff's view of the topics as principles or strategies to "enable the arguer to connect reasons with conclusions for the purpose of effecting a proof" ("The Topics of Argumentative Invention" 25). According to Leff, inferences depend on the connections between propositions taken as whole units relative to the audience addressed and thus arising from and verified by social knowledge in a community (25). Ellen Quandahl considered the topics as part of a method of interpretation. Carolyn Miller in "The Aristotelian *Topos*: Hunting for Novelty," drew on the venetic (hunting) tradition and the spatial metaphor of *topos* (place) to argue that Aristotle's topics can be sources of novelty with generative capacity, functioning within the epistemology of the hunt, which concerns the individual case, not universal knowledge, and probability rather than certainty. She maintained that in "the Platonic realm of Being, invention can only be discovery, but in the Aristotelian world of Becoming, it can also be creation" (137).

Scholars have generally considered the purpose of the special topics to be finding and examining subject matter or analyzing the audience. For example, Grimaldi described the special topics as offering the matter for propositions, the sources to be examined (*Studies* 124-26) in order to find content regarding "the time, the place, the circumstances and the emotional involvement" (133).

Diverse points of view also can be found about Aristotle's conception of rhetorical epistemology. Some examples follow. John Gage maintained that Aristotle's rhetoric was legitimate inquiry into probable knowledge. He stated that for Aristotle knowledge was created through invention in the activity of discourse. The enthymeme brought together the rhetor's search for mutually agreed upon grounds for probable knowledge and the audience's premises ("An Adequate Epistemology for Composition"). Lloyd Bitzer differentiated the rhetorical enthymeme from the demonstrative and dialectical syllogism, arguing that the distinction rested on how the premises were secured. In the case of Aristotle's rhetoric they came from the audience ("Aristotle's Enthymeme Revisited"). According to Eugene Garver, who argued for the modesty of Aristotle's *Rhetoric*, those who think of composition as critical thinking and problem-solving aim to reunite wisdom and eloquence and thus extend rhetoric to things as Cicero did but not as Aristotle would have done. In his view, Aristotle was not interested in creating specialized knowledge but in finding the available arguments. Although Martha Nussbaum did not write about Aristotle's *Rhetoric*, she argued that Aristotle's epistemology was based on "appearances":

the world as perceived, demarcated, and interpreted by human beings and their beliefs. She offered the following translation of a passage from the *Posterior Analytics*: "So goodbye to the Platonic Forms, they are *teretismata* [dum-de-dum-dums] and have nothing to do with our speech" (256). For Aristotle, she contended, truth and appearances were not opposed—but truth existed where we communicate inside the circle of appearances.

Subject Positions

During this Greek period, the position of writer/speaker was largely limited to men, excluding slaves and women, although we now know of some women like Sappho, Praxilla, Aspasia, and Diotima, who occupied that position. (See Snyder; Swearingen, "A Lover's Discourse" and "Plato's Women"; Glenn, *Rhetoric Retold*, "Locating Aspasia"; Jarratt and Rory; and Jarratt, "Sappho's Memory"; Fantham, *Women in the Classical World*; and Donawerth, *Rhetorical Theory*, "Bibliography.")

Review: Greek Rhetorical Invention

As the above discussions of Greek views of invention illustrate, issues abound among the Sophists, Plato, and Aristotle as well as among their interpreters. Differences exist over which inventional acts and arts are included in the texts: *kairos* and *status* as initiators of discourse; special and common topics as exploratory arts; *dissoi logoi*, enthymeme, example or dialogue as forms of rhetorical reasoning; and probability, truth, or certainty as rhetorical epistemologies. They also disagree over the purposes of invention: initiating discourse with questions, issues, or contradictions, creating knowledge, reaching probable judgment, finding arguments to support existing theses, communicating truths or supporting persuasive propositions.

Roman Views

The Romans further codified invention, sometimes placing it under types of discourse. This was a significant move away from topics as a set of alternative prompts across types of discourse to ones that were text bound to develop a type of discourse or a section of the text, (i.e., to provide content). This move blurred the distinction between special and common topics. Further, some Romans complicated the enthymeme, making it less flexible. Interpreters of these Roman rhetoricians, discussing their epistemologies, have often described their concept of rhetorical invention as a practical art concerned with the "how," not the "why." Examples of these interpretations illustrate views on these issues. Further, in this culture, subject positions for rhetors continued to be limited.

Invention in Rhetorica ad Herennium

The first complete Roman rhetoric, *Rhetorica ad Herennium*, became the text used for centuries in rhetorical education. It outlined the inventional strategy of *status* to help the rhetor begin judicial discourse (in the court) by determining the type of issue that was at stake: either the conjectural (an issue of fact); the legal (an issue of the letter and spirit, conflicting laws, ambiguity, definition, or analogy) or the juridical (an issue of the rightness or wrongness of an act). Although the anonymous author did not discuss *status* for deliberative discourse (in the political forum) or epideictic discourse (in ceremonial sites), these two types of writing could nevertheless be initiated with a question or point at issue. Raymond Nadeau traced the changing history of *status*, beginning with Hermagoras, who identified four issues: conjecture, definition, quality, and translation ("Hermogenes' *On Stasis*"). For centuries this inventional procedure directed the first composing act, helping the writer to determine which point at issue needed investigation.

In *Rhetorica ad Herennium*, the topics became text bound topics, losing their power as a set of investigative heuristics for the process of knowledge creation or inquiry. Instead they became a search for material to develop parts of the text. The distinction between common and special topics disappeared. Lists of topics proliferated, intermingled, and were placed under the parts of the discourse: Introduction, Narration, Division, Distribution, Proof, and Conclusion. The topics for the introduction helped to prepare the hearer's mind for attention; for narration, they assisted the rhetor in setting up the events; for division they helped make clear what was agreed upon or contested; and for proof, they offered alternative lines of argument (4). Under the proof, topics were further classified within the types of discourse: judicial, deliberative, and epideictic. Judicial topics were divided into conjectural, legal, and juridical. Deliberative topics were represented under the headings of security and honor. Epideictic topics of praise were grouped into external circumstances, physical attributes, and qualities of character. For the conclusion, topics for amplification were enumerated. The anonymous author cited the purpose of invention as "devising of matter, true or plausible, that would make the case convincing" (3).

The Roman emphasis on arrangement was further reflected in a more complex logical argument structure—the epicheireme, with five parts: the proposition, reason (premises), proof of the reason, embellishment, and resume (*Rhetorica ad Herennium* 107). D. Church and R. Cathgart cited George Thiele, who contended that the epicheireme rejected the enthymeme and tried to accommodate the logical syllogism to the needs of rhetoric. He contended that it doesn't "recognize the true nature of the enthymeme and seriously perverts the purpose and methods of rhetorical invention" (142). The authors claimed that in consequence reasoning lost "the persuasive force of an enthymeme that is derived through rhetorical invention rather than dialectical consideration" (147). It was the epicheireme, Church and Cathgart noted, that prevailed as the "cornerstone of rhetorical argument for fifteen centuries" (147). This text-bound inventional system with its formulaic reasoning process drastically changed the more flexible and nuanced previous views of rhetorical invention.

Cicero's Conceptions of Invention

In Cicero's mature discussion of rhetoric, *De Oratore*, Crassus and Antonius (the two major discussants in the text) treated invention more subtly. Although both of them downplayed their own reliance on inventional strategies in favor of their natural abilities, in a number of places the conversation revealed their knowledge of *status* and the topics. Both showed familiarity with the three types of issues: conjecture (fact), definition, and quality. Crassus referred to the commonplaces for each type of discourse (40) and bemoaned the fact that philosophers had usurped the common topics. Antonius compared the commonplaces to letters in a word, immediately occurring to us and useful only to the experienced person (117-18), holding that if the commonplaces were fixed in the memory and mind, nothing would escape the orator (131). In his discussion of the topics, he mentioned a selection of common topics such as definition, resemblance and difference, cause and effect, greater and lesser (127-30), and topics for epideictic

(94-95). Neither he nor Crassus distinguished between common and special topics.

Donovan Ochs maintained that Cicero's system for speculative inquiry had as its object "the study and understanding of an arguable question or principle of behavior" ("Cicero" 219). He found this system to be coherent, functional, and teachable, reflecting the teaching of various schools, including the Skeptics, Stoics, and Epicureans. Ochs contended that using this system of inquiry gave a rhetor the possibility of both eloquence and wisdom ("Cicero" 227). In "The Topics of Argumentative Invention in Latin Rhetorical Theory from Cicero to Boethius, " Leff described Cicero's early topical system in *De Inventione* as divided into topics of person and act in contrast to Aristotle's system. He explained that these two topics provided raw material for arguments and shifted from "the discovery of inferential connectives to the discovery of the materials for arguments" (29). Leff characterized Cicero's treatment of the topics in *De Oratore* as an inventional process resulting in the discovery of material, giving greater emphasis to logical relationships and creating categories of topics based on the subject of the discourse (30-31). Hence, Cicero's system blurred dialectical and rhetorical theories of invention. Leff also explained that Cicero distinguished between his topics and necessary and probable inference and induction and deduction (29). George Kennedy maintained that Cicero's notion of invention was more Aristotelian than that of *Rhetorica ad Herennium* because Cicero did not place invention under the parts of the oration (*The Art of Rhetoric in the Roman World*).

Discussing Cicero's epistemology, Prentice Meador explained that Cicero's idea of probability stemmed from the Skeptic theory of perception, in which a fallible perception was the source of knowledge upon which man acted. Thus, rhetoric and especially invention were not only socially possible but also necessary. Enos pointed to principles of dialectic and ethics as the philosophical foundation of Cicero's litigation strategies. He explained that Cicero was influenced by the Skeptic's notion of probability and the belief that the dialectic of inquiry was held between the jurors, rhetor, and populace. He also pointed out that the Skeptics held that judgment was suspended and moral commitment to the reasonable obtained (*The Literate Mode of Cicero's Legal Rhetoric*). William Covino called Cicero's epistemology shifting dialogic points of view in a frame of irresolution, ambiguity, and open speculation (34). Cicero's rhetoric, according to Covino, encompassed a range of perspectives across time with multiple constructions of history, tradition, and facts, and layers of recollected narrative. For Covino, Cicero's work as a whole was a collection of contradictory and complementary perspectives. Thomas Sloane argued that both Crassus and Antonius agreed on the nature of invention as pro/con thinking, with even *De Oratore's* form demonstrating this dialogic. In this conception of invention, one had to debate all sides or one would not have fully invented. He noted that when the Renaissance humanists discovered Cicero's work, they thought they had found a new philosophy of practical reasoning in which invention was essentially an analytic process—a process of *stasis* ("Reinventing *Inventio*" 466). (See also Sloane's *On the Contrary*.) Renato Barilli claimed that Cicero overturned Aristotle's model of dialectic over rhetoric because Cicero valued the forum over the chamber. He maintained that Cicero refused to privilege content and meaning over modes, signifiers, situations or contexts and that the probable for Cicero had an historical and temporal dimension (27-28). Michael Mendelson pointed out that Cicero in *De Oratore* dramatized *controversia* (two opposing claims in juxtaposition) in order to show his students argument in action. Mendelson took this to mean that Cicero thought all matters were subject to interpretation and opposing positions. He further argued that for Cicero differences of interpretation were the starting point of argument whose goals were to articulate differences within the dynamic of ongoing discourse and to calculate the degrees of probability to provide grounds for action.

The dialogic format of *De Oratore* enabled Cicero to review several positions on the nature, purpose, and epistemology of invention. As seasoned rhetorical performers, Crassus and Antonius privileged their talent and interaction with the rhetorical situation as causes of their rhetorical success although their rhetorical education in invention was evident in the conversation. Such a position is understandable since as prominent rhetors they had by then internalized their education and had used it to enhance their own powers. Also, as the commentators pointed out, Cicero's probable epistemology reflected the climate of his day and the preeminent position of rhetoric over philosophy in Rome.

Inventional Issues in Quintilian's Rhetoric

Quintilian's twelve-volume *Institutio Oratoria* provided a history of some of the inventional issues prior to his day, especially different views of rhetoric as an art and *status*. He continued the text-bound treatment of the topics used in *Rhetorica ad Herennium* as well as the two superordinate categories of topics found in Cicero's earlier work, *De Inventione*: person and act. Further, he included the enthymeme, the epicheireme, and the example as means of rhetorical argument. His work offered a comprehensive description of invention up to that point but not an original theory of invention.

Quintilian's history traced competing views of *status*. He recounted that his early conception had entailed four issues: conjectural, qualitative, definition, and legal, but that later he had changed to the first three. He defined *status* as the kind of question that arises from the first collision between the parties to a dispute (3.6.4). He also claimed that one could begin discourse by invoking the strategy of *status* in all types of discourse although it was not necessary for all subjects (3.5.3). The use of *status* was consequential for the Romans because the type of *status* that the rhetor selected gave direction to the entire investigative process.

Unlike some aspects of rhetoric like *status* for which he provided long histories of different points of view, Quintilian did not trace the history of the topics nor did he elaborate extensively on their purpose. He instead positioned the topics under the types of discourse—epideictic, deliberative, and forensic, ignoring the distinction between common and special topics. Epideictic topics directed the rhetor to subject matters under the categories of gods, men, cities, and public works (3.7.1-28). Deliberative topics included the resources of the state, the character of people, topics of honor and expedience, various virtues like justice and piety, and general topics including comparison and degree (3.8.14-38). Under forensic discourse, he employed the broad categories of "persons" (e.g., birth, education, occupation, personal ambitions) and "things," which included "actions" such as why, where, how, and by what means; causes, definition, consequences and contradictions (5.8.4-95). He thanked the creators of the art for giving us "a shortcut to knowledge," but warned that if the rhetor only knew the "places," he had "a dumb science" (5.10.119-125) unless he also practiced, had discrimination, and understood the context in which he discoursed (213).

Quintilian's notion of rhetorical epistemology can be found in his discussion of certainties in conjunction with his treatment of the enthymeme and epicheireme. He claimed that something in every case must need no proof, which either was or was believed to be true (5.10.11-12). The person who was to "handle arguments correctly must know the nature and meaning of everything and their usual effects" in order to arrive at probable arguments (5.11.1-35). Furthermore, Quintilian gave considerable attention to the example as an argument, describing historic parallels, past actions, quotes from poets, similes, and analogies (271-93). John O'Banion argued that Quintilian considered narration as "a primary mode of thought" and as "a key to strategy" (325), the most important department of rhetoric in practice. He explained that Quintilian integrated narration and logic into a complex dialectic to serve the arrangement or order in which principles were adjusted to specific cases. Narration provided the link between the major and minor premise.

Subject Positions

During these Roman centuries, the rhetor position was occupied predominantly by a male citizen although we now know of women's discourses such as Cornelia's letters and Hortensia's address to the Roman forum, both persuasive discourses entailing arguments (Glenn, *Rhetoric Retold*; Snyder).

Review: Roman Rhetorical Invention

As the above discussion illustrates, conceptions of invention in these major Roman rhetorical texts differed from those of the Greeks and among themselves and their interpreters. Two rhetoricians placed *status* and the topics (now a mixture of common and special) under parts of the discourse. The epicheireme was added to the enthymeme and example as means of rhetorical reasoning. Invention was largely viewed as finding support for judgments and material for sections of the text. Some scholars commented on the situatedness of the inventional practices and the initiation of discourse with issues. Commentators on Cicero generally agreed on his probable epistemology and rhetoric's preeminence over logic. These conceptions of invention, particularly in the *Rhetorica ad Herennium,* would prevail through hundreds of years. They influenced theory and practice through the Renaissance and still characterize a number of pedagogies and textbooks today: 1) the tendency to multiply topics and restrict them to finding content for parts of a text or only for certain kinds of texts rather than acting as heuristic sets to explore for insights and judgments; 2) a preference for more complex logical frameworks rather than informal reasoning based on the audience's knowledge; and 3) the valuing of natural abilities over the guidance of rhetorical arts. A few textbooks and pedagogies today reflect the Roman use of a *status*-like art to begin the process of discoursing by identifying points at issue in the situation or framing questions instead of starting with a thesis or a subject.

Inventional Issues in Second Sophistic, Medieval, and Renaissance Rhetorics

During the second sophistic period (roughly from the second century CE to the fall of the Roman Empire in 410 CE in the West and to around the sixth century in the East), little new inventional theory was developed. The term *sophistic* was used because it represented in the eyes of the historians of the time some features of Greek sophistic rhetoric: an emphasis on decoration, polish, and stylistic eloquence, preferring discourses with little political or even judicial import over those leading to probable civic judgments and new knowledge. Classical conceptions of invention and rhetoric continued to be taught in the Roman empire in the *ephebia* (two years of higher education) until the fall of the empire. As Christianity spread, rhetorical scholars tried to reconcile rhetorical probability with Christian belief in Divine truth, turning inquiry into interpreting the Scriptures and finding material to promulgate Divine truths. Throughout the medieval period, efforts to save the classical rhetoric texts resulted in preserving shortened versions of rhetorical invention in encyclopedias and stripping the arts of their authorizing and explanatory theory. Invention was also channeled into advice for letter writing, preaching, and writing poetry, not as epistemic guides but as advice for generating content. McKeon argued that rhetorical invention went underground, was often subordinated to logic or philosophy, and eventually contributed to the formation of the scholastic and scientific methods. During the Renaissance, invention took three basic directions: classical rhetorical invention found its way into vernacular rhetorical texts; treatises on schemes (syntactic alternatives) and tropes (figures of speech) nudged

invention out of many rhetorical texts; proclamations by individuals
such as Ramus banished invention from rhetoric, leaving it with style
and delivery; and finally, others like Francis Bacon relegated rhetorical
invention to the non-epistemic process of finding the known.

Second Sophistic Issues

The rise of the Roman Empire drove rhetoric from the courtrooms
and assemblies into ceremonial and academic sites. Invention followed.
Epideictic (ceremonial) rhetoric prevailed, with competitive oratory in
some cases becoming a substitute for the gladiator matches. Kennedy,
drawing from Vasile Florescu, called the period one of *letteraturizzazione*, a time in which style became central and invention functioned
as a means of discovering ethical and pathetic appeals to advance the
values and ideas of the emperor and imperial policies, and hence rarely
served an epistemic purpose (*Classical Rhetoric* 5).

Also during this time, Christianity gradually gained ascendancy.
Latin and Byzantine rhetoricians such as Chrysostom, Jerome, Origen, Tertullian, Gregory of Nazianzus, and Augustine struggled over
the relationship between Christianity and rhetoric, pondering the
connection between faith and argument and between Divine truths
and probability. Here inventional acts took a hermeneutical turn as
they were deployed to interpret the Scriptures and embellish sermons
(La Tourneau). As George Kennedy explained, preaching the Christian *kerygma*, the good news, was a proclamation, where the truth of
the message had to be apprehended by the listener, not proved by the
speaker (*Classical Rhetoric* 145-46). Through God's help, not rhetoric,
the listener was able to believe in the person of Christ and understand
the wisdom of the Scriptures. James Kinneavy investigated the correspondence between the notion of Christian faith and persuasion as
pistis, or proof, where faith was an epistemological state of conviction,
freely chosen and based on trust, assent, and knowledge (*Greek Rhetorical*). For Augustine, invention was an art of exegesis that guided
the discovery of meaning in the Scriptures. He also examined some
inquiry purposes. In Book II of *De Doctrina*, he considered the science of disputation useful for understanding and solving scriptural
questions (31) and noted that ambiguity required faith to unravel. For
Augustine, the purpose of rhetoric with all of its powers was to serve
the communication of the truth. In *Greek Rhetoric under the Christian Emperors*, Kennedy maintained that Augustine developed a set of

commonplaces from the Bible (183). Kathy Eden argued that the basis of Augustine's interpretation was a distinction between the Scriptures and the writer's intention, "regarding the dianoetic (rational) meaning as prior to and privileged above the semantic meaning" (50). Because one who was charitably disposed couldn't lie, Augustine required that an interpreter's grasp of the meaning of the text must entail ethical theory.

In the East, a fifth-century Chinese scholar, Liu Xie wrote a treatise on rhetoric entitled *Wen Xin Diao Long* ("The Literary Mind and the Carving of Dragons"). HePing Zhao explained that one of the meanings of *wen* is writing in a generic sense, indicating that writing is composed of patterns (another meaning of *wen)*, thereby establishing "a powerful analogy in which writing, a human creation, is likened to nature, the creation of some 'primal' force" (73). The text has chapters entitled: "Spiritual Thought or Imagination," "Style and Nature," "The Wind and the Bone," and "Flexible Adaptability to Varying Situations," which "discuss discovering ideas, making judgments about observations, and exploring for supporting materials" (Zhao 148-49). Zhao pointed out that there are interactions between content-oriented inventional acts and form-oriented inventional acts.

Inventional Issues in Medieval Rhetoric

What we understand about medieval theories of invention is based in part on observing what was truncated, omitted, or assigned to another field. During this long period, views of the nature and purpose of invention were often reductive and their course circuitous. As Richard McKeon explained, invention during this period influenced three lines of intellectual development: rhetorical theory, theology, and logic. Rhetorical treatises presented short versions of *status*, thesis/hypothesis arguments about whether rhetoric encompassed both abstract and concrete questions or only concrete cases, and the three types of rhetoric (deliberative, judicial, and demonstrative) in civil philosophy (176). Encyclopedists such as Boethius, Cassiodorus, and Isidore of Seville summarized complex classical treatises on rhetoric, reducing their explanations sometimes to two sentences or brief definitions and often thereby losing more subtle understandings like that of rhetorical reasoning and epistemological invention. These enycyclopedists emphasized *status* over the topics and the syllogism over the enthymeme and the example, moves which eventually gave way to deduction and induction. In Book IV of *De topicis differentius*, Boethius described a four-category *status*, differentiating rhetoric from philosophy. He confined the system of rhetorical topics to the attributes of person and action, assigning the common topics to dialectics and the special topics to rhetoric. He also asserted that the rhetorician had to proceed from the dialectical topics (within the study of logic) but the dialectician could stay with his own topics (Stump 94). Leff maintained that Boethius subordinated the rhetorical to the dialectical topics, asserting that the only difference between the two was the kind of subject dealt with: concrete or abstract issues ("Topics"). McKeon commented that Boethius identified the problem of distinguishing principles as the problem of discovering arguments or things ("Rhetoric in the Middle Ages").

P. Osmund Lewry pointed out that at this time dialectic and rhetoric shared the realm of the probable though one did so in view of the truth and the other in order to play on the emotions (49). According to Joseph Miller, Michael Prosser, and Thomas Benson, Cassiodorus, relying on Cicero and Fortunatianus, discussed such inventional concepts as *status*, the syllogism, and the enthymeme (78). Isidore of Seville divided *status* into the syllogistic and the legal, common places into "before, during, and after," and separated rhetoric from dialectic, identifying the syllogism as composed of induction and rationation (Miller et al. 88). These treatments, as discussed above, began to shift invention to logic.

As three new medieval rhetorical arts developed (letter writing, preaching, and poetry), the topics became means for remembering, amplifying, and describing material for these types of rhetoric. A well-known example of the art of letter writing, Anonymous of Bologna's *The Principles of Letter-Writing (Rationes dictandi)*, focused on securing good will largely through the construction of appropriate salutations and subject matters. Geoffrey of Vinsauf, according to Martin Camargo, linked the arrangement of the letter to the enthymeme, division, and definition (176-77). Robert of Basevorn's *The Form of Preaching (Forma praedicandi)* advocated the invention of themes in the use of topics for preaching. He described a "good invention of a theme as concurring with a feast, begetting full understanding, based on an unchanged Bible text, containing only three statements or less, having sufficient concordances with these statements, and having a theme that could serve as an antetheme or protheme" (Murphy, *Rheto-*

ric in the Middle Ages 348). Murphy recounted that for Alain de Lille, the Scriptures were "a double source book for invention" (*Rhetoric in the Middle Ages* 309): ideas to present to his hearers and direct quotations to prove his ideas. Alain also relied heavily on example and authority (Murphy, *Rhetoric in the Middle Ages* 306). In the art of poetry, inventional practices were transformed. In discussing Geoffrey of Vinsauf's influence on Robert Henryson, Robert Kindrick argued that Geoffrey's "emphasis on deliberation and planning encouraged a more intellectual approach to invention" (61). Kindrick stated that Geoffrey extended grammatical precepts into invention, making invention more content-oriented and genre specific.

According to McKeon, rhetorical invention also influenced theology by offering methods for interpreting Scriptures. For example, formal methods were defined for three approaches to reading sacred texts: allegorical, moral, and analogical. The Augustan distinction between things and signs was used to solve theoretical problems ("Rhetoric in the Middle Ages" 178). Thus, discovery became what should be understood ("Rhetoric in the Middle Ages" 178). Later in the period, rhetorical invention shaped the scholastic method of inquiry. According to this method, one began with questions and apparent contradictions, then used topics to sort out theoretical problems by exploring their causes and effects, definitions, and so forth. The method also stressed the importance of sentences (authorities) ("Rhetoric in the Middle Ages" 197-98). According to McKeon, rhetorical invention also shaped logic during phases of the medieval period. The Old Logic used topics for discovery while analytics provided judgment. The New Logic separated logic and dialectic, making rhetoric the counterpart of dialectic and separating scientific proof from probable proof ("Rhetoric in the Middle Ages" 191). In the later Middle Ages, the topics were used as the inspiration for the scientific method—to discover things, not arguments.

In the East, Arab philosophers and rhetoricians such as al-Farabi, Avicenna, and Averroës, wrote commentaries on Hellenic rhetorics, especially Aristotle's. Averroës used Islamic examples in his commentaries (Schaub). All three discussed religious discourse about the nature of God, the principle of the first cause, and the possibility of bodily resurrection, as well as rhetoric's function to convert the masses and its role in securing consent in the community. However, all three thinkers also viewed "dialectic as a more 'certain' way than rhetoric to attain

and convey truth" (Schaub 241), but Butterworth argued that Averroës stressed rhetoric's investigative capacities (Schaub 242), particularly in getting at what is *presumed* to be true in a community of faith
(Schaub 246).

Renaissance Conceptions of Invention

The Renaissance revived classical rhetoric, re-igniting debates over
the nature, purposes, and epistemology of invention. In *The Arte of
Rhetorike*, the first full rhetoric written in English, Thomas Wilson
restored several classical invention strategies but ignored others. It has
been conjectured that this rhetoric, with its eight editions, was written to educate young gentlemen and noblemen for the Inns of Court
(Ong, "Tudor" 54). In judicial rhetoric, Wilson included *status* not
as an initiating act of question posing, but as the stating of a foundation or principal point that revolved around the classical categories of
conjectural, legal, and judicial (120-24). Under demonstrative (ceremonial) rhetoric, he included the special topics of person, deeds, and
things (54-65), referring his readers to his treatise on logic for the
common topics such as definition, causes, parts, and things adjoining
(30). For deliberative discourse (writing to one's neighbor) he offered a
version of special topics such as honest, profitable, pleasant, easy, hard,
and necessary (70-78). For judicial discourse, he listed various topics
under each type of *status:*

- under conjectural: power, time, presence, etc.

- under legal: definition, contraries, ambiguities, etc.

- under judicial: nature, law, custom, assumption, etc. (125-
  132).

He also included topics for pathos (100-3) and special topics for ethos
in the introduction of a text, especially for the establishment of good
will (133-39). Notable was his omission of the enthymeme, the example, and a discussion of epistemology. Lois Agnew, however, maintained that Wilson's rhetoric served as a vehicle through which individuals could bind wisdom to eloquence to create knowledge.

While Wilson adapted classical and medieval inventional practices
to the circumstances of his day, Peter Ramus argued that invention
belonged to logic. In his treatise, *Logike*, he listed topics from prior
logical texts and outlined the proposition and the syllogism. He also

described his method or organizational schema (a movement from general to specific, followed by the use of definition and examples), a method to be used in all texts and in education itself. In *Rhetorica*, written with Omer Talon, he dealt only with style (see Dudley Fenner's edition). As Fr. Walter Ong explained in *Rhetoric, Romance, and Technology*, Ramus simplified complex discursive arts and emphasized analyzing models to find something to say. In *Ramus, Method, and the Decay of Dialogue*, Ong described this eviscerating of rhetoric and invention:

> This studied maneuvering of his sources enables Ramus to moor one item of his dialectic here, another item there, in classical antiquity. But neither in this passage, nor elsewhere does he explain the cavalier picking and choosing which results in his particular mix. There is certainly no insight into processes of cognition or communication or into logical structure to give his amalgam an interior consistency inviting theoretical explanation. (43)

Ramus's influence, however, prevailed so that as the Renaissance progressed, other rhetorical texts ignored invention and treated only schemes and tropes, including Sherry's *A Treatise of Schemes and Tropes*, Peacham's *The Garden of Eloquence*, and Fraunce's *The Arcadian Rhetorike*.

In 1701, Mary Astell, in *A Serious Proposal, Part II*, provided a method of logic and an art of rhetoric appropriate for women and based on conversation with neighbors. Following Peter Ramus, she placed invention in logic and developed her own method of the reasoning process:

> thoroughly defining and gaining knowledge of the question, subjects, and terms used; setting aside irrelevant issues; ordering thoughts from simple to complex; dividing the subject into parts for examination so that nothing is left unexamined; concentrating on the subject without digression throughout; and treating as truth only what one evidently knows, sometimes settling for probability only. (Donawerth, *Rhetorical Theory* 101)

Her rhetoric aimed at allaying the passions of the audience so that they could ponder the subject without bias (Donawerth, Rhetorical Theory 101).

In the later Renaissance, Francis Bacon in *The Advancement of Learning* assigned finding the known to rhetorical invention, while creating new knowledge became the province of the sciences. He proclaimed (without offering an argument):

> The invention of speech or argument is not properly
> an invention: for to invent is to discover that we know
> not, and not to recover or resummon that which we
> already know: and the use of the invention is no other
> but out of the knowledge whereof our mind is already
> possessed, to draw forth or call before us that which
> may be pertinent to the purpose which we take into
> our consideration. So as to speak truly, it is no inven-
> tion, but a remembrance or suggestion, with an appli-
> cation; [. . .] that it hath already obtained the name,
> let it be called invention. (58)

Subject Positions

Throughout the second sophistic, medieval, and renaissance periods, women increasingly occupied subject positions as writers. Although they did not compose treatises on rhetorical invention, their work exemplified its fruits. During the second sophistic, women writers worked in different genres. The Alexandrian, Hypatia, a philosopher, astronomer, and mathematician, wrote scientific treatises. Pamphilia authored 33 books of historical materials under her husband's name (Anderson and Zinsser). Vida Perpetua recorded her days in an African prison cell leading up to her death in the Roman arena (Anderson and Zinsser and Thiebaux). Egeria composed a travel diary (Snyder; Thiebaux). Amalasuntha of Italy wrote letters to the Roman senate and Justinian, and Dhuoda of Uzes authored a handbook of moral guidelines for her son (Thiebaux). (See also Donawerth, *Rhetorical Theory*; "Conversations"; "Bibliography".)

In the medieval period, women occupied more writer positions. Leola of England and Germany wrote letters and poems (Thiebaux). Hrotswitha (Hrotsvit) of Gandersheim authored lives of the saints, drama, and epics; Marie de France wrote three books dealing with

secular love. Hildegard of Bingen produced drama, lyrics, two b
on her secret language, a book of exegesis on the psalms, letters
kings, archbishops, abbots, and abbesses, and books on the saints'
lives. Heloise composed letters citing the Old and New Testaments,
fathers of the Church, and classical authors as well as *Problemata*, and
included questions on divine law, justice, mercy, and contradictions
among the Gospels. Julian of Norwich produced theological treatises;
Margery Kempe authored a spiritual autobiography; and Christine de
Pizan produced ballads, epistles, and biographies (Glenn *Rhetoric Retold* and "Reexamining"; Sutherland and Sutcliffe; Ward; Barratt; Ferrante; Wilson; Vitz).

During the Renaissance, women found and created more complex
writer and speaker positions. In Italy, Isotta Nogarol authored orations, letters, and poetry; Laura Cereta wrote letters about the death
of her husband and her reactions to male and female critics; Cas-
sandra Fedele delivered public orations and wrote in Latin; Gaspara
Stampa published poetry; and Antonia authored religious plays in the
vernacular. In England, Margaret More Roper wrote a commentary
on Erasmus; Jane Anger sent a letter "To Gentlewomen of England";
and Anne Askew composed an account of her torture and examination. Mary Astell authored political pamphlets, argued for women's
rights and education, and challenged John Locke; Elizabeth Gryme-
ston wrote a collection of meditations offering a scholarly synthesis
of the Church fathers and Scriptures; and Elizabeth Richardson authored three books of prayers. A book on nursing was written by Elizabeth Clinton while Dorothy Leigh authored *A Mother's Blessing*, which
offered advice to her children and argued for the value of women's
roles. In addition, women in the English court like Catherine of Ara-
gon, Queen Elizabeth, Princess Mary, Anne Boleyn, and Catherine
Parr produced many compositions. (Glenn, *Rhetoric Retold*; Herberg;
King; Migiel and Schiesari; Redfern; Sutherland; Tebeaux and Lay;
and Travitsky; Willard).

Review: Invention in Second Sophistic,
Medieval, and Renaissance Rhetorics

During the Second Sophistic period in the Roman empire invention
was narrowed to function largely in ceremonial discourse and rarely
served an epistemic purpose. In Christianity, rhetoricians seeking to
reconcile rhetoric with their Christian faith assigned to invention the

se of interpreting the Scriptures. During the long

se of interpreting the Scriptures. During the long
ıvention splintered and penetrated other fields,
es in new types of discourse. Still, interpretation
nvestigation and logic and dialectic overshadowed
rather than probabilities. The classical *status* and
red for new generic purposes. The epistemic func-
........ıvention virtually disappeared, giving way to theology and the emerging scientific method. During the Renaissance, a
version of classical invention was adapted for the vernacular culture,
as seen in Thomas Wilson's first complete rhetoric in English. Earlier,
Ramus relegated rhetorical invention to logic and left style and delivery in rhetoric. Bacon dealt a final blow to invention by proclaiming
that rhetorical invention dealt only with retrieving the known, while
science created new knowledge through an inductive investigation.

Eighteenth- and Nineteenth-Century Discussions of Invention

These centuries gave rhetorical invention little attention. Vasile
Florescu traced this marginalization through Descartes, Spinoza,
Kant, Hegel, and Croce. Descartes's theory of knowledge was thoroughly antirhetorical, for it based knowledge on self-evidence, clarity,
and the distinctiveness of ideas. For Spinoza, rhetoric was to be a kind
of "naked communication," whose goal was to transmit ideas without
participating in their creation. Kant considered *ars oratoria to be an*
inconsequential, personal art, and finally for Hegel rhetoric was calcu-
lated artifice that contrasted with poetry. Florescu further studied the
fate of rhetoric and invention in the work of Croce, whose concepts of
intuition and expression, he argued, formed an indestructible unity,
thus eliminating rhetoric from "the esthetic problematic" (202).

Eighteenth-Century Invention

In the eighteenth century, Hugh Blair, George Campbell, Adam
Smith, and Gregorio Mayans y Siscar held the epistemological position of common sense realism. Using Ong' s concept of noetic fields,
James Berlin characterized eighteenth-century Scottish common-
sense realism as the apprehension of sense data through an extra-lin-
gual process of induction (*Writing Instruction*). Consequently, most of
these rhetoricians relegated rhetoric to the function of communicating
the results of inquiry conducted elsewhere, although interpreters of

Campbell differ about his epistemic position. In this context, rhetoric was a kind of "managerial" art. Its purpose was not to investigate or create, but rather to organize and present arguments through moral reasoning and empirical evidence. Science and philosophy continued to usurp the role of rhetorical invention.

Hugh Blair in *Lectures on Rhetoric and Belle Lettres* announced that invention's purpose was to convey arguments and subject matter that had been generated elsewhere. According to Blair, "what is truly solid and persuasive, must be drawn '*ex visceribu causae*,' from a thorough knowledge of the subject, and profound meditation on it" (118). "For it is one thing," he wrote, "to discover the reasons that are most proper to convince men, and another to manage these reasons with the most advantage. The latter is all that rhetoric can pretend to do" (117).

In *The Philosophy of Rhetoric* George Campbell delineated the kinds of reasoning that related to the different faculties of understanding, imagination, emotion, and will. He categorized truths into intuitive, common sense, and deductive and placed moral reasoning in the province of rhetoric. Moral reasoning, he claimed, moved from particulars to the general and was more direct and useful in gaining new knowledge (182-83), encompassing several of what he called "tribes": experience, analogy, testimony, and calculations of chance (184). According to Campbell, the aim of logic was to evince truth and the aim of rhetoric was to convince the hearer (73). Lloyd Bitzer pointed out that Campbell borrowed from Hume, stressing the importance of imagination and feeling, the attitudes of empiricism, and the doctrine of association of ideas ("Hume's Philosophy"). Hagaman explained that Campbell's acceptance of empiricism led him to think of invention as "an expression of confidence in the mind's ability to observe the natural world and draw inferences, discern opposing evidence, and draw inductive conclusions that are open to continuing examination" ("Campbell's Philosophy" 148).

As Vincent Bevilacqua explained, Adam Smith held a similar conception of the relationship between logic and rhetoric. Smith believed the two were grounded in a common mental faculty; however, logic was concerned with invention, judgment, and memory; rhetoric with communication ("Adam Smith"). According to Howell, Smith shunned the artistic proofs and topical arguments in favor of non-artistic arguments and direct proof. This attention to the "psychological task of verbal expression " made invention an extra-rhetorical act (564).

Mayans y Siscar's *Rhetórica* also distinguished rhetorical invention from "true" scientific invention. Don Abbott explained that Siscar viewed rhetoric as one of four rational arts and defined it as "the art of Transmitting, or of producing and expressing to others those things which have been invented, judged, and laid up in memory" ("Mayans' Rhetórica," 168). Siscar held that invention preceded rhetoric, and defined invention as "the action with which the understanding looks for useful ideas, arguments, affects, and manners of speaking in order to form a persuasive oration (Abbott, 168-69). He also discussed *status*, the four causes, and rhetorical arguments (topics) (170).

In contrast, Giambattista Vico tried to retain a classical sense of rhetorical invention and probable epistemology. Catherine Peadon in "Language and Rhetoric in Locke, Condillac and Vico" demonstrated that Vico united language and ideas, thus abandoning a Lockean separation of words and ideas and embracing an epistemology resting on "a mutually implicated language and thought" (180). She also maintained that he set his topical invention in opposition to Cartesian critical philosophy in an effort to overcome the dualism of *pathos and logos* and to deconstruct the invention/judgment binary (222). Catherine Hobbs, in *Rhetoric on the Margins of Modernity,* maintained that Vico taught and wrote to unite wisdom and eloquence to serve the social body, with the topics as an inventory of shared consciousness. He viewed language as basically metaphorical and the foundation of common sense in the culture. As an alternative to Cartesian critical thought, he emphasized the faculties of memory, *ingenium*, imagination, and common sense, forming topical thought (66). For Vico metaphorical thought underscored three types of thinking: the hieroglyphic, the symbolic, and the vulgar—corresponding to the ages of gods, heroes, and humans (69), with the movement from metaphoric to conventional language being a "continual, cyclical activity" (70). According to Hobbs, Vico held that "invention and poetic imagination unfold before judgment in both the individual and society" (72). The arts of topics, criticism, and method governed respectively three mental operations: perception, judgment, and reasoning. Considering all knowledge rhetorical, Vico developed a rhetoric of social invention with a logic of status and topics. Hobbs claimed that Vico deconstructed the critical-creative binary and the rhetoric-science binary, with the sublime art of metaphor constructing truths (73) and foregrounding probability rather than certainty (92). Mark Williams and Theresa Enos also pointed to Vico's epistemology of the probable by showing how his conception of triangular invention was contingent on history and context.

In contrast to the general view that the eighteenth century saw the demise of invention, Elizabeth Larsen argued that invention was "less abandoned than transformed over time from a specific act associated with particular features (inventio) to a generic act (invention) associated with pedagogical features" (183). According to Larsen, Alexander Gerard's *An Essay on Genius* viewed invention as a mental capacity, a human process of composing that entailed complex powers: re-visioning, negotiating between judgment and the imagination, and induction (186).

Although Vico's theories of invention had an influence on his immediate context, it was the work of Ramus and Bacon that directed the course of invention until the twentieth century. Just as Ramus's reduction of rhetoric precluded a rhetorical way of reasoning in the realm of probability, so Bacon's view of rhetorical invention robbed it of an epistemic function, two diminishments of rhetoric that continued for centuries.

Nineteenth-Century Invention

In the nineteenth century, epistemic rhetorical invention still took a back seat to logic, inspiration, and observation. For the most part, rhetorical invention served only to find content, proofs, and organization for the products of the mental faculties. Romanticism also contributed to the diminishment of invention by stressing intuition and inspiration as the sources of ideas and motivations for writing. Eventually invention gave way to linguistics and criticism. Finally invention virtually disappeared.

In Britain, Richard Whately's *Elements of Rhetoric* distinguished between rules of inference by which one discovers the truth and rules of proof by which one convinces others of its truth (281). The former belonged to logic, he maintained, while the latter was rhetorical invention's purpose. Lois Einhorn contended that his notion of rhetoric as an offshoot of logic significantly altered his perception of the function of rhetorical invention because he eliminated the process of first becoming aware of something and substituted a process of refinement or an "*inventio* of 'management'" (50). Raymie McKerrow argued that Whately offered a subjective interpretation of probability and advanced a rhetorical conception of proof that depended on using argument ("Probable Argument"). In discussing Whately's notion of the role of the audience, McKerrow said that Whately was subject rather than audience oriented, with the audience functioning as a judge but not as a creator of knowledge ("Ethical Implications" 324). Thus Whately's rhetoric was not seen as epistemic. Berlin argued that Whately was a significant force in shaping "Current-Traditional Rhetoric," the model for teaching writing that dominated English departments in America in the nineteenth and early twentieth century ("Richard Whately"). He also speculated that Whately's rational emphasis might have led to a distrust of persuasion ("Richard Whately").

In the United States, holders of the prestigious rhetorical position, the Boylston Chair at Harvard, represented the various fates that had befallen invention by the nineteenth century. According to Ronald Reid, John Quincy Adams adhered to the classical tradition of rhetoric, refuting Blair's repudiation of invention and modifying the notion of status to fit the American legal system. Joseph McKean, following John Ward's *A System of Oratory*, divided invention into intellectual resources and artificial analyses. Departing from Ward, however, he followed Campbell treatments of understanding, imagination, and memory. While McKean defended the usefulness of invention, he warned against mechanical use of the topics and viewed them as helpful for young, inexperienced orators. He questioned the usefulness of *status* for all types of discourse, but acknowledged its value for judicial oratory (344). Edward Channing identified rhetoric with criticism, while Francis Child ignored rhetoric to focus on linguistics and criticism. Adam Sherman Hill changed the term rhetoric to composition and abandoned oratory for writing. His assistant Barrett Wendell advanced a new idea for pedagogy, based on practice and criticism (not theory), ignoring invention, and subsuming persuasion under argument. Describing nineteenth-century romanticism, Berlin spoke of knowing reality through an interaction of the observer and observed, of interpreting underlying reality, of constructing reality through synthesizing all faculties, and of the analogical method of expressing what transcends material reality (*Writing Instruction*). Berlin pointed out that Emerson's orator was motivated to speak by inspiration obtained from the occasions that arose in a democracy (*Writing Instruction* 53) and had to "rely primarily on his intuition to provide the higher truths which men seek" (*Writing Instruction* 45).

Sharon Crowley described three parts of nineteenth-century invention: 1) the use of prior knowledge and natural ability; 2) disciplined exercise of the mental faculties through reading, conversation, meditation, and observation; and 3) textual order as the method of planning ("Invention"). In *Methodical Memory*, she suggested that some of these conceptions were based on the popular pedagogy known as mental discipline, derived from faculty psychology. These conceptions led to an impoverished view of invention as simply a process of selecting, narrowing, and amplifying. Thus invention was subsumed under the modes of discourse: EDNA—exposition, description, narration, and argument, which became the basis for textbooks and curricula. Crowley also called attention to Henry Day's *The Art of Discourse*, which presented an inventional scheme for expository writing based on informal logic. Invention involved stating a proposition and analyzing and dividing the proposition into its constituent parts ("Invention" 150). Crowley suggested that John Genung's concept of invention, which included preparation, deducing and stating a theme, creating a title, planning, and amplification ("Invention" 151), was the most inventional because it enabled writers to generate arguments for discourse. (See also Arthur Applebee, Michael Halloran, Nan Johnson, Albert Kitzhaber, and William Woods for discussions of nineteenth-century rhetoric, composition, and invention.)

Subject Positions

The eighteenth century saw a number of women assuming writer and speaker positions including Mary Wollstonecraft, Hester Thrale, Hester Ann Rogers, Sarah Crosby, Sarah Mallett, Mary Fletcher, Margaret Davidson, Jane Newland, Sarah Grubb, Mara Edgeworth, and Fanny Burney (see Barlowe; Butler and Todd; Donawerth, *Rhetorical Theory*; Ferguson and Todd; Lorch; Poovey; Conway).

In the nineteenth century, as higher education became more available to women, more positions opened up for them, including the role of rhetorical theorist. At the University of Michigan under the direction of Fred Newton Scott, Gertrude Buck wrote her MA thesis, "The Figures of Rhetoric," which Donald Stewart described as an effort to develop a sound psychological basis for the use of figurative language. Her PhD dissertation was entitled "The Metaphor—A Study in the Psychology of Rhetoric," which Albert Kitzhaber praised for its innovative use of experimental psychology (*Rhetoric* 291). After hiring

Gertrude Buck at Vassar, the English department offered courses that encouraged students to develop "reflective, creative, and critical thinking applicable to society's needs" (Ricks 76).

Many other nineteenth-century women occupied subject positions as writers and speakers: Margaret Fuller, Catherine Beecher, Mary Lyon, Harriet Beecher Stowe, Elizabeth Stuart Phelps, Susan Warner, Maria Cummins, Lydia Maria Child, Lucy Stone, Sarah Hale, Jane Addams, and Anna Cooper. Jacqueline Jones Royster wrote about black women writers including Ida B. Wells, Frances Harper, Alice Dunbar, Maria Stewart, Harriet Tubman, and Fannie Barrier Williams. Shirley Wilson Logan edited a collection of African-American speeches, and a book on the persuasive writing of black women, including Sarah Parker Remond, Frances Ellen Watkins Harper, Lucy Wilmot Smith, Lucy Craft Laney, and Victoria Earle Matthews. Ann Marie Mann Simpkins described the textual strategies of two African-American women publishers, Mary Miles and Mary Ann Shadd Cary. For further discussions of nineteenth-century women rhetors and rhetoricians see Suzanne Bordelon; Karlyn Campbell; Jo Anne Campbell; Gregory Clark and Michael Halloran; Catherine Hobbs, *Nineteenth Century*; Annette Kolodny; Barbara L'Eplattenier; Drema Lipscomb; Shirley Wilson Logan; Bridget O'Rourke; Carla Peterson; Louise Phelps and Janet Emig; Joy Rouse; Nicole Tonkovich; and Joanne Wagner.

Review: Eighteenth- and Nineteenth-Century Invention

During the eighteenth century, Scottish and British rhetoricians, following Ramus and Bacon, considered logic the home of invention while rhetoric was assigned to communication. Invention was also compartmentalized into the faculties of understanding, imagination, emotion, and will. George Campbell considered rhetoric as moral reasoning while Adam Smith and Mayans y Siscar considered invention outside of rhetoric.

In the nineteenth century, Richard Whately continued to hold the view that rhetoric's purpose was to convince others of the truth, constructing a rhetoric of management. In the United States, various holders of the Boylston Chair at Harvard helped to marginalize invention in favor of criticism and linguistics. The very term *rhetoric* was replaced with *composition*, which was devoted to practice and criticism. Genung subsumed invention under the modes of discourse;

description, narration, exposition, and argument. Current-Traditional pedagogy divided into two polar positions, one teaching composition as style and correctness and the other teaching writing as an act of genius, with both positions ignoring invention. During this century, however, women rhetorical theorists brought new interests to composition: metaphor and its psychological bases, creative thinking, new subject matters, and concerns for society's needs.

Part II: Pedagogical Issues

The development of the rhetor has been a long-standing issue in rhetorical history. Since the time of the Greeks, rhetoricians have debated the relative merits of four factors in rhetorical instruction: natural ability, imitation, practice, and art. Eras of discourse instruction have been marked by an emphasis on one or the other of these broad teaching approaches though in some cases all four were integrated. Natural ability pedagogies, what some today call romantic or vitalist teaching, provide encouraging contexts, assignments that motivate students, and feedback on completed texts or drafts, but avoid offering strategies or direct instruction on invention. Students rely for guidance on their native talent and teacher responses to specific texts. Imitation pedagogies provide students with readings and examples, either as stimuli for ideas or as models of invention. The popularity of contemporary readers testifies to the longevity of this pedagogy. Practice pedagogies engage students in frequent, sometimes daily writing, as a way to develop their abilities. Often these practices are decontextualized exercises; some are done in genuine contexts. Art pedagogies provide students with strategies or guides for invention. Richard Young discussed this pedagogy in "Arts, Crafts, Gifts, and Knacks and the Teaching of Writing," contrasting what he called New Romanticism with New Classicism. New Romanticists, according to Young, consider composing as free of deliberate control—imagination is primary and the development of ability is a mysterious growth. The New Classicists emphasize heuristic procedures through which rhetorical knowledge can be carried from one situation to the other, and rational control of the writing processes that can be taught. Lauer also examined this issue in "Instructional Practices: Toward an Integration," arguing for using elements of all four approaches to teach composition.

Greek Discussions of Inventional Pedagogy

The Greeks were interested in the notion of an art as a particular kind of knowledge used to guide activities like rhetoric. A key feature of an art was that it could be taught.

Art (techne)

The Greek concept of art (*techne*) has been at the center of historical discussions of rhetorical pedagogy. Scholars have studied its meaning in different rhetoricians' work and have also researched its history. Janet Atwill in *Rhetoric Reclaimed* traced the concept of *techne* back to the Odyssey, where it signified both implement and boundary, prompting her interpretation that "the accomplishments of art are, paradoxically, tied to its boundaries" (47). She explained that whenever a boundary or limit was recognized, art created a path that transgressed and redefined the boundary (48). Outlining the ancient conceptions of *techne*, she offered the following definition of the ancient concept of *techne*:

1) A *techne* is never a static normative body of knowledge. It may be described as a *dynamis* (or power), transferable guides and strategies, a cunningly conceived plan—even a trick or a trap. This knowledge is stable enough to be taught and transferred but flexible enough to be adapted to particular situations and purposes.

2) A *techne* resists identification with a normative subject. The subjects identified with *techne* are often in a state of flux or transformation. [. . .] Since a *techne* is always transferable, no matter how brilliant the plan or strategy, it is never confined to a specific human or god. In other words, *techne* is never "private" knowledge, a mysterious faculty, or the product of unique genius.

3) *Techne* marks a domain of intervention and invention. A *techne* is *never* knowledge as representation. *Techne* appears when one is outnumbered by foes or overpowered by force. It not only enables the transgression of boundaries but also attempts to *rectify* transgressions. (48)

She explained that in the mythic traditions of the Prometheus accounts, *techne* is depicted as a trick, contrivance, or stratagem, as well as a method of making or doing that is set against nature (*physis*) and force (*bia*). *Techne* is a uniquely temporal and situated kind of knowledge. In discussing the relationship between *techne* and *kairos*, for example, she pointed out that "knowing how" and "knowing when" to deploy an art distinguishes *techne* from "rule-governed activities that are less constrained by temporal conditions" (59). She further used the work of Marcel Detienne and Jean-Pierre Vernant to argue that ancient conceptions of *techne* are identified with cunning intelligence (*metis*), not practical wisdom (*phronesis*). As such, *techne* is a kind of knowledge that is used to challenge given circumstances and create not only new relations of power but also new subjectivities. She maintained, for example, that for Isocrates the art of rhetoric was as concerned with transforming subjectivities as with transferring rhetorical knowledge.

Sophists

Protagoras was one of the first to articulate the relationship between art, endowment, practice, and models in the development of a rhetor. He said that natural talent was a necessary ingredient, but also that "art without practice, and practice without art, are nothing " (Kathleen Freeman, *Ancilla* 127). In the *Graeci-Syrian Maxims*, Protagoras asserted: "Toil and work [practice] and instruction and education [art] and wisdom [talent] are the garland of fame which is woven from the flowers of an eloquent tongue" (Freeman, *Ancilla* 127).

Scholars, however, differ over whether the Sophists really developed an art. Below are some examples. Richard Enos held that it was "the mark of the 5th century BCE that abstraction of notions leading to a *techne* is made conscious and explicit" (*Greek Rhetoric* 60). John Poulakos claimed that Protagoras and Gorgias called their work art not demonstrative knowledge ("Toward a Definition"; see also "Terms"). Susan Jarratt, disagreeing with the idea that the Sophists were vitalists, insisted that they educated for empowerment, allowing anyone who could pay fees to learn rhetoric for the assembly, the council, and the courts ("The First Sophists" and "Performing Histories"). In *Rereading the Sophists*, she viewed this education as having goals similar to the twentieth-century efforts to provide an ethical education in civic virtue and to empower students to participate in democracy (83). She also discussed the critical potential of sophistic rhetoric for today: "Gorgias's apagogic of argument—the exploration of various alternative positions—likewise offers the opportunity to reflect on the contradictory nature of propositions" (103). The technique of antilogic gave the students an ability to gain distance from the hegemony of custom and law—"the ability to stand outside of and perhaps control aspects of it" (104) and to engage in a "critical analysis of popular belief" (104). Bruce McComiskey contended that "the primary goal of Gorgias's *techne* is the desired action of the audience" and that "moving audiences to action is aesthetic, using the emotional response of an audience to the immediate rhetorical context" (*Gorgias* 28). Contesting Socrates's claim that Gorgias's rhetoric was a mere knack, McComiskey argued that for Gorgias, "*logos* could be part of both the content and the articulatory method of a *techne*" (*Gorgias* 30). Moreover, he maintained that Gorgias favored "the topical invention of ethical arguments over the magical invention of false arguments" (*Gorgias* 32). Part of Gorgias's *techne* was to analyze different types of souls and to test the most effective means of influencing them (*Gorgias* 31). In analyzing *Palamedes*, McComiskey divided the arguments from probability into those that "(1) explore past, present, and future probabilities, (2) describe the character of the speakers, and (3) limit the ethical uses of emotion in forensic discourse" (*Gorgias* 31).

On the other side, Thomas Cole argued that there was no art until Plato because for the rhetorician to control the medium of transmission, two developments had to take place: 1) "audiences and composers had to acquire the habit of abstracting essential messages from verbal contexts" (x); and 2) "'written' eloquence had to come into being—that is, a body of prose texts which might be read or delivered verbatim and still suggest the excitement, atmosphere and commitment of spontaneous oral performance or debate" (x). Robert Connors maintained that prior to Corax and Tisias rhetoric was considered a gift, not an art, related to memory and poetic abilities, but they taught poetic devices as a *techne* ("Greek Rhetoric" 41, 48). Edward Schiappa argued that various Sophists, such as Empedocles, Corax, and Protagoras, did not use the term *rhêtorikê*, representing the study of rhetoric as a discrete field focused on persuasion (*RHÊTORIKÊ* 81). Instead the older Sophists taught an art of *logos*, a more comprehensive term that challenged the hegemony of poetic discourse and called for arguing, not telling (*RHÊTORIKÊ* 89-91). (See also Schiappa's *The Beginnings of Rhetorical Theory in Classical Greece.*) H. Marrou claimed that Protagoras's teaching was based on antilogy, which Marrou described as a practice of "low cunning" (51). Freeman stated that Gorgias taught by modeling and practice (*The Pre-Socratic Philosophers*).

Plato

In the *Phaedrus*, Plato defined the characteristics of an art and outlined a conception of rhetoric that met those standards. He compared rhetoric and medicine as arts because they both analyzed the nature of something, either the soul or the body (61); he further insisted that art entailed knowing how to apply it to appropriate situations. He believed that the art of rhetoric centered in *kairos*, knowing different kinds of souls and the appropriate time and circumstances in which to appeal to them (64). He addressed the issue of the development of the rhetor, referring to rhetoric as engaging nature, knowledge, practice and stargazing (60).

Interpretations differ, however, on Plato's conception of a rhetorical art—as the following examples illustrate. Charles Griswold traced Plato's descriptions of rhetoric as being either artful or lacking it, pointing out that Socrates views *techne* as "an intellectual procedure [. . .] that involves a determinate series of steps [. . .] that operates on complexes of elements via division and collection, that is a means to a goal, and that is teachable" (160). For Plato, according to Griswold, *techne* accomplishes part of the complex task of inducing souls to think (167). He further explained that for Plato, "opinion unravels its intuitions unreflectively; *techne* grapples with them and imposes an order, and dialectic forces reflection on them by means of questions" (176). Griswold also pointed out that Plato saw natural ability, episteme, and practice as operative in rhetorical activity (183). David Roochnik argued that the conventional view of Plato that links *techne* with moral knowledge needs to be modified because wisdom cannot be rendered by a *techne* ("Is Rhetoric an Art?"). Atwill argued that Plato separates *logos* from *techne*, "redefining knowledge in terms of subject matter and making *techne* equivalent to social function" (*Rhetoric* 126-27). She explained that in contrast to any sense of knowledge as production, Platonic knowledge is a process of recollection. In Plato's view, art defines one's function, determining one's place in the hierarchy of the state (*Rhetoric Reclaimed* 130).

Aristotle

Aristotle offered a more extensive treatment of art and rhetoric. At the beginning of his treatise on rhetoric, he defined an art as a path based on observations of the "cause why some succeed by habit and others accidentally, and all would at once agree that such observation is the activity of an art [tekhnē]" (1354a). An art, then, for Aristotle, entailed knowledge of effective rhetorical strategies and provided a guide for rhetorical action. Scholars have offered different interpretations of Aristotle's concept of an art, as the examples of scholarship below reveal. E. M. Cope described Aristotle's notion of an art as a process of generalizing from particulars, which provides knowledge of causes, and gives us the power to teach what we know. Cope commented that even though a skill derived from experience may be more useful than an art, that skill is always tied to the particular and acquired by mere repetition. But the master craftsman is wiser than the handicraftsman because he knows why and therefore can teach others (14ff). Cope went on to characterize Aristotle's view of an art as systematic, rational, governed by rules derived from experience, guided by general principles, whose end is act, practice, and the production of a concrete work. Aristotle's art, in his view, was two-fold, a power of mind and a body of principles. Gerard Hauser described Aristotle's conception of rhetoric as an art in terms of "a habit of mind which realizes a capacity to find what in each particular case has the potential to gain accedence ("Most Significant" 14). William Grimaldi explained that Aristotle contrasts art with spontaneity and habit, calling art instead a reasoned method, a path. The principles in an art must be capable of being taught (*Studies*). The artist knows causes, having an established capacity for making, conjoined with true reasoning. J. Dunne distinguished between *technai* that contrive through strategy and talent to bring about a desired outcome and *technai* that work on stable materials in a straightforward process of fabrication. Atwill in *Rhetoric Reclaimed* demonstrated that of Aristotle's three kinds of knowledge (theoretical or *episteme*, practical or *phronesis,* and productive or *techne*), historical interpretations of Aristotle's rhetoric have ignored productive knowledge, situating his rhetoric in a theory/practice binary. She explained that those who have interpreted Aristotle's rhetoric as theoretical (e.g., Grimaldi) relate rhetoric to philosophy; those who ally it with practical knowledge (Cope and Kennedy) treat it within a handbook tradition or a statesman/orator tradition. In contrast, she argued that

Aristotle considered rhetoric productive knowledge so that rhetoric could neither authorize itself as knowledge for its own sake nor be the instrument of a specific social and political objective. Rhetoric as *techne* for Aristotle, then, she explained, is situated wherever values are in conflict, is assessed according to competing situational demands, is epistemologically and ethically indeterminate, depends on the situation and time, and can never be a private possession. Aristotle's notion of productive knowledge, she concluded, is concerned with contingent and socially useful knowledge, originating in the artist, allowing for critique, directed toward the user, and requiring an active use by the receiver.

Roman Discussions of Inventional Pedagogy

Roman rhetoricians paid less attention to the nature and purpose of art but continued to address the issue of what was most important in the education of a rhetor: art, talent, imitation, or practice. *Rhetorica ad Herennium*, a practical treatise with little theoretical commentary, offered succinct directives for the student, reducing art to "a set of rules" that provided a method to follow. In *De Oratore* Cicero assumed the existence of an art and devoted more attention to the relative contribution of talent or practice in the development of the ideal rhetor. Quintilian sketched a history of points of view on rhetoric as an art, including a history of *status*. None of these rhetoricians provided original theories of an art or of inventional pedagogies.

Rhetorica ad Herennium

The author of *Rhetorica ad Herennium* made only passing references to the notion of art: "To avoid prolixity, I shall now begin my discussion of the subject, as soon as I have given you this one injunction: Theory [in Latin *artem*] without continuous practice in speaking is of little avail; from this you may understand that the precepts of theory here offered ought to be applied in practice" (5). Later he commented "All these faculties [invention, arrangement, style, memory and delivery] we can acquire by three means: Theory [art], Imitation, and Practice. By theory is meant a set of rules that provide a definite method and system of speaking. Imitation stimulates us to attain, in accordance with a studied method, the effectiveness of certain models in speaking. Practice is assiduous exercise and experience in speaking" (7-9).

In this text, inventional advice was placed under parts of a text. Thus invention's function was reduced to supplying ideas, subject matter, and arguments to flesh out the introduction, the statement of facts, and the proof or the refutation for judicial, deliberative, and epideictic discourse. The author listed directives and strategies to elaborate the point to adjudicate, the course of action to be taken, and the points of praise or censure.

Cicero

In *De Oratore*, Crassus and Antonius discussed the relative merits of talent, art, imitation, and practice in the development of the ideal orator. Crassus referred to rhetoric as an art of how men of skill have performed, one that gives coherence to widely scattered practices (32-39). He held that art is the offspring of eloquence and that it made talented orators even better. Crassus agreed that there is a single art teachable to all but that different users of the art must adapt it. He gave priority, however, to natural ability, the talent to be swift in invention, copious in exposition, and steadfast in recollection (34). To practice he accorded some benefit if done in genuine situations (45-46), but he was cautious about the value of imitation, preferring the use of freer translations of the best Greek orators (43). Antonius was ambivalent about the value of art, claiming in one place that oratory derives distinction from ability but owes little to art (89-91). He stated that nature comes first but did acknowledge that rhetoric resembles an art of observing the causes why some speak better than others and that artful direction may be given to move feelings and gain favor (91). He explained that there are three requisites for finding arguments: genius, method (art), and diligence (123) and also recognized the value of imitation and frequent and laborious exercise (107-9). It is understandable that both Crassus and Antonius, at the pinnacles of their careers as great orators, would foreground ability and downplay art, even though throughout the text they evidenced knowledge of most of the strategies of the art.

Quintilian later said that Antonius concealed his art, emphasizing that his performance was a knack derived form experience. Examples of other scholars who weighed in on this issue include George Kennedy, who asserted that Cicero makes too much of the inadequacy of rules in the light of the debt of many portions of his text to rhetorical theory (*The Art of Rhetoric*). Thomas Sloane characterized Crassus as advocating extensive learning combined with practical experience while Antonius emphasizes practice in technique ("Reinventing"). Michael Leff maintained that Cicero taught "less by abstract dicta and more by example," that he instructed by *imitatio*, and that readers grasped the principles in a text and reconstructed them in production of another text ("Topics" 119). In other words, according to Leff, *De Oratore* is not a rhetorical textbook but instructs by being what it cannot explain. In "Genre and Paradox in the Second Book of *De Oratore*," he argued that Cicero struggles with "the opposition between a perspective grounded in practice and a perspective oriented toward the abstract principles that define rhetoric as a coherent realm of experience" (308). Leff maintained that Cicero's effort becomes "intelligible as part of a subtle effort to balance conflicting theoretical principles within a single ironic structure" (309). Conversely, Brady Gilleland argued that in all of Cicero's works it is assumed that the orator must know rhetorical principles. These different positions and those on Quintilian illustrate but do not exhaust the interpretations on these issues.

Quintilian

In *Institutio Oratoria*, Quintilian defined art as a power reaching its end by a definite path, that is, by ordered methods. He traced the history of the debate about whether rhetoric is an art, citing several criteria for an art and showing that rhetoric met them:

Criteria	Rhetoric
Arts have their own subject matter.	Rhetoric has its subject matter.
No art acquiesces in false opinions.	The orator deceives others not himself.
Every art has a definite goal.	Rhetoric has a definite goal: the art and artist are independent of the results and the action of speaking well, not results, is the goal.
Artists know when they have attained the end.	Speakers also know when they have reached the end.
No art uses vices to serve its end.	As long as the motive is good, it's all right.
Orators speak indifferently on both sides.	Rhetors reach more or less probability.

Criteria	Rhetoric
Art deals with the known.	Nothing is certain; the reasonable is what is important. (2.17.16-67)

On the question of whether eloquence derives from nature or education, Quintilian said that the ideal orator must have both (2.19.2): "The average orator owes most to nature, while the perfect orator owes more to education" (2.19.2). He went on to assert: "Without natural gifts, technical rules are useless" (1.Pr. 26), but natural gifts are of "no profit in themselves unless cultivated by skillful teaching, persistent study, and continuous and extensive practice" (1.Pr. 27)). He also stated that "everything which art has brought to perfection originated in nature" (2.17.9). He warned, however, that the topics are a dumb science without practice, self-control, and nature (5.10.119).

Scholars have commented on Quintilian's views of art and pedagogy. Important examples include Kennedy, who explained that Quintilian so valued the concept of rhetoric as an art that he used it as a structural principle in *Institutio*, dividing the text into *ars* (art), *artifex* (artist), and *opus* (work) (*The Art of Rhetoric*). Michael Winterbottom recounted that Quintilian criticized those who relied solely on talent, saying ironically: they are eloquent "without work, without method and without discipline" ("Quintilian" 95). David Roochnik argued that Quintilian offered an extended defense of rhetoric as an art. He wondered whether Quintilian viewed rhetoric as "a stochastic *techne*, a set of informal and flexible rules of thumb" rather than of mechanical or systematic rules" ("Is Rhetoric an Art?" 145). James Murphy described how Quintilian prescribed methods for students to learn the art (e.g., memorizing the topics) and to engage in imitation using a seven-step process ("Roman Writing" 41-68). Jonathan Barnes in "Is Rhetoric an Art?" examined four texts on this question: Quintilian's *Institutio*, Sextus Empiricus's *Against the Mathematicians*, Cicero's *De Oratore*, and Phildemus's *Rhetorica*. He agreed with Sextus and Philodemus's arguments that rhetoric is not an art.

Elaine Fantham focused on the role of nature in Quintilian's pedagogy, pointing to four themes in Quintilian's treatment of nature:

1) the relative contributions of nature and art (both theory and training) to the orator's excellence

2) the apparent oppositions between nature and imitation (also part of training)

3) the natural origin of artistic expression in society and the individual

4) the varying roles of externalized nature in prescribing the thought (inventio) and empowering the expression (elocutio) of artistic eloquence. (127)

She argued that Quintilian was uncertain whether eloquence or moral virtue was natural, that is, imparted by nature unaided by education. In Book XII, she found Quintilian holding as axiomatic that "both natural eloquence and natural virtue need professional support [. . .] people need both *doctrina*, theory, and discipline to develop their character and *doctrina* for their intellectual development" (126). Conversely, she pointed to a number of allusions to externalized Nature as the agent directing acts of invention and disposition. She concluded by saying that in the end Quintilian "has vindicated the idea of human nature as the full potential of humanity, and externalized Nature as our ally in developing art. Nature is revealed as the efficient cause of artistic eloquence and the patroness of the *Institutio*" (136).

Review: Roman Inventional Pedagogy

During the Roman period, *Rhetorica ad Herennium* served as the main textbook of rhetorical strategies, including *status*, topics, and enthymeme. Instead of representing these guides as transferable strategies across types of discourse and as sets of alternative perspectives, the anonymous author presented them as rules to follow, positioned under the parts of the discourse, and geared to only one type of discourse, thus limiting their flexibility and epistemic power. Cicero, however, in *De Oratore*, referred to them as more generic strategies but somewhat ambiguously reduced their importance in the development of the ideal orator. Quintilian offered many artistic precepts: common and special topics, *status*, the enthymeme, the example, and the epicheireme. By positioning these guides under types of discourse, however, he restricted their applicability and generative power.

Inventional Pedagogy in the Second
Sophistic and Medieval Periods

During these two long periods, discussions about the development of rhetorical powers, especially invention, were minimal. Instead rhetorical instruction focused more on style because epideictic or ceremonial rhetoric prevailed. Rhetoric continued to be taught in the Greek ephebia. With the spread of Christianity, rhetoricians struggled with the relationship between faith, divine truth, and rhetorical probability. During the long medieval period when instruction in writing was often limited to the clergy, efforts were made to preserve and teach some classical rhetorical theories and practices in what medieval scholars call "encyclopedic" form. Texts were also written to guide minimal inventional practices for new rhetorical genres (letter writing, preaching, and poetry). Scholars paid little attention to the issue of the relative effectiveness of talent, art, imitation, and practice in developing a rhetor.

Second Sophistic Period

In the second sophistic period (around the second century CE to the fall of Rome in 410 in the West and to the sixth century CE in the East), the Roman empire dominated the education of a vast political domain. The pedagogical issues discussed in the classical periods above did not preoccupy rhetoricians even though the teaching of rhetoric crowned the education that young men received in the Roman Empire's *ephebia*, a required two-year military and rhetorical training through which they were prepared for participation in the Empire. Epideictic discourse flourished while deliberative and even judicial discourse withered under imperial rule, despite the fact that some emperors were patrons of rhetoric (Enos, "The Effects"). Discussions of the art of invention were marginalized in the face of an increasing emphasis on written style, narration, personal discourse, and literature (see *letteraturizzazione*, Kennedy, *Classical Rhetoric* 5). Later in this period, rhetorical teachers such as Tertullian, Origen, John Chrysostom, Jerome, Cyprian, Ambrose, and Augustine focused more on the issue of how to reconcile rhetoric with Christianity than on how to teach invention.

A predominant pedagogy during this time was the progymnasmata, graduated exercises for writing different types of discourse that relied heavily on models. These exercises were based on the work of Hermogenes of Tarsus, who recorded an already stereotyped system of techniques, and Aphthonius, who later worked out examples. Students learned to write types of discourse in a developmental sequence of exercises ranging from the fable and proverb to the declamation. Such instruction focused on analyzing, memorizing, imitating models, and recreating these types of discourse, rather than using *status* (deciding what was at issue) and the topics (exploring alternative arguments and subject matters). Yet John Hagaman argued that the progymnasmata, taken as a whole, was a general heuristic (a structured yet flexible system) that engaged students in viewing their subjects from multiple perspectives, progressing from concrete to abstract tasks in various rhetorical situations ("Modern Use"). Frank D'Angelo also claimed that this pedagogy introduced writers to a genuine rhetorical understanding of invention, providing a bridge to real world practices (*Composition* 1). This teaching curriculum remained strong through the Renaissance.

Medieval Period

During the long medieval period, the encyclopedic treatises discussed in Part I occasionally mentioned pedagogy. Boethius referred to rhetoric as a faculty ("An Overview" 70) and Isidore of Seville mentioned the importance of natural ability, training, practice, and studied eloquence in preparing a rhetor (81): "Nature furnishes the bent; training, the knowledge; and practice, the skill" (81). Richard McKeon made an interesting distinction between two medieval tendencies: 1) the tendency to "intellectualize the art and change its orientation to subject matter and its peculiarities into problems of inquiry and understanding" and 2) the tendency to emphasize the orator, "morals and eloquence, concerning the relation of art and wisdom, and concerning the definition of rhetoric as a virtue or an art or a discipline" ("Rhetoric in the Middle Ages" 189). These differences bear some resemblance to the contrasts made between art and knack today (Young, "Arts").

Inventional Pedagogy from the Renaissance
through the Nineteenth Century

After a brief resurgence of classical invention in the Renaissance as
discussed in Part I, a major trend in these periods was the gradual
elimination of the art of invention from rhetorical education.

Renaissance

In the Renaissance, rhetorical pedagogy split into two directions: one
continued the Aristotelian view of art and its importance for education; the other banished invention from rhetoric altogether. Thomas
Wilson's *Art of Rhetoric* extended the classical tradition of combining
art or knowledge, wit and aptness (talent), practice, and the use of
models in the education of a rhetor. Having written the first complete rhetorical treatise in English, Wilson obviously foregrounded art
or *techne*. Russell Wagner commented that Wilson considered an art
to be principles derived from effective speakers in real situations, a
programmatic, dynamic body of principles. Sister Miriam Joseph in
Rhetoric in Shakespeare's Time explained that the "Elizabethan literary
critics and poets, not less than the rhetoricians and logicians, insisted
on the importance of precepts and theory in the creation of literature"
(5). She pointed out that "a lack of art was regarded as intolerable by
Thomas Nashe who said, "Nothing is more odious to the Auditor then
the artlesse tongue of a tedious dolt" (6). She went on to say that a
"thorough training in the arts of language was the fundamental aim of
the grammar schools of Tudor England" (8). Richard Rainholde in his
rhetorical treatise also commented that "art supplements and perfects
the gifts of nature" (6). Don Abbott contended that the major process
for composing themes in the Grammar school was to gather material
for imitation. Ray Nadeau translated the work of Thomas Farnaby,
who discussed the role of practice in Renaissance education, saying:
"The first requisites of Nature and the details of the Art have been
explained. There remains the aids of Practice, without which the other
two attributes rush hither and yon and are helpless" ("A Renaissance"
172).

   In contrast, Peter Ramus, after transferring the art of invention to
logic, developed a "method" for teaching all subjects, a multipurpose
pedagogy entailing an invariant movement from the general to the
specific followed by the use of definition and then by divisions and

examples. Albert Duhamel called this method formulaic and argued that it confused the arts of teaching and performing ("The Logic"). Fr. Walter Ong said that Ramus emphasized the analysis of models in order to find something to say (*Rhetoric, Romance*). In *Ramus, Method and the Decay of Dialogue*, he commented: "Ramus persists here in regarding the order of teaching, and through this, all intellectual order, as reducible by rough analogy to some simple spatial arrangement or rearrangement of intellectual atoms" (247). This method, devoid of any notion of art or natural ability or invention, had widespread influence.

Mary Astell advocated imitation as the primary means of learning to speak and write well (Donawerth, *Rhetorical Theory* 101). She also claimed that

> As nature teaches us logic, so does it instruct us in rhetoric much better than rules of art, which, if they are good ones are nothing else but those judicious observations which men of sense have drawn from nature, and which all who reflect on the operations of their own minds will find themselves. The common precepts of rhetoric may teach us how to reduce the ingenious ways of speaking to a certain rule, but they do not teach us how to invent them; this is nature's best work and she does it best. (Astell 102)

Anticipating faculty psychology, she wrote that the great secret of writing is a just proportion so that the reader's "understanding is enlightened, his affections subdued, and his will duly regulated" (Astell 104).

Eighteenth Century

In the eighteenth century, Hugh Blair foregrounded natural ability in the development of eloquence. "Whether nature or art contribute most to form the orator is a trifling inquiry. In all attainments whatever, nature must be the prime agent" (129). For such development he credited five means of improvement: personal character and disposition, a fund of knowledge, the habit of application and industry, attention to the best models, and frequent exercise in composing." He recommended a strong, lively, and warm imagination; quick sensibility of heart, joined with solid judgment, good sense, and presence of mind; all improved by great and long attention to style and composition" (128). Vincent Bevilacqua explained that Blair's philosophical assumptions were that rhetoric originates in various natural senses and powers of the mind and the improvement of rhetoric entails improvement in the mind (Philosophical Assumptions").

George Campbell in *Philosophy of Rhetoric* spoke of rhetoric as an art that was first developed by the methodization of the natural persuasive abilities of people, then the perfection of the rules of art, and finally the move to general principles. As the art matured, so did the inventional aspect of rhetoric. Campbell paradoxically described a pedagogy that entailed common sense as validated by intuition, scientific inquiry, and moral reasoning based on experience, analogy, testimony, and calculations of chance. This empirical turn also affected American rhetorical education. Michael Halloran pointed out that in the eighteenth century in American colleges "topical invention and deductive argument were de-emphasized, under the influence of the new empirical philosophy" ("From Rhetoric to Composition" 155).

Nineteenth-Century Britain

In nineteenth-century Britain, Richard Whately in *Elements of Rhetoric* returned to what he called the Aristotelian rules drawn from the invariable practice of all (289). He commented that practitioners in his day hid their art (286). Responding to arguments against art, he qualified his view, saying that art could not equalize men of different abilities and that a system should not be judged according to learners (287). He remarked that the general view of his day was that a natural gift and practice, not art, were involved in the development of a writer (287). But he countered by calling rhetoric "'the Art of Composition'—such 'rules as *every* good Composition must conform to' whether the author of it had them in his mind or not" (289). He went on to say, however, that the rules should be constructed on broad philosophical principles. He also commended practice, the use of real occasions and interesting subjects. He advised students to fashion exercises out of their current experiences as opposed to earlier uses of Latin epigrams, recommending that they outline before composing and outline the compositions of others. Whately's *Elements* was widely used as a writing textbook in American colleges in the middle decades of the nineteenth century. James Berlin argued that Whately contributed to current-traditional rhetoric by substituting an invention of management for the invention of classical rhetoric ("Richard Whately" 14). Thus, Whately valued art but a very different one from classical rhetoric.

Nineteenth-Century United States

In the United States, John Genung in an influential textbook, *Practical Elements of Rhetoric,* developed his own version of invention, defining it as finding material by thought and observation, testing that material, and ordering it. He deemed finding material the least invaded by rules and dependent on the peculiar direction of the writer's mind (217-19). He spoke of the inventive attitude that entailed grasping connections between ideas and seeing their power over others. He also asserted that the mark of the inventive mind was an aptitude to discern literary capacities in a subject and a native endowment of imagination to choose effective facts and group them in interesting combinations (221). He also differentiated between originative invention, reproductive invention, and methodizing invention (223-24). Genung's inventional strategies were designed to work within the modes of discourse: description, narrative, exposition, and argumentation. Berlin in *Writing Instruction in Nineteenth-Century American Colleges* argued that textbooks in the nineteenth century presented invention as a managerial process that placed discovery outside the purview of the composing process. Invention was devoted to ways to impact the audience and the faculty being addressed, giving way to an emphasis on genre, form, and arrangement.

In 1888, Sara Lockwood in *Lessons in English* taught invention based on Pestalozzi's work on the importance of children learning from direct observation of objects and personal experience and identified writing topics that came from these "collections of information" (Donawerth, *Rhetorical Theory* 223). Lockwood also maintained that for students between ages fourteen and sixteen composition should be limited to the reproduction of thought and should concentrate on practice, observation, and the paraphrasing of models (Larson 231-32). Older students could begin to invent thought for themselves by exercising the imagination, collecting material, jotting down notes about their thoughts, and consulting authorities without copying their words (Lockwood 236). In 1904, Mary Augusta Jordan published *Correct Speaking and Writing*, arguing that writing correctly (including all aspects of writing) depends on personal and social virtues. She maintained that to write correctly students must think, feel, and act correctly (312). She also advocated literary models for letter writing (315).

Women's Rhetorical Education

In "Women's Reclamation of Rhetoric in Nineteenth-Century America," Robert Connors recounted that with the introduction of women to colleges the male "agonistic rhetorical culture was swept away, and rhetoric itself was changed forever" (74). One result of this change was that oral rhetoric declined and writing ascended, with the women at first only being taught analytic rhetoric. He explained that argument courses slowly gave way to "multimodal" courses that included different types of discourse and that topics changed from abstract to concrete and to personal writing, which had been associated with women. Suzanne Bordelon, writing about Gertrude Buck's rhetoric courses, described how Buck's course in argumentative writing drew on her social Christianity, functional psychology, and progressive realism. It rejected faculty psychology and emphasized the dialectic process, inductive learning from experience and practice, and student interests. Rebecca Burke wrote that one of the three essentials in Gertrude Buck's writing texts was the necessity of a real motive for writing, a desire to communicate. In Buck's teaching of narration, according to Burke, she emphasized finding suitable matter and fixing a point of view by using exercises before the actual writing act. In teaching argumentation, she engaged students in finding "the reasoning in their own and others' thoughts" (16), using exercises to help them analyze arguments.

Vicki Ricks described the writing program at Vassar which encouraged women to develop reflective, creative, and critical thinking. She also described Radcliffe's program, which required women to write their "daily themes." Sue Carter Simmons also explained that at Radcliffe during the last quarter of the nineteenth century, women were required to take a first-year writing course, to write several long papers, and to listen to lectures on style. They could also take an advanced writing course with its daily themes. Sandra Harmon described the curriculum at Illinois Normal College as requiring two final writing projects: a paper discussing the Geology, Botany or Natural History of the region in which the student lived and a paper as a graduation theme. None of these commentators referred to teaching or learning an art of invention.

Current-Traditional Pedagogy

The above pedagogies hardened into what Daniel Fogarty called the "current-traditional paradigm" that governed composition instruction in the first half of the twentieth century and still is prevalent today. Several composition theorists in the 1960s described this paradigm. Richard Young identified its overt features as an "emphasis on the composed product rather than the composing process; the analysis of discourse into words, sentences, and paragraphs; the classification of discourse into description, narration, exposition, and argument; the strong concern with usage (syntax, spelling, punctuation) and with style (economy, clarity, emphasis); the preoccupation with the informal essay and the research paper and so on" ("Paradigms" 31). Young claimed that vitalism, with its stress on the natural powers of the mind and the uniqueness of the creative act, led to a repudiation of the possibility of teaching the composing process, hence the tendency of current-traditional rhetoric to become a critical study of the products of composing and an art of editing. He maintained that vitalist assumptions become the most apparent when one considers what was excluded from the present discipline that had earlier been included, the most obvious and significant being the art of invention ("Paradigms" 31). Albert Kitzhaber noted that at this time studying literature was considered the best way to improve writing ability and that teachers considered the principles of rhetoric to be barren formulas. He also pointed out that in the early to mid-twentieth century the large numbers of students who were enrolled in college necessitated simple dogmatic texts, in which invention was often displaced by lists of topics (subject matters) or titles for papers.

Sharon Crowley referred to the current-traditional paradigm as "full frontal teaching; students don't perform; teachers do" (*Methodical Memory* 147). She described the pedagogy in these terms:

> In the current traditional classroom, teachers required students to read the textbooks they assigned; they lectured about the prescriptions given in the textbooks; they analyzed finished essays to show how their authors had adhered to textbook prescriptions; and they asked students to complete textbook exercises about grammar, diction, and style. Almost never did they

> model the writing process for students; almost never
> did students actually write in class. (147)

The model collapsed the composing process into a neat linear progression of select, narrow, and amplify. Crowley pointed out that the most common assignment was to choose a topic (a subject to write on) from a list, construct a thesis, develop support, organize your ideas, and draft the essay. This pedagogy. she contended, "substitutes discussion of current-traditional arcana for the writing process" (148). Berlin and Robert Inkster analyzed the epistemology of this paradigm, focusing on the ways it constrained the writer and ignored audience. They explained that it foreclosed heuristic processes by failing to discriminate among heuristic, algorithmic and aleatory processes (3). They pointed out that the paradigm was dominated by two polar positions about what should and could be taught in the composition course: those who would teach composition as stylistic correctness or facility and those who would teach composing as an act of genius (13). They went on to say that "Both ignore the problematic character of knowledge and meaning, and hence, of discourse. To view composition as a complex heuristic procedure is to acknowledge—even to embrace—the assumption that knowledge and meaning are tentative, problematic, elusive, and partial" (13).

Review: Pedagogy from the Renaissance through the Nineteenth Century

During these periods, aside from the resurgence and adaptation of classical invention in vernacular Renaissance rhetorics, many treatises gave only lip service to the art of rhetorical invention, placing the onus of creation and discovery on processes outside of rhetoric: intuition, imagination, logic, and scientific inquiry. Genung's textbook did outline modal inventional questions for description, narration, argument, and exposition while Gertrude Buck applied psychology to the study of invention. After the Renaissance, authors placed natural gifts, imitation, practice and art in descending order of importance for teaching students to write.

4

Issues over the Nature, Purpose, and Epistemology of Rhetorical Invention in the Twentieth Century

In the first part of the twentieth century, the dormant state of invention and rhetoric as a whole was manifest in English Studies where literature had eclipsed rhetoric and in the academy at large where philosophy monopolized invention. With rhetoric's loss of life and respect came the loss of power. By the mid-twentieth century, philosophy held sway over the study of reasoning, restricting it to formal logic, even symbolic logic. The study of rhetoric became largely the province of the field of Communication. English Studies held sovereignty over the teaching of written discourse but studied only literary discourse. Within this rhetorical void in English Studies, interest in invention began to emerge in the 1960s. This chapter chronicles that reemergence.

The first part of the chapter will outline some interdisciplinary intellectual developments in the first half of the twentieth century that created a context for the renewal of interest in invention. The chapter will then feature statements of members of English departments who began calling attention to the lack of invention within their departments, demonstrating the vacuum that existed before invention's renewal. That will be followed by early calls for the reinstatement of invention in composition theory and practice. These voices helped to open a path and establish a need for scholarship and pedagogy for invention. The main thrust of the chapter will be to examine inventional

work in Rhetoric and Composition, Communication, and other fields
since the mid-twentieth century.

Interdisciplinary Contexts for the Revival of Invention

During the first six decades of the twentieth century, a wide array of
interdisciplinary scholarship helped to construct an intellectual context for the revival of rhetorical invention. In different fields, scholars began challenging Cartesian epistemology, formal logic, notions
of certainty, discourse as its own end, and decontextualized views of
language and interpretation. While I cannot undertake here an extensive discussion of this work, I will point to some of the theorists whose
work influenced early developments in rhetorical invention.

Philosophical Studies

Two important theorists of this era whom Daniel Fogarty cites in his
influential book, *Roots for a New Rhetoric*, were Kenneth Burke and
I. A. Richards. In the 1940s and 1950s, Kenneth Burke advanced a
number of seminal concepts and theories that impacted work on invention, including *dramatism* (language as symbolic action), the view
that language is primarily a mode of action rather than a mode of
knowledge. In "The Five Master Terms," he proposed the pentad as a
strategy for interpreting the motivation for action in texts. The pentad had five interpretive terms: *Act* (what was the action?), *Agency* (by
what means did it occur?), *Agent* (by whom was it done?), *Scene* (where
did it occur?) *and Purpose* (why did it occur?). Burke also stressed the
ratios between terms, that is, interpreting one term in the light of the
other: for example, the ennobling of a person by an act of heroism
(Agent-Act) or the impact of poverty on the use of riots as a means of
improvement (Scene-Agency). He later added a sixth term, *Attitude*
(one's general view of life and its bearing on action) as another central
factor explaining motivation. In contrast to new criticism's analytic
method, the pentad was intended to help readers analyze motives and
symbolic acts in their fullest contexts. Although Burke intended the
pentad for interpretive purposes, he later acknowledged its heuristic
(generative) viability and stressed the importance of using the pentad
in its *circumference*, the overall scene in which human action is discussed (e.g., the rhetorical situation or cultural context) ("Questions").
Burke's definition of rhetoric as "the use of language as a symbolic

means of inducing cooperation in beings that by nature respond to symbols" (*A Rhetoric of Motives* 43) posited that one of the purposes of language is social cohesion. He also stressed the terms *consubstantiality* or *identification*, by which the rhetor articulates shared experience, imagery, and values.

In the 1930s, I. A. Richards in *The Philosophy of Rhetoric* introduced a conception of rhetoric as the study of verbal understanding and misunderstanding and its remedies, building on a contextual basis of meaning. He argued that language is the means of understanding thought, both forming and formative, and he advanced other perspectives that later would inform the work of some composition theorists, including the notions of ambiguity as the highest thought, of messages in context, and of the power of metaphor to improve understanding and language use. He also discussed the construction of meaning as interpretive choices guided by purposes.

In 1956, Bernard Lonergan, in *Insight: A Study of Human Understanding*, defined the process of inquiry as a quest for the discovery of insight, as an act of grasping the unity of data, of finding a point of significance, and of reaching new understanding. He argued that insight comes unexpectedly as a release to the tension of inquiry and is a function of inner conditions (3-6). Those inner conditions include a heuristic structure: "Prior to the understanding that issues in answers, there are the questions that anticipate answers; [. . .] A heuristic notion, then, is the notion of an unknown content and is determined by anticipating the type of act through which the unknown would become known" (392). This study, along with G. Wallas's *The Art of Thought*, informed some inventional theories that framed writing as a process of inquiry.

In 1958, Michael Polanyi, in *Personal Knowledge* and later in *The Tacit Dimension*, discussed tacit and focal knowledge in the act of inquiry and developed an epistemology of personal knowledge. Maintaining that tacit knowledge undergirds all explicit knowledge, he argued that scientific communities have beliefs and values to which the inquirer must appeal. He also discussed the importance of heuristic action among members of an interpretive community.

In 1965, Maurice Natanson and Henry Johnstone published a collection of essays, *Philosophy, Rhetoric, and Argumentation*, in which a number of contributors characterized invention as the source of rhetoric's vitality. Hoyt Hudson asserted that the loss of invention in rheto-

ric occurred in any period when "subject-matter was conventionalized,
[. . .] the tendency to depend upon tradition or convention for material
and devote oneself wholly to style in writing and delivery in speaking"
(30). In the same volume Donald Bryant lamented that invention had
been removed from its rightful province and placed in the realm of the
sciences. He went on to call rhetoric "the rationale of informative and
suasory discourse" ("Rhetoric" 36), operating chiefly in the areas of
the contingent, whose aim is maximum probability (39). In another
essay in this collection, Albert Duhamel offered a view of the shifting
purposes of invention throughout history. He contended that in the
medieval period systems of invention for the discovery of arguments
were transferred to medieval logics, "where they appear as means of
discovering the sense in which terms are to be understood" ("Function" 81). He noted that in this period they sought to "express more
effectively the truth already possessed" (81). He further explained that
invention disappears in a period which is "convinced that truth is safe-
ly within its grasp" or not worth worrying about (82).

In 1969, Stephen Toulmin, in the *Uses of Argument*, challenged the
dominance of formal logic, questioning the validity of formal or analytic reasoning and theorizing informal or substantive reasoning. He
argued that the two could only be distinguished by looking at the nature of the problem under investigation and the manner in which the
warrants were established, insisting that validity rests in the backing of
the warrants (135-43). Claiming that analytic arguments were either
quite rare or often mere tautologies, he maintained that informal or
substantive arguments account for the most frequently used kinds of
reasoning, which occur in real languages and situations of probability
where the backing for the warrants is field dependent. Although he
did not refer to rhetoric, Toulmin was in fact talking about rhetorical
reasoning, a fact that was not lost on those interested in rhetoric.

Also in 1969, Chaim Perelman and Madame Olbrechts-Tyteca
published *The New Rhetoric,* the result of a study conducted to investigate the kinds of reasoning that were done in fields like law. Motivated by a gap in their education that had introduced them only to
analytic and scientific reasoning, they attempted to catalog, define,
and illustrate the kinds of arguments used in areas of the probable,
grouping them as arguments in the form of liaisons (quasi-logical arguments, arguments based on the structure of the real, and arguments
to establish the structure of the real) and arguments in the form of

dissociation. Their enterprise was similar to Aristotle's in that it catalogued prominent arguments of the day, illustrating them with current
examples. In other words, they were interested in rhetorical invention.
In a later shorter version of this work, *The Realm of Rhetoric*, Perelman
castigated Ramus for eliminating the distinction between analytic and
dialectical reasoning: "It is in relation to this distinction that we can
see how the innovation introduced by Peter Ramus turned out to be
an error that was fatal for rhetoric" (3), depriving rhetoric of its two
essential elements, invention and disposition. Ramus thought to cram
the teaching and theorizing of all types of knowledge into one—analytic knowledge or logic. This over-simplification deprived rhetoric of
its own kind of knowledge, probable audience-based knowledge, and
made it dependent on logic for its inventional functions. Max Loreau
stated at the time that the objective of Perelman and Olbrechts-Tyteca's work was "to produce an instrument capable of achieving in the
realm of values results exactly analogous to those pursued by analogical reasoning in the domain of the exact sciences" (456). Henry Johnstone characterized Perelman's work as "exploring the principles and
important ramifications of the art of allaying philosophical doubts
and hesitations" ("New Theory" 127). Although Perelman and Olbrechts-Tyteca's as well as Toulmin's theories fell outside the parameters
of philosophy's disciplinary power structure, their work influenced developing theories of rhetorical invention.

In "The Methods of Rhetoric and Philosophy," Richard McKeon,
speaking of the historical functions of rhetoric, said that invention was
"the art of discovering new arguments and uncovering new things by
argument," while judgment was "the art of testing arguments, prov-
ing conclusions, and verifying statements" (*Rhetoric* 59). He stated:
"method is needed in invention to define the question and to order the
data pertinent to it" (59).

The above philosophical works called attention to probable reasoning, inquiry in terms of field-dependent and audience-based argument, the importance of values and beliefs in knowledge construction,
and language as motivated action. Because these concepts were essentially rhetorical, they stimulated people in English who were beginning to study invention.

Semiotics and Tagmemic Linguistics

In the 1930s and 1940s, Charles Morris and others, drawing from the work of Charles Sanders Peirce, developed theories of semiotics (signs). Some of their tenets included the idea that signs cannot contain definite meanings; that there are three kinds of signs: the icon (e.g., photograph), the index (depending on associate relationships), and the symbol (depending on social and cultural conventions); and that signs have three parts—the sign, the object, and the interpretant. Peirce had also developed a new trivium: Speculative Grammar, Critical Logic, and Speculative Rhetoric. Charles Morris spoke of the aims of discourse as informative, valuative, incitive, and systematic. Semiotics formed a basis for the work of James Kinneavy.

In 1964, Kenneth Pike developed tagmemic linguistics, which posited that discourse like language is fundamental to human rationality and that sentences and other aspects of discourse had to be understood in the larger context of purposes, audiences, and cultural differences. Pike claimed that certain characteristics of rationality underlay human experience: 1) units had distinctive features, range of variation, and distribution in a class, functioning in a temporal sequence or spatial array, and distributed in a dimensional system; 2) experience could be viewed from three complementary perspectives: as a particle, wave, and field; and 3) language was social behavior in a universe of discourse, with change occurring over a bridge of shared features. This theory demanded attention to the situatedness of language and the importance of the wholeness of a discourse event unlike other sentence-based linguistic theories of the time. Because tagmemic theory focused on entire discourses in their contexts and on epistemological processes of discourse production, some scholars found tagmemics of interest in the development of a modern theory of invention.

Psychological Studies

In *Thought and Language*, Russian psychologist Lev Vygotsky examined how the mind develops within a community and culture. He also posited that the ontogenetic development of children moves from the social to the individual, to inner speech as social, and that writing makes possible the higher mental functions. Based on his study of higher mental functions, he differentiated spontaneous concepts that children acquire naturally from nonspontaneous concepts learned in school. These notions would later impact theories of social invention and composition pedagogy.

In another strand of interdisciplinary research in the 1960s, the study of heuristics, psychologists and others began to investigate a new kind of thinking that was neither formal logic nor scientific induction. As Chapter 2 indicates, they considered heuristic thinking as more flexible than logic and more effective than waiting for the muse. Heuristic strategies guided conscious activity but also entailed intuition, prompting investigators to take multiple perspectives on their questions in order to break through their usual ways of thinking and to stimulate new insights and meanings. These procedures could be taught, adapted, and used in many situations. (Lauer, "Invention," "Heuristics"). G. Polya claimed that no artist could create without a good supply of heuristic methods. These features of heuristic thinking attracted the attention of some scholars in the developing field of Rhetoric and Composition who were trying to formulate inventional strategies for the creative process of writing.

Other works that had impact on studies of invention in the creative process include Jerome Bruner's *The Process of Education* and *On Knowing: Essays for the Left Hand*; Leon Festinger's *A Theory of Cognitive Dissonance*; Arthur Koestler's *The Act of Creation*; Sidney Parnes's and Eugene Brunelle's work on creativity ; William Gordon's *Synectics*; and George Miller, Eugene Gilanter, and Karl Pribram's *Plans and the Structure of Human Behavior*. Also of interest was research on cognitive and ethical development and different ways of knowing (e.g., Jean Piaget, *The Psychology of Intelligence*; William Perry, *Forms of Intellectual and Ethical Development in the College Years: A Scheme*; and Howard Gardner, *Frames of Mind*).

Literacy Studies

The development of literacy and its contrasts with orality also had an impact on composition scholars' studies of the nature of reasoning processes and on writing pedagogy. Both Eric Havelock and Fr. Walter Ong wrote extensively on this subject. In *Preface to Plato*, Havelock argued for the cognitive effects of literacy, characterizing the Greek preliterate society as transferring knowledge and cultural values uncritically through a mimetic spell in contrast to the literate period which fostered questioning, critical thinking, self-consciousness, and abstract and syllogistic thought. In *The Presence of the Word*, Fr.

Ong addressed the impact of alphabetic writing systems on thought, maintaining that writing and print became gradually interiorized into human consciousness, changing ways of thinking. He called contemporary culture a period of secondary electronic orality in which traces of primary orality and literacy mingle with secondary orality. He also discussed two kinds of commonplaces used in rhetoric: cumulative commonplaces (e.g., set phrases) and analytic commonplaces like the topics. (See also the work of Marshall McLuhan and Albert B. Lord.) Anthropological research on literacy also stimulated some inventional theorists. Jack Goody and Ian Watt examined the impact of literacy on modes of thought, work that would be followed later by the studies of A. R. Luria, and Sylvia Scribner and Michael Cole. These studies examined intellectual processes across cultures, including perception, deduction, reasoning, and imagination.

By the 1960s, many ideas from these interdisciplinary studies were circulating: insights into the processes of inquiry, creativity, and heuristic thinking, new conceptions of rhetoric, testaments to the importance of invention, understandings of informal rhetorical reasoning, and the connections between the evolution of literacy and intellectual acts.

The State of Invention at Mid-Twentieth Century

At the time of these interdisciplinary developments, English departments had largely abandoned rhetoric as a discipline, keeping only its application—the teaching of composition. Within composition teaching, invention was neglected or trivialized (James Berlin, "Richard Whately," "Transformation," and *Writing Instruction*; Richard Young, "Arts, Crafts"; and Sharon Crowley, "Invention" and *Methodical Memory*), contributing to the loss of prestige and the power of composition instructors (Susan Miller; Sue Ellen Holbrook). In 1950, James Brown reported in the *Journal of Higher Education* that the most common types of traditional Freshman English (the term at that time) were "the composition course," which was predominantly traditional grammar, and the "composition-readings course," with no inventional component. In 1957, in *College Composition and Communication*, Henry Thoma described the major influences on composition textbooks of that time—General Semantics, linguistics, and communications—with no reference to invention. In 1959 in *College Composition and*

Communication, Harold Dean's ten-year perspective on the communication course gave no treatment of invention. Charles Ferguson's book,
Say it With Words, confined preparation for writing to the unconscious
or the interview. In 1960, in *College Composition and Communication*,
Charles Hoffman traced the fluctuating influences in Freshman
English from an early concern with Western Masterpieces, through
the Communications phase in the 1940s, to the use of the reader and
masterpieces of prose in the 1950s. In 1963, Albert Kitzhaber published his study of the status of Freshman English, reporting that the
content of the standard Freshman English course was expository reading and writing or the study of literature. In 1965, Robert Gorrell provided a similar view of Freshman English at the time, representing the
same emphases: usage, general semantics, logic, language study, forms
of discourse, and literature. In 1967, Janice Lauer's search for invention in 57 composition textbooks showed that most texts incorporated
some version of the classical topics (e.g., definition, cause and effect)
but they were presented as discrete modes of organization or development not as a set of inventional strategies. A few texts helped students
to analyze their audience. No texts were self-conscious about the epistemological function of their directives. No strategies were offered to
initiate inquiry (131-33). In such a climate, there is small wonder that
in English departments composition instruction was considered an
onerous service with little stature or power, while literary studies en-
joyed the prestige and rewards of the academy. As Elbert Harrington,
Richard Young, and others have said: the status and exclusion of invention reflected the status of rhetoric: no inquiry, no discipline.

Awakening Interest in Invention

In the late 1940s and 1950s, however, points of light signaled the
reemergence of rhetorical invention. In 1949, Craig La Driére in
"Rhetoric and 'Merely Verbal' Art" argued that rhetoric had its own
kind of thinking, a rhetorical *dianoia* whose end was in the addressee
(139). In that same year, Albert Duhamel wrote that "The content of
the idea 'rhetoric' [. . .] is dependent upon the epistemology, psychology, and metaphysic of the system in which it occurs" ("Function"
345). In 1953, Manuel Bilsky, McCrea Hazlett, Robert Streeter, and
Richard Weaver in "Looking for an Argument," advocated a topical
approach to college composition. Their course at the University of

Chicago aimed at discovering relevant and effective arguments by using the topics of genus or definition, consequence, likeness and difference, and testimony and authority.

In *Roots for a New Rhetoric*, Daniel Fogarty defined rhetoric as "ways of arriving at mutual understanding among people working toward patterns of cooperative action" (4). In particular he singled out the "thought-word-thing " relationship in Richards and the General Semanticists. Instead of rhetorical invention, he used terms like the "philosophy" of composition that he forecast would characterize the new rhetoric. Also in 1959, Fr. Walter Ong published *Ramus, Method, and the Decay of Dialogue*, in which he explained Ramus's role in renouncing any possibility of invention within a speaker-auditor framework (288). See also John Brereton and Maureen Goggin for discussions of this period.

The 1960s marked a turning point for invention. Discussions of invention were woven with attempts to revive an interest in rhetoric within the academy and in particular within English Studies. At the 1961 Conference on College Composition and Communication, speakers on a panel entitled "Rhetoric—The Neglected Art" argued for the importance of rhetorical invention (Virginia Burke), while others spoke of rhetoric as an intellectual art whose core was invention. In 1962, Elbert Harrington published an important essay, "A Modern Approach to Invention," in the *Quarterly Journal of Speech*, contending that: "Most teachers know that rhetoric has always lost life and respect to the degree that invention has not had a significant and meaningful role" (373). Two years later, Dudley Bailey in "A Plea for a Modern Set of Topoi" challenged composition instructors to develop a new rhetorical invention, claiming that: "The heart of rhetoric has always been 'invention' and disposition" (115-16). In 1965, Robert Gorrell reported on a seminar on rhetoric held the prior December, organized by the executive committee of the College Composition and Communication Conference. The members were Wayne Booth, Virginia Burke, Francis Christensen, Edward Corbett, Robert Gorrell, Albert Kitzhaber, Richard Ohmann, James Squire, Richard Young, and Karl Wallace. Gorrell recounted that they had lamented the state into which rhetoric had fallen, offering as one of the reasons that "invention had become largely a matter of assigning a book of readings, presumably to provoke thought or stimulate ideas for writing" (139).

Also in 1965, numerous publications and interdisciplinary meetings were devoted to rhetoric and invention. Gorrell noted that a "small but probably significant revival of interest in rhetoric is occurring" ("Freshman Composition" 33). In that same year in the *Quarterly Journal of Speech*, Edward Corbett summarized several roots for a new rhetoric: classical rhetoric, General Semantics, linguistics, Kenneth Burke, I. A. Richards, Jerome Bruner, B. F. Skinner, Kenneth Pike, and Marshall McLuhan. Richard Hughes, in a widely read article, "The Contemporaneity of Classical Rhetoric," described rhetoric as "an art of moving an idea from embryo to reality [. . .] an art which rests not at the end of the intellectual process, but an art that lies within the process" (157). He defined invention as the "gradual evolution of a judgment out of disparate and embryonic evidence, the formulation of the realized judgment in the rhetor's own mind, and the propagating of that realized judgment in whatever structures will lead to a duplication of his discovery in the mind of his audience" (158).

In 1966, Robert Dick maintained that the topics, first, were useful not only for developing a proposition but also in arriving at one, and, second, they were not "a procrustean bed to which the subject is fitted but rather a method of analysis originating in the ontological reality of the subject" (314). In 1968, Lloyd Bitzer's "The Rhetorical Situation," published in the first issue of *Philosophy and Rhetoric*, sparked a conversation on the rhetorical situation as the exigency to initiate rhetorical processes. This conversation continued with essays by Richard Vatz, Kathleen Jamieson, and Scott Consigny. At the 1968 Conference on College Composition and Communication, the Rhetoric Society of America was founded, an organization drawing together scholars in Communication, Philosophy, English, and Linguistics. This group, with its newsletter and regular meetings, helped to build a resurgence of rhetoric and a nucleus of people interested in restoring rhetoric to English Studies.

During the 1960s, three important collections of essays appeared, that included discussions of invention: *New Rhetorics*, edited by Martin Steinmann; *Teaching Freshman Composition*, edited by Gary Tate and Edward Corbett; and *Rhetoric: Theories of Application*, edited by Robert Gorrell. Steinmann included Richard Young and Alton Becker's essay on tagmemic invention previously published in the *Harvard Educational Review*. Tate and Corbett included Robert Gorrell's article on freshman composition. Gorrell reprinted Edward Corbett's

"A Look at the Old Rhetoric,'" which asserted that "one of the reasons why there has been no major breakthrough in the formulation of a new rhetoric is that we still have not plumbed the psychology of the composition process" (17). He seconded Dudley Bailey's call for "a system of discovery that will be as sensible, as helpful, as productive as the common and special topics devised by the classical rhetoricians" (17).

All these works helped to pave a path for the development of new inventional theories for rhetoric.

Early Studies of Invention: Mid-1960s to Mid-1970s

The new theories of invention that appeared from the 1960s to the 1970s reflected diverse conceptions of the nature, purpose, and epistemology of invention that were described in Chapter 1. Some theories of invention dealt only with the exploration of subjects; others addressed the search for rational arguments to support theses. Very few treated the initiation of discourse. These theories also varied in their conceptions of the social nature of invention and the purposes for rhetorical invention, which included raising questions for inquiry, identifying points at issue, stimulating text production, generating subject matter for texts, constructing new knowledge, reaching insight, finding arguments for theses already held, interpreting texts, and investigating from different perspectives. These varying purposes often entailed different epistemologies: constructing new knowledge; locating or recalling known information, observations, experiences, and lines of reasoning; knowing oneself; leading to certainty or probability; reaching truth; or playing. This chapter showcases these points at issue among prominent inventional theories in Rhetoric and Composition and Communication from the 1960s to the present. As the discussion proceeds, most of these issues echo those in the account of rhetorical history in Chapter 3.

Rhetoric as Epistemic

A key influence on inventional research in the 1960s and early 1970s was the discussion of rhetoric as epistemic carried out largely in Communication Studies beginning in 1967 with Robert Scott's "On Viewing Rhetoric as Epistemic." Drawing on Stephen Toulmin's distinction between analytic and substantive arguments, Scott argued for the possibility of rejecting "prior and enabling truth as the epistemological basis for rhetoric" (12) and instead proclaimed: "rhetoric may be viewed not as a matter of giving effectiveness to truth but of creating it" (13). He cited Douglas Ehninger and Wayne Brockriede's descriptions of cooperative critical inquiry as asserting that truth is not prior or immutable but contingent, "a process of interaction at any given moment" (13). Rejecting the idea that one first knows the truth and then makes it effective through rhetoric, he invoked Gorgias and the sophistic *dissoi logoi* in his argument that in the face of uncertainty humans create situational truths that entail three ethical guidelines: toleration, will, and responsibility. In the following years, others such as Robert Carlton, Richard Cherwitz, Barry Brummett, Thomas Farrell, Richard Gregg, Richard Fulkerson, Charles Kneupper, and Michael Leff contributed to this conversation.

Work on probability also added to the expanding views of rhetoric's epistemology. Charles Kneupper in "Rhetoric and Probability Theory" discussed three schools of probability theory.

1. Classical Theory which framed probability as a measure of rational expectation or belief, which entailed the principle of indifference: "two possibilities are equiprobable if and only if there is no ground for choosing between them" (292).

2. Frequency Theory was a relative probability empirically derived by "observing what actually occurs and counting" (293), that is, "the proportion of occurrences of any event compared to the total possible occurrences" (i.e., what happens) (293).

3. Logical Implication Theory was based on logical analysis (i.e., finding "a local connection between the evidence and the hypothesis or conclusion based upon it") (294).

Kneupper argued that Logical Theory had a broader range of application than classical and frequency theories and hence the greatest implications for rhetoric.

Wayne Booth's 1973 *Modern Dogma and the Rhetoric of Assent* examined the modern propensity to polarize fact and "mere" opinion, thereby excluding probable claims supported by good reasons. Discussing the tensions between what is and what ought to be and between fact and value, he argued that language is "the medium in which selves grow, the social invention through which we make each other and the structures that are our world, the shared product of our efforts to cope with experience" (135). To Booth, "the supreme purpose of persuasion

[. . .] could not be to talk someone else into a preconceived view; rather it must be to engage in mutual inquiry or exploration.[. . .] The process of inquiry through discourse thus becomes more important than any possible conclusions" (137).

In the early 1970s, the Speech Communication Association's National Developmental Project on Rhetoric published *The Prospect of Rhetoric*, which reported on the Wingspread Conference (1970) and the National Conference on Rhetoric (1970). In this volume, Richard McKeon's essay, "The Uses of Rhetoric in a Technological Age: Architectonic Productive Arts" called on rhetoric to help in the "resolution of new problems and architectonically in the formation of new inclusive communities" (45). A new rhetoric should be "constructed as a productive art and schematized as an architectonic art" (45). He contended that the topics had been "degraded from instruments for discovery of new ideas or arguments to repertories for repetition of old devices and adages" (55). Among several recommendations, he suggested that the new rhetoric should clarify the relationship between judgment and invention. The published conference discussion cited three inventional perspectives: the formal, conceptual, and analytic. In a review of the volume, W. Ross Winterowd, while largely agreeing with McKeon, criticized the conference for failing to go outside its boundaries to other fields in order to create a new rhetoric, contending that new theories of invention will develop from fields like psychology, philosophy, and linguistics ("Review" 58).

New Invention Theories in Rhetoric and Composition

Responding to these discussions of rhetorical invention from the mid-1960s to the mid-1970s, a number of scholars in the emerging field of Rhetoric and Composition within English Studies developed new theories of invention, generating research and pedagogies. The accounts of these theories will include an examination of their treatments of the nature, purpose, and epistemology of invention as well as their social nature.

Prewriting. In 1964, Gordon Rohman and Albert Wlecke published a report on an experiment at Michigan State University: their research launched the term "prewriting," which they called the "initial and crucial stage of the writing process" (12). They argued against "the rhetoric of the finished word" and advanced the notion of prewriting as the "stage of discovery in the writing process when a person transforms a 'subject' into his own categories" (13). They further described prewriting as the discovery of a personal context, of self-actualization through writing. Although later writers would use the term *prewriting* to refer to internal mental processes, the three inventional strategies that Rohman and Wlecke suggested entailed writing: keeping a journal, meditating as a puzzle form, and creating analogies that led to patterns—all discursive ways of helping students escape thinking in clichés and assimilate their subjects to themselves. In 1969, Rohman's essay, "The Workshop Journal, " described the journal as a system of collection (capturing ideas on the fly from every-day experience) and recollection (using these ideas so that they have the freedom to move about and form new associations)—a kind of journal that recorded things to which "writers happen," not things that happen to them. The journal was not meant to initiate a discrete piece of writing but was rather a long-range strategy to help students search for patterns or anomalies that puzzled them. The meditation and analogy were proposed to encourage students to invest themselves in their subjects and to stimulate ideas and organizational patterns. This study's emphasis on using writing in a way other than to create a finished paper led to interest both in invention and the composing process. Rohman had previously explained this emphasis by pointing to a:

> fundamental misconception which undermines so many of our best efforts in teaching writing: If we train students how to recognize an example of good prose, ("the rhetoric of the finished work") we have given them a basis on which to build their own writing abilities. All we have done, in fact, is to give them standards by which to judge the goodness or badness of their finished effort. *We haven't really taught them how to make that effort.* ("Pre-Writing" 106)

The notion of prewriting informed textbooks like Donald Stewart's *The Authentic Voice* and suggested new composition classroom practices.

Classical Invention. In 1965, Edward Corbett's *Classical Rhetoric for the Modern Student* devoted a chapter to the discovery of arguments, including 1) the classical strategy of *status* with three questions students could ask to find a thesis: whether it was a fact, definition, or quality; 2) selections of common and special topics that could be used to find arguments and subject matter; and 3) discussions of the rational, ethical, and emotional appeals to develop a paper. Corbett presented *status* as a strategy for formulating a thesis rather than helping students pose a question for investigation or to identify a point at issue for resolution. His list of common topics and appeals, selected from different periods of classical rhetoric, was designed to help students find support for a thesis already in hand, not to create new knowledge.

Tagmemic Invention. Also in 1965, Richard Young and Alton Becker published their first account of the developing theory of tagmemic rhetoric, foregrounding new inventional strategies that stressed imaginative discovery. They called their exploratory strategy an *epistemological heuristic* based on how we come to know something. Contrasting their heuristic with Aristotle's topics, which they viewed as a taxonomy of arguments already known, they offered a heuristic to help writers go beyond the known. In 1970, Young, Becker, and Kenneth Pike elaborated and expanded this theory in *Rhetoric: Discovery and Change*, based largely on maxims from tagmemic linguistics. Its epistemology emphasized the active role of the observer in discovering pattern and meaning, as well as the importance of complementary perspectives in investigating a subject. The text offered a strategy to help writers initiate inquiry with puzzlements and to frame questions. To guide exploration, they developed a heuristic procedure that they defined as a series of questions or operations to guide inquiry in order to retrieve relevant information, draw attention to missing information, and prepare for intuition. Open-ended and recursive, the heuristic guide was designed to help writers explore their subjects from multiple perspectives (particle, wave, and field) and investigate its contrastive features, range of variation, and distribution. The purpose of tagmemic invention was to assist writers in reaching new understanding and insights. This modern conception of invention, drawing as it did on studies of the process of inquiry and on a tagmemic theory, stressed the importance of invention in probing local cultural differences, the need for context in knowledge construction, and the role of cognitive dissonance as a major catalyst for genuine inquiry. In the 1960s and 1970s, the theory stimulated further research on invention and later spawned variations of the tagmemic exploratory guide.

Research on Invention

In addition to the new specific inventional theories discussed above, scholars also conducted studies of invention itself. In 1967, Janice Lauer, in "Invention in Contemporary Rhetoric," documented the state of invention in English Studies in the mid 1960s. Because new studies of heuristic thinking defined it as more flexible and open-ended than logic and as a guide to creative acts and complex arts, she maintained that heuristics had potential for characterizing new theories of invention. She described a number of these theories, critiquing them with criteria gleaned from a broad range of literature on heuristics: theories based on Aristotle's rhetoric (e.g., Corbett, Hughes, Brockriede, Black, Dearin, and Weaver); Overstreet's behaviorism; Kenneth Burke's dramatism; I. A. Richards's work; General Semantics; tagmemic rhetoric; Rohman's prewriting; the Amherst Experiment; Reid's spectrum model; and Braddock's issues approach. Finally she surveyed composition textbooks, searching for their inventional material. In 1972, Lauer's bibliographic essay on heuristics and composition was followed by a dialogue with Ann Berthoff, who disagreed with Lauer's recommendation that composition theorists use work in psychology to develop new understandings of invention. Their exchange focused on several issues: 1) the introduction of material from another field into English Studies; 2) the humanities/science divide; 3) the explicit theorizing of invention, drawing on interdisciplinary sources; 4) the conception of invention as strategy or art. This last concern over teaching an *art* of invention had been long debated in rhetorical history, as Chapter 3 indicated. The contemporary debates over this issue will be taken up in dealing with inventional pedagogy.

In 1971, Janet Emig's study of the composing processes of twelfth graders made an important contribution to inventional theory. Her research described students' stimuli for composing, prewriting, and planning, which included jottings, lists, and topic outlines. She defined *prewriting* as "that part of the composing process that extends from the time a writer begins to perceive selectively certain features of his inner and/or outer environment with a view to writing about them—usually at the instigation of a stimulus—to the time when he first puts words or phrases on paper elucidating that perception" (39). She defined *planning* as "any oral and written establishment of elements and parameters before or during a discursive formulation" (*Composing Processes* 39). For a field that had taught writing as the production of a finished essay, her study underscored the importance of a process of writing and analyzed a range of inventional acts. Without recognition of a writing process, discussions of invention and their relationship to the classroom were moot. In 1977, Emig argued that writing itself is inventional, a unique mode of learning, because it is active, engaged, personal, self-rhythmic, enactive, iconic, and symbolic, structuring the web of meaning, differing from inner speech, and signaling the center of conceptual relations. In short, she maintained that writing is epigenetic, a record of the journey from jottings and notes to full discursive formation ("Writing"). Emig's study of the composing processes of twelfth graders was followed by several studies of prewriting (e.g., C. Stallard, Sondra Perl, and Sharon Pianko, who examined the time devoted to prewriting, the ways students selected their topics, and how they associated ideas with their subject).

During this decade, there were also meta-theoretical discussions, categorizing and evaluating sets of topics. In 1973, W. Ross Winterowd's "'Topics' and Levels in the Composing Process" positioned inventional guides into two categories: topics that were a closed or finite set and topics that were open, to which more could be added. He maintained that Burke's pentad and the tagmemic guide were finite sets that encompassed all possible perspectives, while the classical topics were an open set. In 1967, Lauer proposed two criteria for evaluating heuristic procedures: whether they helped writers probe all aspects of the rhetorical situation (writer, audience, and situation), and whether they specified a clear set of operations in a direction of inquiry. A decade later, in "Toward a Metatheory of Heuristic Procedures," she posed three criteria: whether they were transferable and portable (able to be used in many situations); whether there was a flexible order to the questions or procedures, and whether they were highly generative, capable of prompting many and diverse ideas and perspectives.

Other theorists in the 1970s foregrounded nonlogical acts and the imagination as central to invention. In 1972, in both "Response to Janice Lauer: Counterstatement" and "From Problem-Solving to a Theory of the Imagination," Ann Berthoff spoke of the imagination as the legacy of the Romantic Movement, of the form-creating powers of the secondary imagination, and of the uses of chaos. In 1974, James Miller argued for the importance of the non-conscious and non-rational in inventional activities. In 1975, Frank D'Angelo's *A Conceptual Theory of Rhetoric* stressed structure in thinking and considered the genesis of discourse to be an intuitive grasp of the end, of the gestalt or the whole. He described the conceptual patterns of extended discourse as topical, symbols of abstract underlying mental processes, including the nonlogical processes of imagining, symbolizing, free associating, repetition, condensation, displacement, and transformation.

The work on invention of this decade was reviewed by Richard Young in a bibliographic essay, "Invention: A Topographical Survey," that not only presented the methods of invention discussed above but also treated historical studies from ancient Greece to the present and studies of the contexts necessary for understanding and teaching these methods.

Review: Early Studies of Invention

In this decade, the first theories to emerge—Rohman and Wlecke's, Corbett's, and Young, Becker, and Pike's—responded to a gap in the composition theory and pedagogy of the day: a lack of invention. Each theory authorized its inventional practices by drawing on different interdisciplinary work: Rohman cited Cassirer, Langer, and existentialism; Corbett deployed classical rhetoric; and Young, Becker, and Pike drew on tagmemic linguistics, phenomenology, and studies of the inquiry process. Each theory treated the initiation of discourse and exploration but provided different heuristics to guide these acts. Young, Becker, and Pike also offered a guide for the verification of insight. But the purposes for invention were different in these theories: Rohman and Wlecke's goal was a writer's self-actualization; Corbett's was support of a thesis; and Young, Becker, and Pike's was new insights and understandings. These guides were also informed by different epistemologies for writing: reaching self-knowledge, locating known arguments and support, and constructing new knowledge. The decade also spawned different conceptions of prewriting and the composing process. None of these theories explicitly dealt with the social dimensions of rhetoric, but the nature of Corbett's and Young, Becker, and Pike's heuristics did not exclude the social. Their guides could be used collaboratively, as was demonstrated later in some textbooks. Further, these strategies had a social cast because the very nature of a heuristic is that it codifies effective practices in the community, helping students participate successfully in these communities. Although differences existed among prewriting, classical invention, and the tagmemic guides, the theorists proposing them were not in conflict with each other, attempting to discredit each other's inventional practices. Instead they saw them as complementary, accomplishing different ends. Disagreements were strong, however, over the value of heuristics versus reliance on the imagination, the nonlogical, and the unsystematic.

During this period, the writer was generally considered to have a unified coherent subjectivity and a powerful agency that could be enhanced by inventional practices. Most theorists constructed their practices for a writer who occupied a nongendered student position primarily in an introductory writing class. They proposed general heuristics that could function for different types of discourse, including expressive, persuasive, and expository.

New and Elaborated Theories of Invention:
Mid-1970s to Mid-1980s

In the second decade of work on invention, new theories emerged, previous theories and practices were studied, and rhetorical epistemology was further discussed, with some issues becoming more contentious. Linda Flower and John R. Hayes developed cognitive rhetoric, studying composing processes through the use of protocol analysis. Others like Ann Berthoff continued to emphasize the imagination and the use of nonrational heuristics. A number of studies proposed Kenneth Burke's work, especially the pentad, as an inventional strategy. More discussion occurred about classical rhetoric, tagmemic rhetoric, and rhetoric as epistemic. Some scholars introduced invention as the interpretation of texts, as hermeneutic, while still others mounted various critiques of previous inventional theories. Finally this period saw some meta-theoretical work, efforts to review and categorize theories of invention.

Cognitive Invention

Cognitive studies spawned a new model of writing and research on invention. In 1980, in two essays in *Cognitive Processes in Writing*, Linda Flower and John R. Hayes offered an early description of their cognitive writing theory and outlined dynamics of composing, such as setting priorities, drawing on routines, and juggling the constraints of knowledge and written speech through strategies like partitioning problems. In 1981, in "A Cognitive Process Theory of Writing," they described their cognitive process model as a set of distinctive thinking processes that are orchestrated during composing. They demonstrated that these processes are hierarchical (one embedded in another) and goal-directed (guided by a network of goals). Using evidence from protocol analyses, they challenged the common sense view that knowledge of topics or text directs the process, arguing instead that goals direct the process. Their model included 1) the task environment (rhetorical problem: rhetorical situation, topic, audience, and goals); 2) long-term memory (knowledge about the topic and audience, writing plans, and problem representation); 3) planning (generating ideas, organizing, goal-setting, exploring and consolidating, stating and developing, writing and regenerating); 4) translating, 5) reviewing (evaluating, revising); and 6) the monitor that directs the processes. In "The Cognition of Discovery," they further delineated the nature of rhetorical problems, as situated, shared, and unique problem representations stemming from exigencies or assignments and from the audience. They described goals as the reader, persona or voice, meaning, and features of the text, contending that good writers respond to all aspects of their rhetorical problem. In "The Pregnant Pause: An Inquiry into the Nature of Planning," Flower and Hayes argued that writers pause to rhetorically plan, an hypothesis that they again demonstrated using protocol analysis and research on episodic structures. In "Plans that Guide Composing," they distinguished between ill-defined and well-defined problems, exploring the meaning and power of plans to help writers make large situations manageable. They also offered a sequence of procedures to enable writers to set priorities. In "Images, Plans, and Prose," they showed a range of ways that writers represent their composing plans, using semantic and other symbolic notations and abstract networks, including schemas, concepts, and metaphors that vary from one field to another. Flower's textbook, *Problem-Solving Strategies for Writing*, implemented their cognitive process model for technical writers.

During this period, many other cognitive studies were conducted on aspects of invention. For example, Marlene Scardemalia, Carl Bereiter, and Hillel Goelman studied how three conditions of text production influence cognitive processes in composition: 1) short-term memory loss of the products of planning slows down writing; 2) interference from mechanical demands of the written medium competes for mental resources with the higher-level demands of content planning; and 3) the lack of directional signals, production signals such as to keep on going, and discourse schemata effect a general lack of coordination of language production. Several collections of essays also featured cognitive studies, some of which considered invention. In *Research on Composing*, edited by Charles Cooper and Lee Odell, some essays devoted attention to inventional theories and needed meta-rhetorical research on invention. In *Cognitive Processes in Writing*, edited by Lee Gregg and Erwin Steinberg, essays presented work on writing development, information-processing loads in writing, reflective thinking leading to epistemic writing, idea production, and writing as discovery. In *What Writers Know: The Language, Process, and Structure of Written Discourse*, edited by Martin Nystrand, some essays dealt with subjects like production factors; scripts, plans, goals, and themes; and knowledge of topics and audience. In *Research on Writing: Principles and Methods*, edited by Peter Mosenthal, Lynne Tamor, and Sean Walmsley, a few essays dealt with research practices for studying writing processes and the teaching of writing.

Non-Rational Invention, Shaping, Imagining, and Forming

In 1979, James Kinney argued for intuitive invention and non-systematic inventional practices. Toby Fulwiler and Bruce Petersen further advanced this discussion, proposing mumbling (low-level articulation), staring, moving, doodling, and noise. In 1980, James Britton, in a collection of essays from the Ottawa conference, offered another perspective on invention that he termed "shaping at the point of utterance," arguing that writing itself is heuristic. Working from a comparison of speaking, Britton held that once writers' words appear on the page, they act primarily as a stimulus to continue writing. Movements of the pen capture the movements of thinking in a moment-by-moment interpretive process. The act of writing becomes a contemplative act revealing further coherence and fresh patterns. This conception of a heuristic echoes Isocrates who, according to Richard Enos, defined writing as a heuristic that guided creativity and intellectual complexity ("Literacy in Athens"; see also William Benoit).

In 1981, Ann Berthoff proposed some inventional practices in *The Making of Meaning: Metaphors, Models, and Maxims for Writing Teachers*. As a way of "rediscovering the power of language to generate the sources of meaning" (70), she introduced learning the uses of chaos as the source for alternatives for the writer. In her discussion of invention, she said that in addition to such devices as heuristics, which she characterized as helping students to take inventory of what they knew, another way of getting started was to question what the reader needs to know. As an important way of forming concepts, she mentioned specifying and called for a reclaiming of the imagination, the active mind, which she argued finds or creates forms.

Burkean Invention

During this decade, a number of people advocated the value of the pentad for heuristic purposes and the importance of many Burkean concepts for composition. In 1978, Kenneth Burke himself, in "Questions and Answers about the Pentad," provided a short account of his development of dramatism as a view of language as a mode of action rather than a mode of knowledge, of his extension of this concept to symbolic action in general, and then his move to theorize humans as symbol-using animals. In this account, he also spoke of symbolic action as public and social in contrast to the realm of non-symbolic motion in which we live and die as individuals: "No symbolic action is possible without a grounding in non-symbolic motion" (330). In terms of the pentad as a heuristic, he pointed out that he had intended an interpretive role for the pentad but that a heuristic purpose had its place as well. He explained: "My job was not to help a writer decide what he might say to produce a text. It was to help a critic perceive what was going on in a text that was already written" (332). He ended his discussion by insisting: "Not just the Pentad. But the ratios and circumference" (334). Several theorists interpreted some of Burke's concepts and their relevance for composition. In 1979, Charles Kneupper, discussing Burke's dramatistic theory in terms of discourse production, explained the heuristic function of the pentad and its ratios as well as language itself as a motive for discoursing. In the same year, Joseph Comprone discussed several of Burke's key notions (the pentad, terministic screens, perspective by incongruity, and identification) as means of writing critical essays. In 1983, Winterowd explained Burke's dramatistic view of meaning, pointing out that Burke used a non-Aristotelian conceptual pivot, the representative anecdote, which does not lead to closure in contrast to the enthymeme. He argued that both Burke and many of our students are appositional writers who should be understood and valued. Such writers do not start their essays with theses followed by supportive material but rather begin and continue with anecdotes, examples, and stories that build toward a final point.

More on Classical Invention and Tagmemic Invention

During this decade, aspects of classical invention were further analyzed. In *Essays on Classical Rhetoric and Modern Discourse*, for example, several pieces addressed invention. John Gage argued that concepts of dialectic, enthymeme, and *stasis* support the view of rhetoric as a means of discovering and validating knowledge. This epistemic conception entailed mutual construction of knowledge between the audience and the writer, with the audience supplying the question or issue to be pursued and the premises for arguing toward probable truth. Janice Lauer examined three issues concerning the nature of invention in rhetorical history: differences in conceptions of the genesis of discourse, treatments of exploratory acts and their relation to judgment, and disagreements over the province of invention. James Raymond's essay offered a way of helping students to better understand Aristotle's enthymeme and example, renaming them assumptions and paradigm. In 1986, James Kinneavy argued for the importance of the neglected sophistic concept of *kairos,* the right measure and opportune time, explaining that *kairos* entailed an epistemology that brought timeless ideas into time, emphasizing values and involving free decisions. In the next decade, R. Gerald Nelms and Maureen Goggin surveyed this revival of classical rhetoric in Composition Studies.

In 1980, Charles Kneupper, critiquing the tagmemic heuristic's terminology and its apparent redundancy, offered a revised version with six directives instead of nine. In 1979, Bruce Edwards published "The Tagmemic Contribution to Composition Teaching," which offered a comprehensive commentary on tagmemic invention.

Further Discussions on Rhetoric as Epistemic

At this time, several interdisciplinary scholars further debated the concept of rhetoric as epistemic, the relationship between rhetoric and philosophy and between language and thought. In 1976, Scott published a second essay, "On Viewing Rhetoric as Epistemic: Ten Years Later," that attempted to clarify several questions: "Is there one way of knowing or many? What sort of knowing does rhetoric strive to achieve? Is rhetorical relativism vicious?" (259). He answered these questions by saying that there is a plurality of ways of knowing, that rhetoric is a constituent of any act of knowing (260), that rhetoric "aims at knowledge that is social and ethical: it has the potential of creating commitment" (259), and that rhetoric has an epistemic role in seeing and choosing possibilities for creating knowledge in specific situations. Scott also argued that rhetoric makes its contribution to knowledge in "understanding how human action is *decisive*" (261). He acknowledged that he held that reality is socially constructed (261), stating that the kind of knowledge rhetoric seeks is to "understand what it means to be persuaded and to persuade" (263). In response to the charge that rhetorical relativism is vicious, he offered two "common-sense" counter-arguments. In the first, he used the example of religious wars to illustrate that certainty can enable extreme actions. If one has recourse to standards outside the individual conscience or the interests of an immediate community, then one doesn't feel responsible for making decisions. "Contingency is much less to be feared in creating chaos, wantonly or whimsically, than the spirit of axiomatic detachment" (264). In the second argument, he maintained that "rather than a standard-less society, or a maze of differing standards" (264), relativism identifies situations in which "standards have to be established cooperatively and renewed repeatedly" (264). Relativism would thus stimulate a responsibility for establishing agreement based on one's traditions, seen only as traditions.

In the same year, Barry Brummett argued for an epistemic notion of rhetoric that entailed process and intersubjectivity. He critiqued the mechanistic point of view for its incompatibility with everyday experience, its faith in objective truth, its lack of concern with values, and its simplification of phenomena. In contrast he advocated an intersubjective reality characterized by ambiguity that he defined by this equation: sensation plus meaning equals experience. He asserted "only if reality is shared, that is, created by discourse, can it be changed or altered by discourse" (31). Echoing Scott, he argued for an ethic of rhetoric based on intersubjectivity, which entails more responsibility than idealist ethics. Finally he proposed a process methodology for joining experimental methods and rhetorical criticism.

In 1978, Michael Leff, Thomas Farrell, and Henry Johnstone also addressed aspects of rhetoric as epistemic. Leff reviewed and categorized four notions of rhetoric as epistemic that had been circulating in the 1970s: 1) a rhetoric that clarifies the relationship between a par-

ticular problem and a fixed standard of truth; 2) a rhetoric that generates an autonomous form of knowledge based on social consensus; 3) a
rhetoric that adjudicates between the first principles of science and/or
speculative philosophy; and 4) epistemology as rhetoric ("In Search").
Farrell, in "Social Knowledge II," argued that rhetoric constructs
knowledge in social fields through attributions of consensus that act
as preconditions for the validity of a theory. Distinguishing between
social and technical fields, he explained that social knowledge depends
on personal relationships between advocates and their audience. Such
knowledge, he argued, carries a normative force demanding that decisions be made or action taken. Johnstone asserted that Heidegger conceived of philosophy as fundamentally a rhetorical enterprise because
he viewed the concept of destruction (an awakening, a recall from
forgetfulness) as a primary task of philosophy. This interpretation,
Johnstone argued, leads us to no longer consider rhetoric as an art of
persuasion but rather as an art to totally reorient hearers.

In 1980, Charles Kneupper and Floyd Anderson noted that the
field of Speech Communication had a need for rhetorical invention.
They pointed out that a minimum inventional theory would concern
itself with retrieval of information and ideas germane to a subject matter, while a more powerful conception would consider invention as
playing a role in inquiry and discovery of new knowledge (321). In
1981, Richard Gregg, in "Rhetoric and Knowing: The Search for Perspective," reviewed distinctions current at the time, such as between
technical and social knowing, between explicit and implicit knowledge, between knowledge including and precluding rhetoric, between
what we know and the processes by which we know, and among critical, personal and social thought. He argued instead for a perspective
that maintains a focus on how we come to know that begins with real-
izing that all knowledge is symbolic activity: "Perception moves with
a generative activity to join physical or 'real world" information with
cognitive purpose to create patterned experience" (142). He maintained that cognitive processes are tinged with affective states and that
comprehension is linked with purpose and intention. He theorized
that "inherent in all symbolic activity is the function of inducement"
(143) to symbolize at all levels. He concluded that the study of rhetoric
is "the study of symbolic inducement however it occurs within these
realms of cognitive, systemic, and social activity " (144).

In 1982, Richard Cherwitz and James W. Hikins, in "Toward a Rhetorical Epistemology," posited that rhetorical discourse is "the description of reality through language and that knowledge is justified true belief" (135). They discussed truth, belief, and justification as conditions for having knowledge. They also defined several premises of a rhetorical epistemology: "that matters of epistemology are both conceptually and logically *prior* to matters of ontology " (140), that a reality exists independent of individual attitudes and beliefs, and that a "definition of knowledge is useful and productive if it affords linguistic and conceptual classification of the ways in which epistemic judgments and their terminology are employed" (141). These notions helped to separate definitional from methodological issues. They held that "the propositionality of all knowledge rests in the fact that it is conceived, understood, transmitted, and employed *via language*" (148). Finally, they described rhetorical discourse as differentiative, associative, preservative, and perspectival. In 1986, in *Communication and Knowledge*, they argued that coming to know something is, at least in part, a rhetorical activity. They investigated how epistemic judgment can be assessed philosophically using a theory of rhetorical perspectivism in which derived meanings, although linguistic, are tied to a real and knowable world.

These different positions on rhetoric as epistemic strengthened such claims for the importance of rhetorical invention as: 1) rhetoric constructs all that there is to know, 2) rhetoric constructs knowledge in social worlds, 3) all knowing is symbolic activity, 4) philosophy is rhetorical, and 5) rhetoric adjudicates between competing disciplinary paradigms. The differences among these conceptions would continue to be argued, prefiguring advocates and critics of postmodern theories of invention in the next period.

Rhetorical Invention as Hermeneutics

In this period, the long-standing historical debate continued over whether invention's purpose was primarily heuristic, to help speakers and writers construct knowledge and produce discourse, or whether its role was hermeneutic, to help writers interpret texts already written. As discussed previously, Augustine had emphasized the latter role of invention to guide the interpretation of the Scriptures, and Kenneth Burke had contrasted these two roles in his discussion of the uses of the pentad. A number of scholars espoused a hermeneutic view of invention, particularly scholars with a background in literary studies.

In 1985, Steven Mailloux proposed rhetorical hermeneutics as "historical sets of topics, arguments, tropes, ideologies, and so forth, that determine how texts are established as meaningful through rhetorical exchanges" (629). He maintained that interpreters neither discover nor create meaningful texts, but engage in interpretive work that "attempts to convince others of the truth of explications and explanations" (630). He further argued that rhetorical hermeneutics provides histories of how particular theoretical and critical discourses have evolved because persuasion always takes place in changing contexts of disputes. In "The Structure of Textual Space," Martin Nystrand also discussed invention as hermeneutical, considering interpretation as the construction of meaning and stating that language production can be viewed as interpretation in a sphere of meaning.

In 1987, Lynn Worsham, in "The Question Concerning Invention: Hermeneutics and The Genesis of Writing, " set out a theory of invention based on Heidegger's philosophy of Being and critique of technology. She advanced Heidegger's interpretation of *techne* as meaning "bringing forth" and "to make manifest" and thus related to *"aletheia,* or the truth-process in which something comes into unconcealment" (207). She proposed an hermeneutical understanding of writing that focused on the experience of questioning not *what* but *how* (218). She explained that Heidegger's Typology of Being, rather than providing strategies for effective guessing, provided "hints, clues, indications of the places where the event of meaning localizes itself" (219). She also found important Heidegger's understanding of "truth as a happening in human existence" (219) as well as his theory that the interaction between being and language was one of undergoing an experience, entering into it, submitting to it, yielding to it, being owned, possessed and appropriated by it. This appropriation was "the highest and most profound play" (227-28). The essence of art for Heidegger was, she explained, disclosure; "it recovers our sacred connectedness to the earth and remembers for us that 'upon the earth and in it, historical man grounds his dwelling in the world'" (230). She turned to Cyril Welch's hermeneutic interpretation of writing as an art: "Reflective writing says *how things are* and, moreover, *how things might be"* (232). It is a kind of writing" whose topos and ethos are potentiality and possibility" (232). For Worsham, then, the task of writing is to "subtract the familiarity and alreadiness of what has been said" (233). She claimed that "writing happens first of all as a hermeneutic process, as an event of disclosure" (235).

Critiques, Cautions, and Rejoinders

During this decade, critiques and cautions about previous work on invention were mounted. In 1977, Susan Wells asserted that the field must find tools to evaluate invention procedures, tools that are "grounded in some sense of the value of the information and attitudes that invention procedures generate" (469). Critiquing Christensen's work and the tagmemic model, she claimed that popular heuristics in composition were empiricist in their epistemology and contemplative in their ethos. In 1978, James Kinney also criticized tagmemic theory, saying that its exploratory heuristic did not provide total or in some cases significant knowledge, was epistemological in contrast to the classical topics, and did not offer adequate treatment of arrangement. Lee Odell responded to Kinney's critique, stating that Young and Becker claimed only that using the procedure would increase the chances of discovering the solution to a problem, not that it would supply knowledge. Odell further rejoined that systemic inquiry was not precluded even by those who emphasized writing itself as an act of discovery. Odell also raised important questions about heuristic procedures that needed to be answered: Is training in systematic inquiry equally useful for all? Are such procedures equally useful for all types of writing? At what point does systematic inquiry fit into the composing process? What form should systematic inquiry take? And how do the various heuristic procedures compare and contrast?

In 1980, Mike Rose further cautioned that heuristics could be turned into formulas. He distinguished between algorithms, heuristics, sets, and plans, pointing out that several factors cause writer's block: treating heuristics as algorithms, using inappropriate sets of questions or disciplinary methodical orientations, and setting too many rules. In 1985, Gary Olson put forth two diagnostic instruments for detecting problems students had with invention: one based on the work of Lee Odell and the other based on Michael Polanyi's idea of tacit knowledge.

At this time, scholars in other fields were also debating these matters. Responding to common sense points of view that heuristics interfered with the natural and mysterious processes of creativity, David

Perkins, in *The Mind's Best Work*, argued that heuristics were only one type of numerous behaviors that humans had developed to help with thinking. He further pointed out that heuristics ("Plans Up Front") like education cut deep into the course of thought, are used by experts to solve open-ended problems without guarantees, and are teachable. He reviewed debates about whether general or discipline-specific heuristics are preferable and more effective, concluding that both types had advantages. He explained that creators need particular knowledge and experience to function in a field, knowing the informal rules of the game. On the other hand, when they operate in unfamiliar areas, general strategies provide an initial approach to an inquiry (213). Perkins and Gavriel Salomon offered another perspective on this issue in "Are Cognitive Skills Context-Bound?" reviewing thirty years of research on the subject. They concluded that general strategic knowledge and specialized domain-specific knowledge function in close partnership and stressed the importance of teaching general heuristics in a contextualized way and helping students to transfer them to a range of situations (152). From the perspective of Rhetoric and Composition, Michael Carter also tackled the question of general versus specific heuristics, arguing for a pluralistic theory of human expertise that entails both kinds of heuristics. He explained that expertise develops through five stages. In the early stages, writers use context-free heuristics while in later stages they use more local writing knowledge. Expert writers, however, still use general strategies when they write in new areas. Agreeing with Perkins and Salomon, he suggested that this theory of expertise implies that instruction in general writing heuristics has value, but that it needs to be situated and modeled.

Overviews of Inventional Theories

In 1980, Virginia Underwood completed a study of theories of heuristics in place at the time, comparing the theories' epistemological claims, controlling metaphors, heuristics, conceptions of the purpose of discourse, goals of the pedagogy, assumptions about the writer, and treatments of arrangement and style. Her study focused on the classical topics, Rohman's and Wlecke's pre-writing, Zoellner's behavioral pedagogy, Burke's pentad, tagmemic rhetoric, and D'Angelo's conceptual theory. In 1987, Elizabeth and William House reviewed different conceptions of problem-solving, arguing that the theories fall on a continuum based on the ideas of internal and external validity and claiming that both types are necessary in a search for truth. In 1989, Terry Beers discussed the "new classicist" and "new romanticists" theories of invention, asserting that "contrasting perspectives suggest the possibility of *dialectical* rather than exclusive relationships" (25). Engaging in an axiological analysis of these theories, Beers urged a consideration of their value and the relative permanence of these values, thereby doing justice to their interdependence. At the end of this decade, Winterowd, in "Rhetorical Invention" in *Composition/Rhetoric: A Synthesis*, discussed some of the previous work on invention, stating that "rhetorical invention concerns the generation of subject matter; any process—conscious or subconscious, heuristic or algorithmic—that yields something to say about a subject, arguments for or against a case" (35). He represented different positions on heuristics, putting them into the framework of what Paulo Freire called "problematization" (38-46).

With the development of so many inventional theories and practices, Richard Young, in "Paradigms and Problems," argued that the field needed research to make reasonable judgments about the adequacy of these theories of invention. He suggested that researchers should ask two general questions of each theory:

1. Does it do what it claims to do? That is, does it provide an adequate account of the psychological processes it purports to explain? And does it increase our ability to carry out these processes more efficiently and effectively?"

2. Does the theory provide a *more adequate* account of the processes and *more adequate* means of carrying them out than any of the alternatives?" (40).

He called for different kinds of investigation of questions: empirical, bibliographic, philosophical, historical, and meta-rhetorical.

Review: Elaborated Theories of Invention

During this period, earlier heuristics were tested, adapted, applied, and critiqued. New theories extended the range of invention from cognitive to nonrational to hermeneutic, with the divide widening between inventional claims for heuristics and hermeneutics. Empirical studies, including protocol analysis, were used to develop and test cognitive inventional theories. Arguments escalated over rhetoric as epistemic. Much of this work differed from that in the previous de-

cade in that studies revolved around neither specific heuristic strategies nor instructional practices, but instead focused on epistemological matters. This decade of inventional studies closed in 1987 with
Richard Young's second bibliographic essay, "Recent Developments In
Rhetorical Invention," which clustered its entries under the following
headings: composing process; rhetoric as an epistemic activity; situational context, including audience and ethos of the writer; heuristics, pedagogy and methods of invention; and the history of invention.
These headings bespeak the expansion and complication of inventional studies during this decade. The conception of the subject position of
the writer in theory and practice changed little during this period.

Diversified Invention: Mid-1980s to the New Millennium

In this third period, studies of invention migrated to many sites, including writing in the disciplines and the rhetoric of inquiry. Larger
theoretical movements also influenced studies of invention. The rise of
social construction, deconstruction, poststructuralism, postmodernism, and cultural studies challenged conceptions of writers' agency,
individual invention, certainty and the advisability of general strategies. These theories posited multiple writer positions, writers written
by language, social conceptions of invention, the importance of local
knowledge, discourse communities, and the role of readers and culture
in inventional acts. Theorists also foregrounded the hermeneutical, interpretive, and critical purposes of invention while previous theories of
invention were modified.

Invention in the Disciplines

As the field of Writing in the Disciplines emerged, scholars began to
study invention in diverse fields. Carolyn Miller provided an extensive bibliographic essay, "Invention in Scientific Research in Technical
Communication," in which she treated invention as encompassing "all
the means by which writers come to their matter, whether consciously
and systematically or intuitively and routinely," involving "presuppositions, premises, values, inspiration, work activities—anything that
leads to or is taken as a 'good reason'" (123-24), including both writing
as a process and also criticisms of writing as a product (124) as they
illuminated invention. She divided invention into three areas. In the
first, "Invention As Scientific Inquiry and Technical Problem-Solving,"

she examined the arguments over whether rhetoric participated in the context of discovery (the intellectual environment in which ideas originate), discussing Popper's view; the hypothetico-deductive view; the acquiescence to inspiration; Hanson's work on the reasoning processes of a scientist; Wartofsky's theory of heuristic thinking; Polyani's notion of tacit knowledge; the roles of special and pictorial thinking; Black's work on models, often expressed in analogies and metaphors; Fleck's idea of a thought-collective; Holton's account of the nascent moment of scientific discovery; and various problem-solving models, including Herbert Simons's and the Delphi method. In her second area of invention, "Contexts, Constraints, and Forums for Presentation," she discussed the perspective that persuasion is crucial for science, not for discovery but for justification. She cited Charles Bazerman's analysis of the arguments in formal scientific literature; work on the *ethos* of science; discussions of the effect of the working environment on rhetorical invention (e.g., James Watson, Francis Crick, Bruno Latour and Steve Woolgar); the literature on decision making in organizations; and lists of special topics in areas of technical decision making. In her third area of invention, "Applications, Heuristics, and Teaching Methods," she explored the limited accounts of instruction in developing the art of invention for science and technical discourse.

Other scholars also studied the inventional practices of scientists, engineers, philosophers, musicians, economists, and so on as the following examples illustrate. Charles Bazerman, in *Shaping Written Knowledge*, studied research articles in physics, particularly those using spectroscopy as a primary technique, demonstrating that this discourse was linked to epistemology; "beliefs about what can be known, how it can be known, in what form it can be expressed, and how it should be argued" (174). Among his many findings, he demonstrated that the arguments in the articles gave insight into how graphic features (e.g., spectral lines and the substances that produce characteristic patterns) connect with epistemological and intellectual changes in the field: as the work advanced in the field, the articles become "more theory based and ultimately more self-conscious about their constructed theoretical character" (177). Greg Myers examined the grant proposals and journal articles of two biologists, including their efforts to define their problems. Michael Halloran studied the work of James Watson and Francis Crick, describing their use of *stasis* and the topics ("Birth"). Rodney Farnsworth and Avon Crismore analyzed Darwin's use of the visual in *The Structure and Distribution of Coral Reefs,* illustrating how he employed drawings, diagrams, and maps at "points of tension between his audience's preconceptions" and his new theory, establishing his ethos and argument (11). They also examined Darwin's meta-discourse about these visuals.

Other studies included John Lyne's investigation of bio-rhetorics, which he defined as "a strategy for inventing and organizing discourses about biology" (38), giving the example of the term *selfish gene* in the study of insects. Referring to invention as "the art of determining the 'sayables'" (49), he contended that "the task for rhetoric goes beyond interpretive understanding, or hermeneutics. In guiding the creation of discourses, not just the interpretation of existing texts, the work of rhetoric is to invent language strategies that bring about change" (37). John Angus Campbell in his study of Darwin's notebooks stated that another way of looking at the notebooks was to see them as following "an informal logic, a logic of rhetorical invention" (59). He explained that each of Darwin's theories was grounded in a central reproductive metaphor and that Darwin's efforts to support his insights started with a specific example and continued with a logic of implication. He further concluded that scientific discovery and rhetorical invention became united in a logic of inquiry.

Carolyn Miller and Jack Selzer examined the special topics used by engineers in writing reports, asserting that Aristotle had intended a kind of special topic based on the specialized knowledge of disciplines. They defined special topics as "patterns of thought deriving from specific genres, institutions, or disciplines—patterns that are material to gaining the assent of the audience within a particular discourse community" (316). In engineering reports, they analyzed the function of generic special topics (e.g., transit development plans and the proposals that won the contracts for those plans); institutional topics (e.g., systems analysis, computer modeling, values of organizations, definitions of efficiency, productivity, and cost control); and disciplinary special topics, such as those for transportation engineering: memory scheduling, coordinate scheduling, pulse scheduling, and headway and streamlining. Miller also studied the role of *kairos* in science, quoting Eric Charles White's definition of *kairos* as " a passing instant when an opening appears which must be driven through with force if success is to be achieved" ("Kairos" 313). She reviewed the time aspect of *kairos* in the work of such figures as Francis Bacon, Karl Popper, Thomas

Kuhn, and Stephen Toulmin and the space aspect of *kairos* in the work of James Watson and Francis Crick and Oswald Avery. In 1994, Richard Brown argued for the importance of studying the "contexts for discovery" in the sciences—'the practices of representation in the texts and contexts of presentation" (3), explaining how these contexts could be examined through narratives of conversion and illustrating these narratives in fiction, travelogue, and ethnography. He concluded that these narratives exhibit such features as a construction of the self, ontological development from doubt to certitude and from the material to the spiritual (26), and epistemological obsessiveness.

The "Rhetoric of Inquiry," an important interdisciplinary movement, was described in several essays by John Nelson, Allan Megill, and Donald McCloskey. In "Rhetoric of Inquiry: Projects and Prospects," Nelson, a political scientist, and Megill, an historian, set out the background for this movement, identifying the theorists whose work set the stage for it: Nietzsche's assault on the subject/object dichotomy; Heidegger's imposition of severe limits on the subject/object oppositions and his notion of "*Dasein,* [as] constituted 'always already' by the situation in which it finds itself" (24); Dewey's renunciation of certainty as a modern aim and his engagement in public life; Wittgenstein's reconception of certainty and his rhetorical approach to language in actual practices; Gadamer's rhetorical attention to dialogue and communication and his resolving of argument and epistemology into the science of interpretation, hermeneutics; Rorty's replacing of epistemology with hermeneutics and his turn from certain truth and coercive argument; Habermas's endowing philosophy with the problematics of rhetoric, his critique of distorted communication, his more directly political version of the rhetoric of inquiry and his self-conscious rhetorical treatments of inquiry; Derrida's recognition that reality is rhetorically constructed; and Foucault's account of the devices of language and argument which defend modern power (24-27). Nelson and Megill also noted that Perelman, Toulmin, and Thomas Kuhn anticipated the rhetoric of inquiry. According to them, the Rhetoric of Inquiry opposes modern epistemology that considers only two main images of science: "science as formally demonstrative and science as empirically compelling" (23). They went on to argue that inquiry allows scholars to accept uncertainties that lead to "a richer appreciation of questions and complexities" (25) and helps them to understand the "diverse standards and strategies of science on their own levels"

(25), connecting them to their logics, methods, aesthetics, econom-
ics, histories, and sociologies (25). They explained further that this
interdisciplinary field explores inquiry as "networks of cases, stories,
metaphors, measurements, experiments, seminars, and publications"
(31), involving "more subtle and sympathetic attention to discovery,
meaning, persuasion, and sociology" (31), and encompassing psychological studies of inference, communication studies of dialogue, and
anthropological studies of institutions and symbols of inquiry. The
University of Iowa Project on Rhetoric as Inquiry (POROI) has been
the site for this movement [http://www.uiowa.edu/~poroi/].

Social Construction and Invention

In 1982, Patricia Bizzell challenged what she argued was the individual cast of inventional theories and practices, categorizing theorists
as inner-directed or outer-directed. She described the latter as those
interested in the social processes whereby thinking powers are shaped
and used in communities (215), stating that the thrust of composition writing instruction should be the analysis of the conventions of
particular discourse communities. She concluded that in order to have
a complete picture of the composing process, we need answers from
both theoretical schools to explain the cognitive and the social factors
in writing development and the relationship between them. In 1986,
Kenneth Bruffee—drawing on the work of Kuhn, Richard Rorty, and
Geertz—advocated the social construction of knowledge, which included cognition, emotion, motivation, perception, imagination, and
memory. He maintained that this theory characterized knowledge as
non-foundational, generated by socially justified beliefs about reality,
and non-problematic with language at the center. It viewed thought as
constructed within a community of knowledgeable peers and vernacular language. (See also Bruffee, "Writing and Reading".)

   Also in 1986, Karen LeFevre, in *Invention as a Social Act*, explained
that "invention is conceived broadly as the process of actively creating
as well as finding what comes to be known and said in the discourse of
any discipline" (33). She characterized invention as a dialectical process in which the individual and the socio-culture are coexisting and
mutually defining, explaining that invention is "enacted by inventor
and audience" and that "the act of invention can be thought of as having "two parts: the initiation of the invented act and the reception
and execution of it" (38). The execution or completion may be by a

number of others (e.g., another part of the rhetor, the perceived actual audience, a collaborator, or a reader) because inventing over time entails transactions and intertextuality. She identified several versions of social invention: 1) as the self being socially influenced or even constituted; 2) as using language which is socially created and shared by discourse communities; 3) as building on knowledge accumulated from previous generations; 4) as internal dialogue with imagined others or a construct of audience that supplies premises as structures of belief; 5) as involving others as editors and evaluators; 6) as influenced by social collectives; and 7) as the reception, evaluation, and use of discourse dependent on the social context. She also categorized existing theories of invention, placing them on a continuum from Platonic, to Internally Dialogic, to Collaborative, and to Collective. In 1988, Bennett A. Rafoth and Donald Rubin edited a collection of essays, *The Social Construction of Written Communication*. In the opening essay, Rubin identified four types of social constructive processes: 1) writers' constructions of mental representations of the social contexts in which their writing is embedded; 2) writing as a social process that creates or constitutes social contexts; 3) writers creating texts collectively in discourse communities; and 4) writers assigning consensual values to writing (2).

Counterstatements and Socio-Cognitive Invention

Several scholars critiqued some of the social constructivist assumptions. In 1991, Joseph Petraglia challenged the notion that knowledge is constructed by consensus, that it is discovered through discourse, and that reality changes as discourse changes. He argued that these ideas lead to a relativist theory that collapses under its own weight and involves a dualism between the mental and the physical.

In response to critiques of cognitive rhetoric, in "Cognition, Context, and Theory Building," Linda Flower argued for an interactive theory between cognition and context, for the value of a grounded theory (based on observation), a theory that helps us to learn something we didn't know about the individual and society, helps us to teach, acknowledges the pressure and potential of social context, and addresses the ways writers negotiate the context and create goals. The principles she articulated included

1. context cues cognition: dictates the problem; offers a repertoire of conceptual frameworks; provides cues to action (goals, criteria, strategies); and sets criteria;

2. cognition mediates context: there are individual differences in task representation; different goals; and tacit meditation; and

3. a bounded purpose is a meaningful rhetorical act with constraints, choices, and a web of purposes (goals, plans, intentions, and ideas). (287-94)

Flower's 1993 essay," Cognitive Rhetoric: Inquiry into the Art of Inquiry," outlined several premises for a socio-cognitive stance: 1) meaning is made for a purpose; 2) purposes are made, not given; 3) the networks of intentions that writers construct are part of a larger rhetorical, social, and cultural situation; 4) meaning-making as a negotiated activity reveals tensions between personal agency, social influence, and received knowledge; 5) understanding meaning-making as a rhetorical action will entail more than a single dimension of an event; and 6) a fully specified, grounded observation-based theory that links cognition and context is based on an educational need for informed accounts of individual and group differences. She pointed out that cognitive rhetoric always asks for evidence and considers claims as statements about greater or lesser probability. She identified ways in which this rhetoric fits into epistemic rhetorics, emphasizing that it is "a set of questions and a repertoire of interdisciplinary methods for trying to answer them—it is a scaffold for inquiry" (174). Its method is interplay between observation and inference.

In 1994, Flower, in *The Construction of Negotiated Meaning: A Social Cognitive Theory of Writing*, further outlined a socio-cognitive theory of writing, which features an inventional heuristic called collaborative planning, distinguishing between schema-driven, knowledge-driven, and constructive planning that tailors a plan to the rhetorical situation. In collaborative planning "the writer (as planner) explains and elaborates his or her plan (or partial text) to a partner (as supporter). The supporter listens, asks questions, and encourages the writer to develop his or her plan" (142). Flower identified strategic knowledge as an example of the kind of inventional thinking her theory supported, defining strategic knowledge as understanding in action characterized by three elements: setting goals, using strategies, and having meta-cognitive awareness. Identifying three current metaphors for how meaning is made—reproduction (reproducing existing meaning), conversation (e.g., consensus reaching, meaning as a product of interaction, and combative dialogue), and negotiation—she critiqued the first, pointing out that students transform and elaborate meanings and that this position entails textual determinism; she faulted the second, showing that conversation often excludes the marginalized and has difficulty with the notion of individual cognition and agency; and she adopted the third metaphor, negotiation, as the position of socio-cognitive rhetoric in which meaning is made not only in conversation but also in the minds of conversational partners in the socially situated but often solitary acts of writers. She characterized negotiation as a dilemma-driven, goal-directed effort to construct meaning in the face of forces such as disputes, competing interests, and patterns of power, arguing that negotiation is a response to multiple voices or kinds of knowledge that can shape action, arbitrate power relations, navigate through problems, avoid difficulties, and satisfy some goals.

Further Cognitive and Creativity Studies

During this decade, cognitive studies continued to investigate the relationship between thinking and learning. In 1987, Judith Langer and Arthur N. Applebee, in *How Writing Shapes Thinking*, reviewed many studies on this subject and conducted their own research on how writing works in support of learning. They demonstrated how different kinds of writing lead students to "focus on different kinds of information, to think about that information in different ways, and in turn to take quantitatively and qualitatively different kinds of knowledge away from their writing experiences" (135). In *Cognition and Instruction*, edited by Ronna Dillon and Robert Sternberg, essayists focused on cognition in different fields. Dillon posed the overall question: "What do experts know that novices do not?" (2) His essay examined the types of requisite knowledge underlying successful problem solving, differentiating declarative, procedural, and self- knowledge. Marlene Scardemalia and Carl Bereiter discussed higher order abilities in writing, arguing that they require more educational direction than natural endowments and skills learned though social interaction. Raymond Nickerson addressed the reasoning process, discussing automatic versus deliberate inferencing, closed versus open problems, development of beliefs, and evaluation of informal arguments.

In 1994, Cheryl Geisler, in *Academic Literacy*, argued that educators need to help students go beyond accepting textbook knowledge into questioning and intersecting their own knowledge with new information. She contrasted the literacy of those who write with domain knowledge and those who write rhetorically. In 1995, Mary Murray, in *Artwork of the Mind: An Interdisciplinary Description of Insight and the Search for It in Student Writing*, reviewed the literature on insight and developed an insight scale to measure the degree to which a writer resolved a dissonance in an expressive essay. In 1996, Mihaly Csikszentmihalyi published *Creativity: The Flow and Psychology of Discovery and Invention* in which he discussed a long-range research project that examined how creativity develops over a lifetime. He defined creativity as an "interaction of a system composed of three elements: a culture that contains symbolic rules, a person who brings novelty into the symbolic domain, and a field of experts who recognize and validate innovation" (6). To analyze these three aspects, Csikszentmihalyi interviewed 91 exceptional individuals.

Deconstruction, Poststructuralism, Postmodernism, and Invention

During this period, theories of deconstruction, poststructuralism, and postmodernism offered new perspectives on the relationship between knowledge and discourse, impacting work on invention. Sharon Crowley, in *A Teacher's Introduction to Deconstruction*, provided a useful overview of some of deconstruction's tenets with import for composition and invention. She explained that this theory deconstructs the ideas that the composing process begins with the originating author, that writing *re*presents or repeats the student's knowledge, that language is a transparent medium, that the author is the center of writing, and that the absence of readers is a necessary condition for composing. According to Crowley, these challenges to the writer's agency raise questions about the sources and nature of inventional acts, the role of readers in invention, and about inventional theory more broadly.

In 1986, Lester Faigley assessed three competing theories of process, including their inventional theories: 1) the expressive, valuing integrity (believing what is said), spontaneity (stressing processes of the creative imagination), and originality (the innate potential of the unconscious mind and self-actualization); 2) the cognitive, valuing heuristics and recursive processes; and 3) the social, valuing discursive communities and language development as an historical and cultural process. He concluded that a disciplinary basis for the study of writing would include the best of these theories. In 1988, James Berlin situated composition theories within three ideologies: cognitive, expressionistic, and social-epistemic, critiquing the first two by arguing that cognitive rhetoric centers on the individual mind whose structures are considered to be in perfect harmony with the structures of the rational, invariable, material world, and expressionistic rhetoric whose epistemology stresses the power of the inherently good individual and whose writing process seeks self-discovery. He advanced social-epistemic rhetoric, which, he contended, is a self-critical dialectal interaction among the writer, society, and language.

In an essay in *Rhetoric Review*, Berlin explained that poststructuralism considers the subject (the writer) as the construction of various signifying practices and uses of language in a given historical moment. The inventional work of rhetoric, then, he continued, is to study the production and reception of these signifying practices in a rhetorical context and to study cultural codes that operate in defining the roles of writer, audience, and the construction of matter to be considered. (See also Clifford and Schilb.)

In 1993, Lester Faigley, in *Fragments of Rationality: Postmodernity and the Subject of Composition*, summarized several postmodern tenets that impact theories of invention. The first was that nothing exists outside contingent discourse: no master narratives of human progress, no universal experience, no human rights. Postmodernism rejects the primacy of consciousness, with knowledge instead originating in language and with the subject being the effect of discourse. Postmodernism also challenges agency and with it a conscious and directed view of invention. It pushes composition to surrender its beliefs in the writer as autonomous self and instead to view the writer as written by the discourse. Also in that year, in "Rhetoric as Epistemic: What Difference Does that Make?" Robert Scott argued that "some version of the claim that rhetoric is epistemic (along with the corollaries that unmediated Truth is impossible and that the seeming priorness of Truth is but the arbitrariness of punctuating episodes) is vital to a sense of rhetoric as genuine and important" (128).

Expanding postmodern implications for invention, Victor Vitanza in "Three Countertheses" contrasted invention with paralogy, drawing on Lyotard's *The Postmodern Condition*. He deemed traditional invention as "smooth, continuous, and controlled and accounted for by a system or a paradigm of knowledge and which is used to promote the capitalistic, socialistic, scientific 'efficacy' of that system or paradigm" (147), in contrast to paralogy in Lyotard's terms as "'discontinuous, catastrophic, nonrectifiable, and paradoxical.' It (re) turns—that is, radically tropes—against the system, or paradigm of knowledge, 'changing the meaning of the word *knowledge' (Postmodern* 60)" (147). He went on to further differentiate the two: "Whereas invention is used for traditional or modern science, paralogy is used by postmodern science" (147). Vitanza explained that instead of consensus, Deleuze and Guattari focus on 'outsider thought', 'nomad thought', and schizo-dissensus'" (148). Contrasting the purposes of invention in Flower and Hayes's model with those of Deleuze and Guattari, he maintained that "What appears to be writing as discovery is only—unbeknown to its unself-conscious mystified self—writing that uncovers what had already been predetermined by the modes, or the social codes, or production and representation" (150). On the other hand, he explained that Deleuze and Guattari had developed an anti-model based on "desire and schizoexcess, on capitalism and schizophrenia cum schizoanalysis" (150) whose antipurpose is to critique the modes of representation, decoding them "to free the libidinal energy or, rather, desire" (150). Vitanza pointed out that Deleuze and Guattari find rational consensus suspiciously like political oppression and that commonplaces "have an insidious way of only fostering the dominant discourse" (151).

Also in 1998, Michael Bernard-Donals characterized the postmodern antifoundational world, saying that the "antinomian divisions implied by the Cartesian cogito—subject/object, mind/world, materiality/cognition—have been thrown over in favor of a discursive world where certainties are themselves the products of human invention, and where our language shapes our lives" (436). He contended that teaching writing now entails helping students to see that their writing engages them in hermeneutically remaking their life-worlds (437). He advanced Roy Bhaskar's theory of transcendental realism that provides, he maintained, a stronger theory of human agency, allowing "a connection between the situatedness of human activity and the material constraints," and that "connects human activities like observation and work to the possibility of real social change" (447).

In response to some of these postmodern positions, Barbara Couture in *Toward a Phenomenological Rhetoric* addressed what she called the "exclusion of truth from writing that now marks our textual scholarship [reflecting] a critical turn that has been accomplished in two moves: first, in our acceptance of philosophical relativism as the basis of all truth claims; and second, in our acceptance of personal resistance as *the* method of securing a true and valued self-identity" (2-3). She proposed a phenomenological rhetoric of writing that "considers writing as an activity that is consonant with the view of people as purposeful beings" (3). She posited three central premises of this rhetoric: 1) all essences or truths are located in subjective experience; 2) truth is an outcome of intersubjective understanding; and 3) intersubjective understanding progresses toward truth through writing (4). She argued that in such a rhetoric, practices guided by phenomenological principles can be validated as conscious, public, and collaborative efforts to know the truth of the world. Further, she introduced three standards for evaluating the truth and rightness of discourse: congruence, consensus, and commensurability.

Critical Rhetoric

Within the field of Communication Studies, a group that came to be known as Critical Rhetoricians fostered hermeneutical inventional acts that have interested some composition theorists who were developing poststructuralist and postmodern composition theories. In 1989, Raymie McKerrow presented a theoretical rationale for a critical rhetoric, elaborating eight principles to guide the act of criticism. He argued for critique as a transformative practice that

> recognizes the materiality of discourse, reconceptualizes rhetoric as doxastic as contrasted to epistemic and as nominalistic as contrasted to universalistic, [that] captures rhetoric as 'influential' as contrasted to 'causal,' [that] recognizes the importance of absence as well as presence, [and that] perceives the potential for polysemic as opposed to monosemic interpretation, and as an activity that is 'performed.' (91)

He explained the critique of domination and the critique of freedom. The first focuses on the discourse of power, of ideologies as rhetorical creations. The second entails a nontraditional historical analysis that seeks differences and discontinuities, not privileging the options it raises for considerations, but remaining free to open new possibilities for thought and action (96). According to McKerrow, critical rhetoric's task is to "undermine and expose the discourse of power in order to thwart its effects in a social reality" (98). In 1991, Robert Hariman critiqued McKerrow's characterizations of *doxa* and *episteme* and argued that McKerrow's writer of critical rhetoric was a disembodied modernist thinker having no identifiable social location, matched by a universal audience.

Michael McGee also discussed critical practice as invention, calling attention to the "formation of texts" in their original fragmented form. He theorized that the critic as inventor interprets for the consumer the meaning of fragments collected as a text. He also offered eight principles for defining critical rhetoric: 1) critical rhetoric is not method but a practice; 2) the discourse of power is material, existing in and through language; critical rhetoric aims at transformation; 3) rhetoric constitutes doxastic rather than epistemic knowledge, focusing on how the symbols come to possess power, bringing the "concealed to the forefront;" 4) naming is the central symbolic act of a nominalist rhetoric, directed against universalizing tendencies; 5) influence is not causality; 6) absence is more important than presence in understanding and evaluating symbolic action; 7) fragments contain the potential for polysemic rather than monosemic interpretation; and 8) criticism is performance, focusing on the activity as a statement and the critic as arguer or advocate for an interpretation of collected fragments (108) .

In 1990, Dilip Gaonkar critiqued McGee for problematizing the character of the critical object. He felt that McGee viewed rhetoric as a "globally constitutive agency," in which rhetoric is a material social process that constitutes a wide range of objects—beliefs, attitudes, actions, events, text, selves, and even communities" (290). He considered McGee to view rhetoric as "a process ontologically prior to its products" (291). Gaonkar pointed out that McGee's essay, "A Materialist's Conception of Rhetoric," presented a variation on the dialectic between object and method (303), constructing a materialist process model in which rhetoric is a global object and criticism becomes an object of study instead of a means of study" (305). Further Gaonkar argued that Michael Leff's textual criticism, which studies exemplary texts in order to find the possibilities of rhetoric as an art, seeks to understand these discourses in terms of how they work, how they are constructed, and how they respond to the situation, thereby pushing rhetorical criticism into hermeneutics. He maintained that Leff," through the process model was inclined to habitually defer the text" (310), considering rhetorical criticism as an interpretive discipline.

In 1990, Carole Blair and Mary Kahl applied some of these theories to historical studies. In their essay on revising the history of rhetorical theory they identified the inventional choices that historians make, arguing: "to the extent that we take the history of rhetoric seriously, we must take the historian's inventional choices as seriously" (148). Blair in "Contested Theories of Rhetoric" examined some of these inventional choices and their consequences in two major approaches. The first traced influence through scorning departures from ancient doctrines, focusing on one theorist's influence on another at the expense of what they said about rhetoric, dismissing or overlooking theories that did not fit a pattern of continuity, and minimizing documentary evidence. The second approach inscribed rhetorical theories within their own temporal contexts, using standard period divisions and often obscuring internal differences within periods.

Epistemic Rhetoric, the Third Discussion

During this period, the dialogue about rhetoric as epistemic resumed. Barry Brummett lamented that "the idea of rhetoric as epistemic has faded as a scholarly inspiration because its followers failed to link theoretical principles to actual criticism or analysis of 'real life'" (69). He maintained that failure to apply theoretical arguments is "failure to be grounded in a discipline" (70), but that two new sub-disciplines, argument theory and the rhetoric of science, were extending the principles of epistemic rhetoric. Responding to Brummett, Cherwitz and Hikins contended that what was called for was more epistemological musing by rhetoricians, not fewer. What was necessary to resolve difficult epistemological questions was to lay out and debate premises, question terms, and discuss consequences. Farrell entered the discussion, stating that Brummett failed to mention an earlier stage of the history of this issue—the centrality of rhetorical invention. He also asked what would happen if we acknowledged, "that not all positions (covert or overt) are equal in rigor and plausibility" (81). He suggested that rhetorical and communication theory are not identical because rhetoric is a "collaborative manner of engaging others through discourse so that contingencies may be resolved, judgments rendered, action produced" (83). He concluded that Brummett and Cherwirz and Hikins see rhetoric "as something critic-theorists do, rather than something that is produced in and through other people" (83). Farrell also concluded that there is no reason why epistemic rhetoric should provoke a dispute between theory and practice because: "the real mission of rhetoric as tradition and theory has always been to invent and to enrich rhetorical practice" (84). Scott averred that the "rhetoric as epistemic" claim came from a concern with argument that considered the nature of invention. He objected to explaining the term "epistemological" as asking the question, " How can I be certain?" He wondered:" If rhetoric is simply finding effective words to adapt Truth to those unable or unwilling to recognize it as such can we truly *invent* arguments?" (301). He proposed that theoretical work go forward in different areas including "the further development of invention on the grounds that argument is more fundamentally substantive than formal" (302).

Cultural Critique

In this decade, many composition theorists began to advocate work in cultural studies as a way of theorizing the cultural function of written discourse. Some of these advocates offered inventional strategies to guide cultural critique. In "Composition and Cultural Studies," Berlin created heuristics for a composition course that focused on cultural studies. These analytic guides combined the methods of semiotic analysis with those of social epistemic rhetoric in order to study the relationship between signifying practices and the structuring of subjectivities, such as race, class, and gender. The three acts that he proposed as a heuristic guide were: 1) locating binary opposites in texts; 2) discovering denotation and connotation that involve contestation; and 3) invoking culturally specific patterns (51). In "Marxist Ideas in Composition Studies" Patricia Bizzell maintained that cultural critique should include positive analysis. She argued that engaging students in Freirian critical consciousness entails studying how meaning-making processes are culturally constituted. She called attention to Fredric Jameson's point that in addition to demystifying ideology, instructors need to engage in "utopian" analysis and that analysis needs to be both deconstructive and constructive, thus incorporating ethical commitments. As a model, she described Jameson's three-part interpretive process: the study of forms, which reveals that symbolic configurations grow out of changing social pressure; the study of ideologies, which views the text as an utterance in the discourse of a particular class; and the study of discourse which reveals the way social classes struggle for discursive hegemony (56-57). (See also John Schilb, "Cultural Studies, Postmodernism, and Composition"; Diana George and Diana Shoos; John Clifford.)

Invention and Civic Discourse

In the 1990s, theory and research were also directed toward the role of discourse in the public realm. In 1991, Thomas Farrell argued that rhetorical practice allows anyone to participate effectively in public discourse by exercising practical wisdom in real-life settings where matters are in dispute. He asserted an inventional function for enthymemes (194-95), claiming that "rhetoric is practical reasoning in the presence of collaborative others" (189) and its "whole emphasis is toward action and the agency of others" (188). Farrell's 1993 *Norms of Rhetorical Culture* aimed to "rethink practical reason rhetorically, through its characteristic *manner* of engaging collective thought" (225). His examination of practical reason concluded that "to the extent that we envision at least the possibility of a rhetorical practice which might be informed by a sense of justice, solidarity, the particularity of audience interest, the forums of distance and disturbance, and the critical publicity of judgment, a rhetoric informed by practical reason remains a live civic option for our age " (229). He also made strong claims about the function and importance of inventional heuristics:

> the formal technai of rhetoric may be able to generate new dimensions of practical consciousness while working within the received opinions, appearances, and conventions of everyday life. This inventional process . . . typically involves an intersection between the rhetorical speaker's suggested interpretive horizon and the audience's received opinions, cultural norms, or [. . .] conventions and rules. (257)

He thus argued that invention could be both topical and enthymemic. He also demonstrated how rhetorical practice could be inventional because it recombines and individuates received opinions and convention in order to interrupt everyday policy and practice (273). He also refocused attention on the role of exigence in the rhetorical situation, which, he suggested could take the form of a disturbance or a contested issue or perspective (287). He concluded that rhetoric is "more than the product, more even than practice; it is the entire process of forming, expressing, and judging public thought in real life" (320).

Others have conducted research on the practices of those writing public discourse. For example, Jay Satterfield and Frederick Antczak, in "American Pragmatism and the Public Intellectual: Poetry, Prophecy, and the Process of Invention in Democracy," described inventional theory in the pragmatic tradition, as post-foundational, as politically effective knowledge constructed in a public space. Haixia Wang examined the discursive construction of the Tian'anmen Square incident in the *People's Daily*, the official Chinese newspaper. Karen Dwyer analyzed the way writers for Amnesty International construct the subject positions of international discourse publics and human rights activists. Karen Griggs conducted an historical case study of the complex authorship of an environmental policy. Thomas Moriarty studied the role of discourse in the peaceful removal of apartheid in South Africa. See also Martha Cooper, *Analyzing Public Discourse*; Gerard Hauser, *Vernacular Issues: The Rhetoric of Publics and Public Spheres*; William Craig, *Public Discourse and Academic Inquiry*; Manfred Stanley, "The Rhetoric of the Commons: Forum Discourse in Politics and Society;" and Paul Collins, *Community Writing: Researching Social Issues Through Composition*.

Feminist Invention

During this period, feminist studies paid some attention to women's inventional practices. Scholars such as Carol Gilligan, Nell Noddings, and Deborah Tannen investigated women's ways of knowing and communicating. Describing creativity and communication as a "situated, embodied process," Philippa Spoel argued that "a feminist approach to embodied rhetorics opens up possibilities for re-integrating bodily emotional ways of knowing into the process of invention" (201-2). Marianne Janack and John Adams discussed two presuppositions of feminist standpoint epistemology: the one who theorizes is a prime criterion for evaluating theories and one's social position influences one's theorizing (215). This research has been applied by rhetoric and composition scholars like Elizabeth Flynn, Karyn Hollis, Elizabeth Daumer, and Sandra Runzo, and Lillian Bridwell-Bowles, who have outlined various models of women's ways of composing: playing with language; using language close to the body; personal and emotional discourse; writing personal narrative over argument; foregrounding concrete particularities instead of abstract generalizations; emphasizing the nonlinear, associate, and inchoate as opposed to the hierarchical and argumentative; and viewing persuasion as the construction of matrices or wombs rather than an exercise of force. Feminist scholars have also advocated specific inventional strategies such as journaling (Cinthia Gannett); collaborative planning (Lisa Ede and Andrea Lunsford; Linda Flower, 1994); dialoguing and interviewing for ideas (Janice Hays); naming oneself through women's narratives instead of being defined by others (Daumer and Runzo; Bridwell-Bowles); and playing the believing game as connected learning (Hays). This work has been critiqued at a number of points. Diana Fuss, Teresa de Lauretis, Joy Ritchie and Gesa Kirsch have charged models like these with essentialism, arguing that they obscure differences in race, class, sexual preference, and ethnicity. Jarratt pointed out that some models of feminism overstress the avoidance of conflict ("Feminism"). Evelyn Ashton-Jones suggested that some feminist pedagogies offer an uncritical emphasis on collaboration. Finally, Janice Hays expressed concern that some feminist pedagogies focus on less complex forms of reasoning.

Another area of feminist research that bears on invention is revisionist historiography. In "Border Crossings: Intersections of Rhetoric and Feminism," Lisa Ede, Cheryl Glenn, and Andrea Lunsford discussed the rhetorical canons of invention and delivery, pointing out that they are "hardly natural methods but rather socially and historically constructed—and constructing—language games [. . . constraining and shaping] both who can know and what can be known" (411). They asserted that feminists have to challenge traditional understandings of the rhetor and what counts as knowledge, particularly the public/private distinction that has devalued personal and lived experience. Women should also include the intuitive, paralogical, and thinking of the body as sites of invention (412-413). See also Barbara Biesecker, "Coming to Terms with Recent Attempts to Write Women into the History of Rhetoric;" Miriam Brody, *Manly Writing: Gender, Rhetoric, and the Rise of Composition*; Cheryl Glenn, *Rhetoric Retold*; Catherine Hobbs, *Nineteenth-Century Women Learning to Write*; Susan Jarratt, "Performing Feminisms, Histories, Rhetorics;" Andrea Lunsford, *Reclaiming Rhetorica*; Louise Phelps and Janet Emig, *Feminine Principles and Women's Experience in American Composition and Rhetoric*; Jane Snyder, *The Woman and the Lyre*; Christine Sutherland and Rebecca

Sutcliffe, *The Changing Tradition: Women in the History of Rhetoric*; and other women writers in rhetorical history in Chapter 3.

Inventional Diversity

Several investigations of racial and ethnic discursive practices bear on rhetorical invention (e.g., Beverly Moss's collection of essays on how literacy is achieved in different communities; Victor Villanueva's and Mike Rose's personal narratives about literate ways of knowing; Jeanne Smith's account of the role of narrative among Lakota students; Villaneuva's discussion of the distinctive features of Hispanic/Latino writing; and Jacqueline Jones Royster's study of the tradition of black feminism among nineteenth- and early twentieth-century black women). Henry Louis Gates, Jr. extensively analyzed what he termed conscious rhetorical strategies: signifyin[g] as the master black trope, subsuming multiple subtypes such as talking smart, putting down, playing the dozens, shagging, and rapping.

More on Hermeneutics

During this decade, attention continued to be paid to hermeneutics and invention. In 1997, Alan Gross and William Keith edited a collection entitled *Rhetorical Hermeneutics: Invention and Interpretation in the Age of Science*. A central issue in the essays was the binary between production and interpretation—heuristics and hermeneutics. In the initial essay, Dilip Gaonkar argued that classical rhetoric gave priority to the "rhetor as (ideally) the conscious deliberating agent who chooses and discloses the capacity for prudence, who invents discourse that displays an *ingenium,* reducing the agency of the rhetoric to the conscious and strategic thinking of the rhetor" (26-49). In contrast, he asserted that contemporary rhetoric "extends the range of rhetoric to include discourse types such as scientific texts and gives priority to rhetoric as a critical/interpretive theory" (26). Concluding that contemporary rhetoric has moved from a vocabulary of production to a vocabulary of reception, he wondered:

> Is it possible to translate effectively an Aristotelian vocabulary initially generated in the course of "theorizing" about certain types of practical (praxis) and productive (poesis) activities delimited to the realm

> of appearances (that is, "public sphere" as the Greeks
> understood it) into a vocabulary for interpretive un-
> derstanding of cultural practices that cover the whole
> of human affairs, including science? (30)

Several authors in this text debated Gaonkar's production/inter-
pretation binary. Michael Leff critiqued Gaonkar's equivocal view of
agency, arguing instead for a notion of agency as the "circulation of
influence, something that remains fluid as one positioned subject engages the work of another, alternating the work while being altered by
it" (94). Leff pointed out that classical *imitatio* was not the mere reproduction of something in an existing text but rather a complex process
that allowed texts to serve as resources for invention, thus permitting
interpretation to play a role in the formation of rhetorical judgment
(97). Deirdre McCloskey critiqued Gaonkar's lack of evidence from
the works he discussed, his lack of familiarity with research in the philosophy of science since 1934, and his case of "theory hope." Carolyn
Miller challenged Gaonkar on a number of points. She maintained
that production and interpretation are not mutually exclusive, and
she pointed to the inconsistency in his claim that our vocabulary is
primarily Aristotelian and at the same time "fashioned for directing
performance" (Gaonkar 32). She also questioned Gaonkar's historical analysis, arguing that the classical tradition is not as univocal as
Gaonkar would have it. She also suggested that the idea of author as
subjective origin was more indebted to modernism than to pre-En-
lightenment humanism. (See also Gross, "What if We're Not Producing Knowledge?")

In 1989 and also in 1999, Thomas Kent proposed a paralogic rhetoric in which both discourse production and analysis are hermeneutic
acts that, he claimed, cannot be codified or learned. These acts, he asserted, are dialogic—open-ended and nonsystematic.

Review: Diversified Invention

In this third period, work on invention dispersed into many sites.
Scholars investigated the role of discourse in the construction of knowledge in the disciplines, including their inventional practices. Studies
in cognitive invention continued, leading to socio-cognitive theories of
rhetoric. Scholars influenced by critical rhetoric and social construction, deconstruction, poststructuralism, postmodernism, and cultural

studies critiqued the notions of unified coherent subjectivities and individual agency, theorizing that discourse constructs writers. They argued for social conceptions of invention and introduced collaborative practices. Others, propounding the importance of cultural critique, developed inventional strategies to investigate cultural codes, signifying practices, and ways in which students and others are constructed and commodified by race, class, and gender. Some theorists rejected the use of general strategies and advocated local heuristics based on the role of discourse communities in the construction of texts and knowledge. Multiple writer positions were advanced, encompassing gender, race, and class differences and expanding well beyond students in introductory writing classes to writers in the disciplines, the workplace, and the public sphere. Conflicts between the hermeneutic and heuristic escalated. Debates about rhetoric as epistemic continued. Invention migrated to various sites of study, e.g., feminism and diversity.

Invention in the New Millennium

In 2000, Victor Vitanza, in "From Heuristic to Aleatory Procedures; or Toward 'Writing the Accident,'" argued that the conditions of rhetorical invention are changing and the foundation—*stasis* theory—is dispersing, even imploding (188). He discussed the conditions for "thinking" in terms of a third term, the possible (that has been excluded by the terms of the ideal and the real). These imminent conditions for "aleatory procedures, with their general economy of excess are emerging through the shift from literacy that Ulmer calls 'electracy,' a shift to 'chance as hazard or to the monstrous'" (189). He pointed to Ulmer's theory of heuretics (heuristics + heretics) involving ubiquitous anagrams. This new theory of invention entails grammatology, exploring the "non-discursive levels—images, puns, or models and homophones—as an alternative mode of composition and thought applicable to academic work, or rather play" (191). Vitanza contended that this was a theory of invention defining "how 'to play' on the road to Serendip(ity)" (192). Heuretics' principle of invention operates "not by way of negation but by way of nonpositive affirmations" (193). Ulmer offered an acronym, CATTt (Contrast, Analogy, Theory, Target, and tale) as an antimethod, which Vitanza elaborated. He also explained a second heuristic, anagrammatic writing, facilitated by Internet Anagram Server/I, Rearrangement Servant, which he called an Invention-Discovery Machine. As Vitanza stated, these are aleatory practices based on a postmodern epistemology. He does not discuss their social nature or purpose.

In 2002, Janet Atwill and Janice Lauer's edited collection, *New Perspectives on Rhetorical Invention*, offered a range of points of view on rhetorical invention, some of which are represented in the essays discussed below. Lauer, in "Rhetorical Invention: The Diaspora," illustrated that studies of invention, rather than focusing directly on it, migrated into a number of areas in Rhetoric and Composition: writing in the disciplines, writing across the curriculum, cultural studies, feminist studies, technology research, and genre studies. She concluded that this scholarship treated invention as localized to these specific sites and as largely theoretical with only occasional mention of the implications for practice and pedagogy. Debra Hawhee's "Kairotic Encounters" examined the postmodern critiques of traditional rhetorical conceptions of subjectivity and invention, especially the dual conception of invention as discovery and creation of a unified subject. She argued for reconceiving invention and subjectivity drawing on sophistic notions and "invention-in-the middle, an idea from the work of Deleuze and Guattari. Arabella Lyon, in ""Rhetoric and Hermeneutics: Division Through the Concept of Invention," discussed the disappearance of rhetoric's public function because of privileging interpretation over rhetorical production. Yameng Liu, in "Invention and Inventiveness: A Postmodern Redaction," addressed the discovery/creation binary, examining the modernist values that bolster this opposition and proposing the term, *inventiveness*. Louise Phelps, in "Institutional Invention: (How) Is It Possible?" pointed out that rhetorical invention helps us to understand the difficulties of institutional change in academia, suggesting that academic institutions can fashion invention as a practical art. Linda Flower and Julia Deems, in "Conflict in Community Collaboration" wrote about the use of heuristics in community problem solving, especially scenarios, in a rhetoric that is generative and nonadversarial. Haixia Wang, in "Invention and the Democratic Spirit in the Teachings of Zhuang Zi," explained that Zhuang Zi, a Chinese philosopher, considered invention to be in analogical and dynamic relation with context.

Michael Carter's *Where Writing Begins: A Postmodern Reconstruction*, as its title indicates, addressed the earliest aspect of invention: beginning to write, the act that *stasis* in classical rhetoric was intended to guide. Carter noted that whereas stasis theory suggested a starting point for a chronological process of rhetorical invention, he questioned the notion of a chronological starting point for any act of writing and, further, the very idea of a beginning in the chronological sense. He argued that any point we could designate as a beginning of writing is ultimately arbitrary and does not help us determine where writing begins. Carter redefined beginning in terms of an ancient Greek philosophical conception of beginning, *arché*, the point at which opposing forces intersect and generate the potential for creativity. He used this alternative understanding of creativity as a basis for questioning the standard academic division between creative and, by inference, not-creative writing, by which the former devalues the latter. Carter also deployed Whiteheadian metaphysics and process theology to establish an understanding of creativity that is ongoing and discontinuous. He linked that understanding to invention, in particular the spatial metaphor of topos which implies a threshold or border between knowing and not-knowing, the familiar and the unfamiliar. For Carter, then, writing is creative not when it produces a special "literary" object but when it places the writer on that borderline of inventive openness, which he associated with beginnings.

In 2003, Anis Bawarshi, in *Genre and the Invention of the Writer: Reconsidering the Place of Invention in Composition*, defined invention as the "site in which writers act within and are acted upon by the social and rhetorical conditions we call genres—the site in which writers acquire, negotiate, and articulate the desire to write" (7). She claimed that writers "write within genres and themselves are invented by genres" (7). Describing the ecology of invention, she maintained that genres enable us to situate "a writer's motives to act within typified rhetorical and social conditions" (11). She also characterized genres as "situated topoi" (13) and argued that there is room within genres for transformation and resistance (93).

Chapter Synopsis

All of these inventional theories since the 1960s have rested on epistemologies ranging from phenomenology to postmodernism. Theorists have also differed over what acts comprise invention (e.g., initiating discourse, exploring subjects and situations, constructing texts or arguments, and interpreting texts). Further, they have disagreed over the purposes for these inventional acts, positing goals such as raising questions; reaching self-actualization; constructing new understanding, meaning, or judgments; finding subject matter; supporting theses; critiquing cultural codes; learning and creating disciplinary knowledge; interpreting texts; and playing. They have also argued over the types of strategies, tactics, heuristics, or guides that best facilitate invention, including the pentad, the tagmemic guide, the classical topics, freewriting, the double-entry notebook, journaling, collaborative planning, cultural code analysis, and playing with anagrams. As the decades have passed, scholars have disagreed more intensely over whether hermeneutics or heuristics were more effective as inventional approaches. Finally, over the years, conceptions of the subject positions writers occupy have become more complex and sites of inventional activity and its facilitation have multiplied. Thus, debates over invention's nature, purposes, and epistemologies have continued.

5

Issues over Invention Pedagogies

In contrast to other fields of scholarship that separate basic research from its application, research on rhetorical invention in the 1960s and 1970s was motivated by the desire to address the problems students faced with selecting subjects, framing a thesis, and getting ideas and arguments to support their theses. This close pedagogy/theory relationship in the field of Rhetoric and Composition was described by Lauer in "Dappled Discipline" and "Cross-Disciplinarity in Rhetorical Scholarship?" This chapter describes instructional approaches to teaching invention from the mid 1960s to the present. and then relates them to five issues that have circulated around invention pedagogy both historically and recently: 1) the relative importance of four formative factors in the development of a writer's inventional powers; 2) the merits of different inventional strategies; 3) the social nature of invention; 4) the character of invention as interpretive or productive; and 5) the role of rhetoric in either constructing or conveying knowledge. Each of these issues is explained below.

Issues

The Relative Importance of Four Formative Factors

One of the long-standing issues in rhetorical education since the Greeks continues today in discussions of composition instruction: What is most important in helping students to investigate their subjects and get ideas? Is it relying on their natural ability? Is it examples and models of invention the instructor provides for imitation? Is it extensive practice through many assignments? Is it strategies the teacher offers to guide invention? Each of these factors described briefly below has played a role in teaching invention. The natural ability pedagogy, what some today call romantic pedagogy, avoids teaching strategies or giving direct instruction on invention but instead provides students with congenial settings and suggestions for subjects that interest them and offers feedback on completed texts or drafts. The teacher tries to set motivating assignments, leaving students to rely on their native talent to produce a piece of writing, and then responds to a specific text. In imitation pedagogies, teachers provide students with readings and examples, either as stimuli for ideas or as models of inventing activity. The popularity of the Reader in composition courses testifies to the ubiquity of this pedagogy. In practice pedagogies, teachers engage students in frequent, sometimes daily, writing, including exploratory activity as a way to develop their abilities. Many of these writings are exercises; a few are done in genuine contexts. In art pedagogies, teachers provide students with strategies for invention and give guidance throughout the composing process. Eras of discourse instruction have been marked by an emphasis on one or the other of these broad teaching approaches as Chapter 3 illustrates. Sometimes today, as in prior periods, instructors integrate all four pedagogies. Richard Young discussed the relative merits of two of these pedagogies in "Arts, Crafts, Gifts, and Knacks and the Teaching of Writing," contrasting what he called the New Romanticism and the New Classicism. In his view the New Romanticists consider composing as free of deliberate control, the act of writing as a mysterious growth, and the imagination as primary. The New Classicists emphasize heuristic procedures, a generic conception of the composing process through which rhetorical knowledge can be carried from one situation to the other, and rational control of some processes that can be taught. Lauer also examined this issue in "Instructional Issues: Toward an Integration," arguing for the value of including elements of all four of these approaches to teaching composition. As invention pedagogies are discussed in this chapter, they will be related to these four approaches.

The Merits of Different Inventional Strategies

A second issue in teaching invention centers on two questions: Which acts of invention can be guided by strategies? Which strategies are most effective? One way of thinking about these questions is to compare strategies on a continuum. As defined in Chapter 2, inventional strategies are heuristic procedures and hence can be positioned on a continuum that ranges from almost algorithmic (rule-governed and highly formulaic) to almost aleatory (trial and error). We can, therefore, differentiate those that are more highly structured from those that have little structure. Algorithms, rule-governed formulas leading to right answers, can stifle inventional creative efforts. Aleatory procedures offer little guidance to students. Because all inventional strategies offer some direction to writers, they will fall somewhere on the continuum. This chapter, then, positions inventional guides on this continuum.

Several lists of these guides have been published. In 1979, David Harrington, Philip Keith, Charles Kneupper, Janice Tripp, and William Woods compiled "A Critical Survey of Resources for Teaching Rhetorical Invention," which annotated an extensive list of inventional practices in textbooks, categorized under the headings of "Neo-Classical Invention, Pre-Writing School, Tagmemic Invention and Linguistic Theory, Burke's Dramatistic Method, and Resources in Speech Communication." In 1993, Vicki Byard examined a range of heuristics procedures in "Considering Heuristics as Symbolic Acts: Their Relevance to Epistemic Rhetoric." Several textbooks and handbooks include catalogs of these invention strategies: *The St. Martin's Guide to Writing, Writing with a Purpose, Four Worlds of Writing: Inquiry and Action in Context,* and *Writing: A College Handbook.*

The Social Nature of Invention

In the last two decades, instructors have become interested in a third issue: whether invention is social or individual. Does a writer engage in invention in a solitary fashion, mentally gathering ideas, or is invention essentially a social act? As recounted earlier, Karen LeFevre argued for the social nature of invention, categorizing it into three types: internal dialogue, collaborative, and collective. She described internal dialogue as dialectic with another self, including internalized constructs influenced by social forces and other people, collaborative invention as the interaction of people, and collective invention as a supra-individual entity like institutions, societal prohibitions, and cultural expectations. The inventional approaches presented below will be interrogated as to whether they encourage, admit of, or preclude the social in any of its manifestations.

Invention as Interpretive or Productive

A fourth issue springs from the question of whether students should be engaged in interpreting texts or investigating questions and subjects. Some advocate that students should use inventional guides to read and critique texts, both written discourse and cultural productions. Others engage students in using heuristic procedures to generate ideas, insights, subject matter, or arguments. Still others give students guidance in both hermeneutic and heuristic acts. (See Chapter 4 for more on this issue.) This chapter will investigate which purposes of invention each pedagogy foregrounds.

Rhetoric as Constructing or Conveying Knowledge

As Chapter 3 has shown, this issue also has a long history. The present chapter will ask two question of each pedagogy: Is this pedagogy designed to help writers to create new knowledge (epistemic) and reach new insights and judgments? Or is its purpose to help writers find and deploy existing information and lines of argument to support theses or judgments already known?

Issues over Inventional Pedagogies

The rest of the chapter provides an account of inventional pedagogies that have been devised for teaching composition since the 1960s. As in Chapter 4, these approaches will be introduced chronologically and examined within the light of the above issues.

Prewriting Pedagogy

One of the first proposals for teaching invention in writing courses was the work of Gordon Rohman and Albert Wlecke, who introduced the concept of prewriting. They advocated several approaches to prewriting: keeping a journal to discover personal contexts and a point of urgency, engaging in meditation to transform an event into a personal experience, and creating analogies to generate and organize aspects of the subject. Each of these invention activities was proposed to help students reach self-actualization through writing. While such actualization included new understanding of one's self, the pedagogy did not stress an epistemic purpose. These strategies lean toward the aleatory side of the heuristic continuum because each can be practiced with minimal direction and can be done in any order, although the journal's purpose was to find subjects for writing investigation while the analogy played both a generative and organizing role. The pedagogy underscores the importance of enhancing natural ability with some guidance and emphasizes the "self," (ignoring invention as a social act, imitation, and interpretation). This approach initiated a widespread use of the journal in classrooms and informed textbooks, such as Rise Axelrod and Charles Cooper's *The St. Martin's Guide*, Clinton Burhan's *The Would-Be Writer*, Joseph Trimmer and James McCrimmon's *Writing with a Purpose*, Michael Paull and Jack Kligerman's *Invention: A Course in Pre-Writing and Composition*, and Donald Stewart's *The Authentic Voice*.

Pedagogy for Classical Invention

As Chapter 3 illustrated, during the Greek and Roman periods, strategies were taught to help rhetors initiate discourse (*stasis, status*); explore for lines of argument (common topics); gather subject matter and create ethical and emotional appeals (special topics); and develop frames of reasoning (enthymemes and examples). During the early part of the twentieth century, some vestiges of the common topics remained in textbooks (e.g., definition, cause and effect), but they functioned as discrete methods of development of an essay not as a *set* of inventional guides (Lauer, "Invention"). Composition theorists since the 1960s have created strategies and textbooks based on these classical heuristics as illustrated below.

   Textbooks. In 1959, Francis Connelly's *A Rhetoric Case Book* introduced some classical topics to be used as a heuristic set for examining and developing a subject. In 1965, Edward Corbett's *Classical Rhetoric for the Modern Student* modernized several classical strategies. He proposed *status* to help students decide on a thesis by defining their subject as a question of fact, definition, or quality. He garnered a selection of classical topics to guide students' explorations (e.g., definition, comparison, circumstance, and testimony). He showed students how to use rational appeals (the syllogism and example) and appeals to emotion in order to support a thesis, and he also provided readings and examples of these strategies as models for imitation. Thus, Corbett's text emphasized art and imitation, and directed inventional activity in a flexible order, positioning itself at the center of the heuristic continuum. Invention was presented as largely non-epistemic (i.e., to support a thesis).

Following Corbett's lead, a number of later composition texts featured *status,* the topics, and the appeals of classical rhetoric, including sets of classical topics as either investigative guides, catalogs of arguments, or methods of developing types of discourse. Winifred Horner, in *Rhetoric in the Classical Tradition*, introduced the three questions from *status* (fact, essence, and quality) as a strategy for exploring the student's subject. Her text also gave students advice on establishing their credibility, appealing to their audience, and finding good reasons. The book also proposed topics of definition, classification, comparison and contrast, and cause and effect that were designed to help students find ideas. Sharon Crowley and Debra Hawhee, in *Ancient Rhetorics for Contemporary Students,* included *stasis* (asking the right questions about rhetorical situations) by focusing on Hermagoras's four questions: conjecture, definition, quality, and procedure. Crowley and Hawhee also provided common topics (the sophistic topics, Aristotle's common topics, and "formal" topics), ethical, pathetic and extrinsic proofs, and types of reasoning. Assigning a different purpose for invention, Frank D'Angelo's *Composition in the Classical Tradition* is based on the *progymnasmata,* "a graded, cumulative sequence of writing tasks, [. . .] within an explicit rhetorical framework" (xiii). He positioned invention topics to develop the types of discourse that were part of this tradition (e.g., Refutation, The Commonplace, Praising and Blaming, and The Thesis), listing, defining, and illustrating these topics. John Hagaman argued for the value of the *progymnasmata* in teaching rhetorical invention as a way of integrating free and structured inquiry. He described the *progymnasmata* as "general heuristics that train students to view their subjects from multiple perspectives" (25), guiding them through patterns of thinking.

Collections of Essays. Several collections of essays also presented accounts of using classical inventional practices (e.g., Robert Connors, Lisa Ede, and Andrea Lunsford's *Essays on Classical Rhetoric and Modern Discourse*; Rosalind Gabin's *Discourse Studies in Honor of James Kinneavy*; Jean Moss's *Rhetoric and Praxis;* Kathleen Welch's *The Contemporary Reception of Classical Rhetoric;* Marie Secor and Davida Charney's *Constructing Rhetorical Education;* Neil Nakadate, Roger Cherry and Stephen Witte's *A Rhetoric of Doing;* and James Murphy's *The Rhetorical Tradition and Modern Writing.*

Specific Pedagogies: The Enthymeme. A number of scholars suggested the enthymeme for teaching invention. In 1991, John Gage articulated a general theory of the enthymeme for advanced composition. Asserting that argumentation is the process by which people come to knowledge, he referred to the enthymeme as "an architectonic rhetorical structure valuable in the invention process" (167). He illustrated how the enthymeme could be a heuristic. It could serve as a guide to help students think through the kinds of questions they are trying to answer and offer them a stance toward these questions, a strategy for approaching that stance, and a way of investigating the assumptions they share with their audience. Also with an epistemic purpose, Barbara Emmel developed a pedagogy of the enthymeme, describing it as "a rich set of relationships with the potential of being expressed in a multitude of ways" (132). She discussed processes through which the enthymeme could be used in the classroom: discovering and shaping claims (the realization of intention) and discovering relationships among claims (the realization of function). She also proposed dialogue to familiarize students with the enthymeme as a heuristic. Jeffrey Walker, countering the prevailing notion that the enthymeme is a shortened rhetorical syllogism, argued for a view of the enthymeme that entails "the inference-making of the heart" and the "strategic intentionality of 'forming plans,' including 'kairotic inventiveness'" and style (49). Referring to Anaximenes and Isocrates, he pointed out that between them we might derive a reasonably full picture of the

> sophistic, non-Aristotelian notion of the enthymeme that is pervasive in the Hellenistic rhetorical tradition: the enthymeme is a strategic, kairotic, argumentational turn that exploits a cluster of emotively charged, value-laden oppositions made available (usually) by an exetastic buildup, in order to generate in its audience a passional identification with or adherence to a particular stance, and that (ideally) will strike the audience as an 'abrupt' and decisive flash of insight. (53)

He noted that what continues to mark the enthymeme today is a "stylistically intensified argumentative turn that serves not only to draw conclusions but also, and decisively, to foreground stance and motivate identification with that stance" (55). He contended that enthymematic skill is crucial for rhetoric and dependent on all other skills or means of persuasion, including knowledge of the "topoi of a discursive field," "various discourse-level gambits, schemes, and strategies," the ability to analyze and adjust to the rhetorical situation, and a "fluent command of the stylistic resources of the language" (62). He concluded that "a trained excellence in enthymeming requires what Isocrates would call an extensive 'discourse education' that cultivates not only advanced literacy but also *phronesis* (judgment and intelligence) and *sophia* (wisdom, skill) through critical argumentative engagement with the argumentation of others in many discursive genres" (62).

Specific Pedagogies: Topics. Others pointed out the contemporary benefits of the topics. In 1987, Carolyn Miller bemoaned the loss of the special topics in pedagogy, which emphasize the "diversity and complexity of rhetorical practice" (65), in favor of the common topics. She proposed that we teach the special topics drawn from specific disciplines. Walter Jost, drawing on the work of Cicero and Wayne Booth, suggested turning to the "special topics—ideas, terms, distinctions, value propositions in all fields, literary works, histories, the civil law, 'all antiquity' *not as determinate and fixed facts and truths*, but as more or less negotiable, interpretable possibilities for argument" (8). He pointed out that for Booth the rhetorical topics are means for building community within and among specialties, training students to function as generalists who can connect fields by addressing issues within larger ethical and political contexts (13). Eugene Garver argued that a theory of writing should include a structure that gives thinking a direction without predetermining results. He proposed the topics as complex sets that could direct thought, discover the unknown, argue a case, or locate clichés (commonplaces). He also discussed the value of *stasis* in classifying issues in order to respond precisely to assignments and in determining the point at issue as a direction.

How do these classical strategies relate to the issues discussed above? Because these inventional guides are based on ones that had been used for centuries, they embody the collective aspect of invention as social. Students are not left alone to figure out how to begin, to explore, or to develop arguments. The use of *status*, however, varies in its epistemic power. Those that suggest *status* as a way of forming a thesis, exploring a subject, finding ways to persuade the audience, framing arguments, or marshalling subject matter generally advise it as a way to communicate and develop the known. Those that suggest it as a way of defining

a question for investigation in a context emphasize its epistemic potential. Most of the treatments of topics, *status*, and the enthymeme are
proposed for a heuristic purpose—to help students produce a text—
not interpret one. Because each strategy has a set of flexible moves or
directives, it can be positioned in the center of the continuum from
aleatory to algorithmic. In terms of the pedagogies for teaching such
inventional strategies, the textbooks deploy a combination of instruction in invention (art), use of examples (although not often of the acts
of invention themselves), and practice through assignments.

Tagmemic Inventional Instruction

In 1965, tagmemic rhetoricians, Richard Young and Alton Becker
provided the first modern set of heuristic strategies to guide students
throughout the writing process: for invention, audience, arrangement,
and style. In 1970, Young, Becker, and Kenneth Pike published *Rhetoric: Discovery and Change*, which detailed inventional strategies to
guide writing as a process of inquiry: for framing questions to pursue,
for exploring, and for stating and verifying emerging judgments and
new understandings. They characterized these strategies as epistemological heuristics to help students construct new knowledge and to
reach new insights. The first strategy helps students make explicit a
problematic situation and pose a well-framed question to direct their
inquiry by classifying their unknown as a fact, a process, or a relationship. A second heuristic procedure helps them to explore their subject
using multiple perspectives: viewing their subject as a particle, wave,
and field, and investigating its contrastive features, range of variation,
and distribution. A third heuristic strategy guides students in verifying their emerging insights by testing them for correspondence with
their experience, consistency with their own image, usefulness, and
simplicity. Because these strategies offer flexible directives and rely on
intuition, they can be positioned centrally on the continuum of heuristic procedures. Even though the textbook foregrounds an art of invention, it also insists upon the natural abilities of intuition, incubation,
and the imagination. Readings in the text act as models of the inquiry
process as well as texts for analysis and imitation. Finally, the textbook
engages students in writing as a process of inquiry numerous times,
thus encouraging practice based on students' own questions. Although
the text does not foreground the social, it does not preclude it. As a
heuristic, it embodies perspectives active in the culture.

This pedagogy has been researched, critiqued, and used in a number of textbooks. In 1973, Lee Odell, in "Piaget, Problem Solving and Freshman Composition," examined the role of dissonance in initiating writing, arguing that according to Piaget all creative processes and analytic thought stem from a sense of dissonance or disequilibrium. Odell described a course engaging students in the process of posing and resolving dissonance. In a 1980 *CCC* article, Charles Kneupper critiqued the terminology and apparent redundancy of tagmemic heuristics and offered his own revised version with six directives instead of nine. (See also critiques by Kinney and Wells in Chapter 2). Studies of tagmemic rhetoric were done by a number of researchers, including Lee Odell ("Discovery Procedures"), Richard Young and Frank Koen, Catherine Lamb, Nancyanne Rabianski, George Hillocks ("Inquiry"), and Sandra Katz. Textbooks have offered versions of the tagmemic exploratory heuristic (e.g., Rise Axelrod and Charles Cooper's *The St. Martin's Guide*, William Irmscher's *The Holt Guide to English*, Janice Lauer et al.'s *Four Worlds of Writing*, Joseph Trimmer and James McCrimmon's *Writing with a Purpose*, Dean Memering and Frank O'Hare's *The Writer's Work*, Tilly Warnock's *Writing Is Critical Action*, Joseph Williams's, *The New English*, and W. Ross Winterowd's *The Contemporary Writer*).

Freewriting

In 1973, Peter Elbow's *Writing Without Teachers*, introduced the concept of freewriting as an inventional practice. Freewriting consists of writing continuously for 10, 15, or 20 minutes without evaluating or editing what is produced. Elbow argued that this practice helps a writer find subjects, clear the mind, bring out voice, and reach a center of gravity. In his discussion of the process of writing as "cooking," he recommended interacting with others about one's writing, encouraging conflicts or contradictions in one's thinking, moving back and forth between ideas and words, and constructing metaphors, comparisons, and examples. In an appendix essay, he introduced the doubting and believing game, explaining that the activity of truth seeking could be analyzed into two essential processes—doubting and believing. The doubting game entailed assessing competing ideas by subjecting them to rigorous doubt. The believing game involved assessing competing ideas by refraining from doubting or searching for shortcomings, trying to see these ideas as true (147-91). Elbow advanced other inventional practices in subsequent books. In 1981, in *Writing with Power*, Elbow described "looping," which entails freewriting followed by selecting, organizing, and revising parts of what was produced in the freewriting (59-77). In 1986, in *Embracing Contraries*, he explained that through writing he taught two kinds of thinking: 1) first-order thinking, which is intuitive, creative, and control free; and 2) second-order thinking, which is conscious, directed, and controlled. He also offered a revised version of his original thoughts on the doubting and believing games, claiming that: "Methodological doubt is only half of what we need. [. . .] but thinking is not trustworthy unless it also includes methodological belief: the equally systematic, disciplined, and conscious attempt to *believe* everything no matter how unlikely or repellent it might seem" (257). He went on to explain that because they are methods, "they help us see what we would miss if we only used our minds naturally or spontaneously" (25). He described methodological doubt as individual, entailing rhetorical propositions, while methodological belief involved the rhetoric of experience (264). Writing, he contended, is a movement from disciplined belief to disciplined doubt (286). The last part of his essay was devoted to suggestions for believing both in the absence of good reasons and on the basis of evidence (270-84).

The freewriting pedagogy has an aleatory cast to it, while the doubting and believing games stress the value of methodology. Elbow's pedagogy also relies strongly on natural ability and frequent practice. Because during invention he encouraged writers to interact with others, some of his heuristics have a collaborative social character to them.

In 1977, Joseph Brown, Jean Colburn, Peter Elbow and others compiled *Free Writing! A Group Approach*. In 1980, Thomas Hilgers published "Training College Students in the Use of Prewriting and Problem-Solving." In 1991, Pat Belanoff, Peter Elbow, and Sheryl Fontaine edited a collection of essays on freewriting entitled *Nothing Begins with N: New Investigations of Freewriting*, that included essays by Elbow, Pat Belanoff, Sheridan Blau, Diana George and Art Young, Richard Haswell, and Ken Macrorie. These essays explored subjects such as a phenomenology of freewriting, freewriting's connection to organization, critical thinking, writing across the curriculum, individual psychological and physical health, and the relationship between freewriting and ideas of theorists such as Berthoff, Emig, and Britton. Elbow also wrote a number of essays related to his pedagogy including "In

Defense of Private Writing: Consequences for Theory and Research."
In addition, researchers have tested freewriting's effectiveness, studies
which are noted in Hillocks's meta-analysis (the results of these studies
are discussed later). The practice of freewriting has been included in a
number of textbooks, including Joseph Trimmer and James McCrimmon's *Writing with a Purpose* and handbooks like Andrea Lunsford
and Robert Connors's *The St, Martin's Handbook.*

Burkean Invention

Kenneth Burke's pentad (discussed in Chapter 4) has been used as
an invention strategy in composition pedagogy. In 1977, Philip Keith
described a set of Burkean terms as dialectical exercises through
which students could develop an argument: Etymology, Thesis as
Dialectic, the Complex in the Simple, Expansion of Circumference,
and Translation. In 1979, he again discussed the use of Burke's pentad
in teaching, stating that Burkean invention interested him because
of its athleticism in discourse, maintaining that it helped the writer
control and develop strategies of stance and reference. He also examined the pentad against the backdrop of Burke's notion of dialectic. In
1978, Joseph Comprone indicated how Burke's theories could become
a heuristic for teaching writing as a process. Prewriting activities could
concentrate on agent and scene as the text evolved toward purpose.
The notion of terministic screen could be turned on the audience;
action could entail asking what is happening as far as readers are concerned. Comprone also discussed Burke's dramatism as a way of teaching writing.

As a flexible yet directive strategy, the pentad stands centrally in
the continuum of heuristic procedures. Burke himself, as mentioned
above, agreed that the pentad could be used for producing as well
as interpreting texts. He also argued that as a guide the pentad is a
grammar of basic human motives, engaging the writer in investigating
broadly acknowledged dimensions of action and thus possessing the
collective feature of social invention. The pentad has been included
as a heuristic procedure in many textbooks such as Rise Axelrod and
Charles Cooper's *The St. Martin's Guide,* William Irmscher's *The Holt
Guide to English*, Tilly Warnock's *Writing Is Critical Action*, and W.
Ross Winterowd's *Rhetoric and Writing* and *The Contemporary Writer.*
Most of the textbooks that include it in their catalogs of planning only
explain it. A few show the heuristic in action, offering examples.

One text that does apply and extend the pentad in a wide variety of contexts for writing and interpretation, with stress on its epistemic function, is David Blakesley's *The Elements of Dramatism*. In this book, Blakesley described dramatism, of which the pentad is but one aspect, as "an analytical method of rhetorical invention" (189) The pentad is "a philosophical grammar [. . .] capable of generating an infinite variety of equations or meaningful relationships, just as the grammar of a language enables us to generate an infinite variety of sentences. In its capacity for generating that variety, the pentad functions much like an Aristotelian general topic" (8). The purpose of dramatism is" not to dispose of ambiguity, but to study and clarify the resources of ambiguity." Aligning dramatism and rhetoric, Blakesley explained,

> it becomes possible to extend the definition of rhetoric from "the art of finding the available means of persuasion" to "the art of elaborating and exploiting ambiguity to foster identification." We elaborate ambiguity in the interest of identifying the margin of overlap midway between identification and division. We exploit ambiguity by reifying particular meaning, hoping that we have found a meaning somewhere in the middle that can be used to persuade others or foster their identification. From this perspective, rhetoric is a multipurpose art of both producing knowledge in social situations and applying that knowledge discretely and strategically to teach, delight, and persuade. (189)

The Elements of Dramatism provides extended examples of how the pentad (and dramatism) can keep us alert to ambiguity in the symbolic action of texts, films, social movements, and other situations, as well as to ways the pentad can help writers multiply perspectives as they construct arguments and take stances.

Larson's Heuristics

In 1968, Richard Larson developed "A Plan for Teaching Rhetorical Invention" that featured over 200 questions categorized into 1) Topics That Invite Comments: Single Items, Single Completed Events or Parts of an Ongoing Process, Abstract Concepts, Collections of Items, and Groups of Completed Events, including Process; and 2) Topics with Comments Already Attached: Propositions and Questions. He stated that the task of invention is to help students "see what is of interest and value in their experiences, to enable them to recognize when something they see or read or feel warrants a response from them, [. . . and] to stimulate active inquiry into what is happening around them" (146). He pointed out that students could use these questions alone or working in small groups. After the students finish applying the questions, he advised that they evaluate what they had generated by comparing their subjects to another one, determining whether or not they liked the subject, and by detecting conflicts or inconsistencies. This heuristic leans toward the algorithmic side of the continuum, becoming less portable with its numerous questions. Because Larson indicated that the strategy could be used alone or with others, it has a social dimension. The discussion accompanying it suggested that its purpose was to find subject matter to develop papers.

The Double-Entry Notebook, The Uses of Chaos, and Shaping

In 1981, Ann Berthoff, in *The Making of Meaning: Metaphors, Models, and Maxims for Writing Teachers*, outlined the method of the double-entry notebook as a guide to critical reading and to encourage habits of reflective questioning, observation (students looking and looking again), shaping, and abstracting both discursively and non-discursively. One side of the notebook would hold reading notes, quotations, and images and on the other side would be notes about these notes, summaries, formulations, and editorial suggestions. She explained that the format provided a way for students to conduct a "continuous audit of meaning" (45). She also encouraged observation as visual thinking and shaping or forming in two modes of abstraction: the discursive mode (successive generalizations) and the presentational mode (direct, intensive insight). In order to help students rediscover "the power of language to generate the sources of meaning" (70), she proposed learning to write by "learning the uses of chaos," contending that meanings are made "out of a chaos of images, half-truths, remembrances, syntactic fragments, from the mysterious and the unformed" (70). In *forming, thinking, writing*, Berthoff offered students assisted invitations to explore the composing process. These included observing and interpreting the observations, as well as a set of exercises: 1) Getting Started: listing, classifying, and determining presuppositions; 2) Forming Concepts: making statements, generating, and interpreting; and 3) Developing Concepts: naming the classes and articulating relationships. For all of these inventional acts, she provided copious examples and exercises. She also elaborated on her inventional strategies in many articles, including "Abstraction as a Speculative Instrument," "Dialectical Notebooks and the Audit of Meaning," "From Dialogue to Dialectic to Dialogue," and "Learning the Uses of Chaos." Her inventional heuristics call into play an interaction among natural abilities, art, imitation, and practice, giving flexible direction to students. The exercises largely engage students in working individually.

Journals

Following Rohman's introduction of the journal as part of the writing process in 1964, many types of journals have been used for different inventional purposes. In *Gender and the Journal*, Cinthia Gannett described the diary and the daybook used by Donald Murray. She also addressed different uses of the journal for writing across the curriculum, including Toby Fulwiler's academic journal as a critical writing tool. Fulwiler, in "The Personal Connection: Journal Writing Across the Curriculum," listed such journal functions as helping students to make connections, summarize material, and do problem solving (18-24). In Fulwiler's collection of essays, *The Journal Book,* contributors offered both theoretical and pedagogical discussions of using the journal in different disciplines. These essays also advanced the idea of journals as not only personal but social writing. Whether the journal has an epistemic character or not depends on its purpose.

Inquiry Strategies

In 1982, George Hillocks in "Inquiry and the Composing Process: Theory and Research" maintained that invention should focus on immediate concrete data. He described inventional strategies as consciously adapted procedures such as observation, description, generalization, and the generation of hypotheses. His argumentative strategies included analyzing scenarios to generate theses, deciding on relevant information, and predicting opposing arguments and dispatching them. To guide the development of definitions, he proposed such guides as setting criteria for a range of target concepts and differentiating them from others, giving examples of the concept, and creating contrastive examples. Because of their flexible yet systematic character, these inquiry strategies can be positioned centrally on the heuristic continuum. Hillocks described their purpose as epistemic and their operation as often social. In addition, they foreground art, imitation, and practice.

Discussing a somewhat different conception of inquiry in 1982, Lauer argued that the purpose of writing as a process of inquiry is to seek insights and new understandings. Such a process is initiated by raising questions about subjects and experiences that puzzle writers in real contexts and then exploring these questions using heuristic guides to stimulate multiple perspectives. Teaching writing as a process of inquiry, she asserted, entails helping students to initiate their writing not with theses but with questions or dissonances, to use heuristics to explore, and then to frame emerging insights into focuses. She pointed out that this conception of writing might entail helping students overcome a number of obstacles: their fear of going beyond the known, their comfortable biases that preclude investigation, and their tendency to succumb to an overdose of common sense that deters them from investigating anything beyond immediate concerns (see Bernard Lonergan's *Insight*). In *Four Worlds of Writing*, Janice Lauer, et al. constructed inventional heuristics to guide students working alone or in groups to engage in writing as a process of inquiry, helping them to frame guiding questions based on their own compelling puzzlements in genuine writing contexts; assisting them in taking different perspectives on their questions, in exploring ideas extensively, imaginatively, and critically; and in encouraging them to construct focuses that represent their new understandings. These heuristics for inquiry are intended to have an epistemic function, helping students to create new knowledge and reach new insights in their everyday experience, public contexts, academic courses, and workplaces, which would require a range of genres. Thus, this inventional pedagogy involves art, models, practice, and natural ability, and falls centrally on the heuristic continuum.

Another form of inquiry is teaching writing as a reflective practice, which was discussed by Kathleen Yancey in *Reflection in the Writing Classroom*. Yancey defined reflection as "processes by which we know what we have accomplished and by which we articulate accomplished products of these processes" (6). She put forward that this method is dialectical, bringing multiple perspectives into play in order to produce insight. Writers look forward to goals and backward to where they have been. Reflection entails for Yancey a process of developing and achieving specific goals and strategies to reach these goals and determining whether the goals have been met.

Problem-Solving Strategies

In 1977, Linda Flower and John Hayes published an early article on their emerging cognitive problem-solving model (see Chapter 4), identifying a number of heuristic procedures consonant with that model: 1) playing the writer's thoughts (turning off the editor and brainstorming, staging scenarios, playing out analogies, and resting and incubating); 2) pushing ideas (finding cue words, stating a key point in a nutshell, organizing ideas by using tree diagrams, testing against an editor); 3) setting up goals; 4) finding operators (setting direction as part of plans); 5) constructing an audience; 6) anticipating roadblocks; 7) using rhetorical strategies; and 8) testing on live readers. Some of these strategies informed the composing process in Flower's *Problem-Solving Strategies for Writers*. Later in Flower's socio-cognitive theory, *The Construction of Negotiated Meaning*, she presented collaborative planning as a social heuristic to engage students in exploring the problems they faced. In *Learning to Rival*, she, Elenore Long, and Lorraine Higgins presented another heuristic strategy called rival hypothesis thinking or "rivaling," which they defined as a "literate practice in which people explore open questions through an analysis of multiple perspectives and evidence" (4). They studied how students learned to rival in order to deal with culturally charged open questions. The planning activities they observed were "deeply embedded in complex patterns of hierarchy and power" (16). Flower explained that rival hypothesis thinking was characterized by three features: 1) a bold attitude toward inquiry that tolerated uncertainty and open questions; 2) a set of strategies for inquiry that helped the writer seek out alternative voices and interpretations and to generate strong rival hypotheses; and 3) a constructive process that tried to build a consensual conclusion (30).

Students can use these problem-solving heuristics either to reach new solutions to problems or to find ideas and material to convince readers. Because in their early model Flower and Hayes stressed the recursive and embedded nature of the composing process, their strategies can be positioned centrally on the heuristic continuum, although this model does not make explicit an epistemic function. In the earlier work there was also little mention of the social character of the strategies, but nothing in their nature prevents them from being used that way. Their later work stressed the social contexts and characteristics of invention.

Invention in Writing Across the Curriculum

In 1984, Anne Gere's *Roots in the Sawdust: Writing to Learn Across the Disciplines* differentiated between writing to learn and writing to show learning. Among the purposes of writing to learn, Gere cited getting the course material right (Britton), creating webs of meaning (Vygotsky), moving from concrete to formal operations (including cause-and-effect relationships), comprehending propositional statements, discriminating between observations and inferences, drawing inferences from evidence, visualizing outcomes, and drawing analogies. She pointed out that this kind of learning entails finding knowledge as well as assimilating it.

Many textbooks in writing across the curriculum (WAC) have given inventional advice and sometimes strategies for invention. In 1981, an early proponent of WAC, Elaine Maimon, with a number of co-authors in different disciplines, published the textbook *Writing in the Arts and Sciences*, which presented inventional strategies, such as problem-solving, private writing, freewriting, the journal, brainstorming, lists, treeing, analogies, tagmemic invention, Burke's pentad, and seeing and diagramming. A collection of essays edited by Maimon, Barbara Nodine, and Finbarr O'Connor provided models for discussing thinking and reasoning from interdisciplinary perspectives, including such topics as thinking, formal operations, reflective judgment, dialectical thinking, informal logic, and meaning making. In *Language Connections: Writing and Reading across the Curriculum*, edited by Toby Fulwiler and Art Young, several researchers described how students used journals to learn a wide range of subject matter. Later WAC textbooks continued to discuss invention, often under the term "inquiry." In *Researching and Writing across the Curriculum*, Christine Hult discussed the inquiry processes in science, technology, social science, and the humanities, describing practices such as observation and hypothesis formulation. In *Research and Writing in the Disciplines*, Donald Zimmerman and Dawn Rodrigues presented task analysis and generation of ideas about a topic using freewriting, brainstorming, patterned notes, and tree diagrams. They also explained how to define a problem and develop research questions. Judy Kirscht, Rhonda Levine, and John Reiff advocated teaching the rhetoric of inquiry, which they argued can link composing to learning and writing in the disciplines so that writing instruction becomes a way not only to "interact with declarative knowledge, but also to develop procedural knowledge concerning the field—to learn *how* knowledge has been constructed as well as *what* that knowledge is" (374). Lloyd Wilson explained the relationship between teaching writing and features of legal reasoning, including the adversarial system, the burden of proof, and case law reasoning. John Warnock, addressing lawyers and law students, advised that a good plan entails having a clear sense of what they want "writing to DO, for whom, and how. One study of professional writers showed them spending over 60% of their writing time in planning, and thinking by means of writing that *preceded* drafting" (10).

Scholars have also critiqued aspects of teaching invention in WAC. In "Rhetorical Invention: The Diaspora," Lauer pointed out that the focus of many WAC courses has been on writing to learn the material in a field rather than to create new knowledge in a discipline. She cited Judith Langer and Lee Odell, who underscored this point. Langer lamented that many teachers in different disciplines focus on content, not on higher-level intellectual skills (71). In contrast, in several classes in biology, history, and literature that Langer visited, teachers were starting to introduce invention, stressing active questioning and interpretation (72), questioning the independence of method and observation, and considering the most appropriate methods of inquiry (73). Langer noted, however, that when teachers tried to introduce students to the process of science, they did not give students any procedural knowledge to apply such methods themselves (75). Odell concurred, pointing out roadblocks to teaching inventional strategies: teachers may have so internalized their thinking strategies that they can't make them explicit, or they may prefer to discuss the content of their disciplines rather than the analytic strategies needed to generate or reflect on that content (97). Donna LeCourt noted another problem facing inventional instruction across the curriculum—that teaching knowledge-making practices may "serve to reinforce the ways of thinking and status of a particular knowledge" (392). LeCourt contended that WAC's goal was usually to initiate students into a "certain way of thinking valued by the discipline" (393), causing "the discourse to appear natural and pragmatic, and thus ideologically free" (395). Arguing against such critiques, Charles Bazerman contended: "Rhetorical criticism, especially if it is carried out with broad sweeps of condemnation, makes disciplines purveyors of hegemonic univocality rather than the locales of heteroglossic contention that they are" ("From Cultural Criticism" 63). He argued for a rhetorical analysis that "makes visible the complexity of participation by many people to maintain the large projects of the disciplines" ("From Cultural Criticism" 64). Further he explained that discourse studies of this kind can build "the intellectual foundations for courses that enable students to enter into disciplines as empowered speakers rather than as conventional followers of accepted practice" ("From Cultural Criticism" 67).

Online Inventional Practices

As the computer became a commonplace writing technology, instructors began to offer online heuristics. One of the first to develop inventional software was Hugh Burns, who in 1979 wrote and programmed three computer-assisted instruction strategies derived from Aristotle's topics, Burke's pentad, and the tagmemic matrix, an inventional tool that later would be developed by the Daedalus Group. These programs systematically prompted students to ask questions, clarify heuristic perspectives, answer questions, store responses, seek additional insights, and attend to their purpose. Burns discussed this software in subsequent essays in 1980, 1983, and 1984. Other early invention software included: Schwartz's "ORGANIZE," "SEEN," and "PREWRITE," Ruth von Blum and Michael Cohen's "WANDAH," William Wresch's "Writer's Helper," Jay Bolter, Michael Joyce, and John Smith's "STORYSPACE,"and Cynthia Selfe's "Wordsworth." In 1982, Helen Schwartz catalogued available computer programs into four areas, including tutorials that helped students to explore their topics using prompts. She also published a textbook, *Interactive Writing: Composing with a Word Processor.* In 1984, in "Computer Assisted Invention: Its Place and Potential," Dawn and Raymond Rodrigues discussed the advantages of having teachers present when students use these guides. They also pointed out several values of computer-based invention: providing individualizing instruction in invention, supporting the recursive use of activities in writing, and accommodating differences in student writing styles. They offered another inventional guide, "Creative Problem Solver," as a supplemental tutoring system that engaged students in dialogue. Also in 1984, Frederick White and Mary Ann Aschauer examined the connections between the word processor and the habits of mind deployed in invention.

Taking stock of the prior work on computer-assisted invention, in 1986 Diane Langston contrasted "old paradigm" computer aids for invention with "new paradigm" ones. She described the old paradigm aids as attempting to transfer paper-based strategies for invention to the computer and critiqued the question-asking and systematic heuristics as well as other programs. She outlined criteria for a "new paradigm" of computer-assisted heuristics. A new paradigm would permit different heuristics to interact as well as produce new strategies. It would also include domain-specific heuristics. Third, it would provide heuristics that could be modified by both teachers and students. Finally, it would stay on the leading edge of technology. In Michael Spitzer's 1989 review of prewriting software and writing programs, he cited the work of James Strickland, who compared structured and unstructured heuristics like freewriting and showed how these early programs could assist invention. He also identified other software programs: Ruth Von Blum, Michael Cohen, and Lisa Gerard's "HBJ Writer," Fred Kemp's "Idealog," and Strickland's own "Invent." Strickland also in "Prewriting and Computing" showed how these early programs assisted with invention. In 1990, Carol Cyganowski offered suggestions for creating a collaborative pedagogy for invention using word processing. Cynthia Selfe in "The Electronic Pen" studied how students adapt prewriting to their use of word processing technology. Thomas Barker refuted the argument that there is no need for invention in technical writing, mentioning the use of collaborative writing, task analysis, usability testing, audience analysis, format paths, argumentation forms, fact finding, on-site observations, and sampling procedures.

In 1991, Wallis May Andersen published a review of computerized invention strategies that included rubrics or template files and outliners that offer hierarchic structures for prompts and responses and the capability to collapse and expand the levels. She also discussed hypertext software that featured text and graphics useful for brainstorming ("STORYSPACE") and software that allowed users to deploy various heuristics ("HBJ Writer," Writer's Helper," "Brainstorms," and "ORGANIZE"). In 1992, James Strickland provided an annotated bibliography of software for writers that included such programs for invention as "Fine Lines," "Daedalus Invent," "ORGANIZE," "Rhizome Project," "STORYSPACE," "Success with Writing," "Thought-line," and "Writer's Helper." In "Structuring Argumentation in a Social Constructivist Framework," David Kaufer and Cheryl Geisler described their "Warrant" project, which identified data structures of written argument and aided in the reading and writing of argument. The project shifted invention strategies to argumentation as a social task, engaging students in analyzing characteristics of their discourse community. Kaufer and Geisler also gave students strategies to transform information from others' texts into discourse, to provide a characterization of a socially constructed argument, to describe teaching strategies for such arguments, and to identify computer software that facilitates this pedagogy.

Visual Rhetoric and Invention

Technology that could alter text and integrate images heightened interest in visual rhetoric. Previously, Gabrielle Rico had advocated visual invention practices, based on brain hemisphere research, including clustering and blocking. Linda Flower and John Hayes had also identified planning modalities for writing that included charts, networks, maps, and tree building ("Images, Plans, and Prose"). In 1989, Ron Fortune pointed out how computers stimulate visual and verbal thought processes. Citing Arnheim's classic work on visual thinking as intuitive cognition, he illustrated the use of visual thinking in the prewriting and planning stages of a student. Patricia Sullivan studied the visual markers for navigating texts and argued that in published documents both words and images contribute to meaning, pointing out that through technology writers must learn how to "take control of the page" (44). Stephen Bernhardt and B. F. Barton and M. S. Barton made other contributions to the discussion about the rhetoric of visual texts and the means for teaching visuals. Anne Wysocki demonstrated how the visual elements of texts construct meaning, countering the word/image distinction and critiquing arguments about hypertext and visual texts. In *Opening Spaces: Writing Technologies and Critical Research Practices*, Patricia Sullivan and James Porter proposed postmodern mapping as a heuristic. Overall, those doing work on visual rhetoric have paid more attention to analyzing the features of visual texts than to studying and teaching heuristics for creating such texts.

Feminist Inventional Practices

Composition theorists have advocated feminist practices for teaching invention. These practices include keeping journals (e.g., Cinthia Gannett); collaborative planning (e.g., Lunsford and Ede, *Singular Texts*, and Flower, *Construction*); dialoguing, interviewing, using the believing game as connected learning (Hays, *Intellectual Parenting*); and generating experimental writing (Bridwell-Bowles, "Discourse and Diversity"). Kathleen Parvin described the connections between teacher action theory, feminist critical theory, and liberatory writing pedagogy. Karyn Hollis proposed using feminist theory in writing workshops ("Feminism"). Several collections of essays have described gendered strategies and ways of writing (e.g., Joanne Addison and Sharon James McGee's *Feminist Empirical Research: Emerging Perspectives on Qualitative and Teacher Research;* Cynthia Caywood and Gillian Overing's *Teaching Writing: Pedagogy, Gender and Equity;* Elizabeth Flynn and Patrocinio Schweickart's *Gender and Reading: Essays on Readers, Texts, and Contexts;* Francine Frank and Paula Treichler's *Language, Gender, and Professional Writing;* and Kristine Blair and Pamela Takayoshi's *Feminist Cyberspaces: Mapping Gendered Academic Spaces*).

Pedagogies of Deconstruction, Cultural Studies, and Postmodernism

In the late twentieth century, several systems of thought influenced the teaching of composition. This section points out a number of pedagogical implications of these developments for invention. Compositionists have devised courses to engage students in reconsidering their positions as writers, their concepts of readers, their analyses of immediate situations and larger cultural contexts, and their deployment of inventional strategies.

Deconstruction Pedagogies. In 1989, Sharon Crowley outlined a deconstructive pedagogy. This pedagogy posited the writer as audience; viewed writing as continuous, dynamic, and collaborative; and engaged students in social and political issues. Crowley argued that a deconstructive pedagogy redirects the notion of genre to its suitability to the rhetorical situation and incorporates the needs of audience into the writing process. This view of pedagogy has a number of implications. Among them, it suggests that inventional acts should be located in specific rhetorical situations and that writers and readers may need to interact during invention.

Cultural Studies Pedagogies. In 1987, Ira Shor advocated a Freirean approach to teaching composition that stressed problem-posing through dialogic teaching and problematizing all subjects of study in students' cultures (105-6). Donald Lazere in "Teaching the Political Conflicts" asserted that the primary aim of teaching should be to broaden the ideological scope of students' critical thinking, reading, and writing capacities in order to empower them to make their own judgments on ideological positions (195). He offered an inventional scheme for guiding the preliminary stages of researching and writing a term paper, including exploring 1) political semantics: using definition, connotation, and denotation to study racism and sexism; 2) psychological blocks to perceiving bias: examining culturally conditioned assumptions, closed-mindedness, prejudice, stereotyping, authoritarianism, absolutism, and inability to recognize ambiguity, irony, and relativity of point of view; and 3) modes of biased and deceptive rhetoric: studying the possible causes for bias, understanding the distinct patterns of rhetoric in different ideologies, and locating and evaluating partisan sources. In "Invention, Critical Thinking, and the Analysis of Political Rhetoric," Lazere argued that the ability to analyze public discourse is crucial in helping students to engage in public rhetoric. He also offered invention strategies for constructing public arguments.

In "Composition and Cultural Studies," Berlin described inventional practices in a composition course that focused on cultural studies. He advocated combining the methods of semiotic analysis with social epistemic rhetoric in order to analyze cultural codes. His heuristics were designed to help students study the relationship of signifying practices to structuring subjectivities such as race, class, and gender. These strategies included locating binary opposites inscribed in texts and analyzing culturally specific patterns, such as the Cinderella story. He claimed that this pedagogy makes teachers and students equal learners and empowers students to become agents of social change. In a 1992 essay, he described other heuristic procedures to help his students engage in cultural critique. Students begin by locating points of resistance in their experience and negotiating the cultural codes they encounter. In texts (print, film, television) related to these experiences, students locate key terms and position them in binary opposites. They next place these terms in narratives related to the text, situating the narratives within economic, political, and cultural formations (26-31). After using these heuristics to analyze texts, students deploy them to analyze their personal experiences, locating points of dissonance for further investigation.

Others who have written about cultural studies pedagogy include Richard Penticoff and Linda Brodkey, who described the difficulties in teaching writing about difference, and John Trimbur, who discussed the contribution of cultural studies to composition ("Cultural Studies"). Essays on other cultural studies pedagogies for teaching invention can be found in such collections as *Cultural Studies in the English Classroom*, edited by James Berlin and Michael Vivion; *Composition and Resistance*, edited by C. Mark Hurlbert and Michael Blitz; *The Politics of Writing Instruction: Postsecondary*, edited by Richard Bullock, John Trimbur, and Charles Schuster; and *Contending with Words*, edited by Patrica Harkin and John Schilb. Textbooks that feature heuristics for cultural critique include John Trimbur's *A Call to Action*, James Heffernan, John Lincoln, and Janet Atwill's *Writing: A College Handbook*, and Lauer et al.'s *Four Worlds of Writing: Inquiry and Action in Context*.

Postmodernism Pedagogies. Postmodernist thought has also impacted the teaching of invention. In 1991, Victor Vitanza described a counterpedagogy that desires to escape what he called the "pedagogical imperative" (161). He spoke about sophistic counterstrategies that are discontinuous, random, and filled with fragmented thoughts and digressions. In this pedagogy, argument is reconceived as *dissoi paralogoi* (165), and processes of invention are paralogic and counterinductive with the goal of innovation. In 1989, Thomas Kent also discussed a paralogic post-process pedagogy that is dialogic, collaborative, and hermeneutic. Countering some of Kent's ideas in 2000, Bruce McComiskey, in *Teaching Writing as a Social Process*, developed a social-process pedagogy that included a heuristic aimed at guiding students to analyze the cycle of cultural production, contextual distribution, and critical consumption. Discussing the postmodern character of this heuristic, he explained that the real work of production is the creation of desire in consumers and the creation of social values that "manifest themselves in institutional practices and cultural artifacts" (21). Discussing the post-process movement, he argued that his social-process pedagogy extends rather than rejects existing conceptions of the composing process. McComiskey illustrated how students could

construct their own postmodern subject positions in the "aporia between identity and difference" (70). Discussing his students' position
papers about culture, he showed how they negotiate the middleground
between competing texts and construct the semiotic significance of
their own experiences. He recommended dual writing assignments: a
critical essay on the competing discourses in an institution and a proposal offering resolutions to the problems identified in the first essay.
He pointed out that the two types of writing drew on students' active reading strategies and their rhetorical heuristics. In 2002, Thomas
Rickert argued for a pedagogy that entails post-oedipal forms of subjectivity, deploying "strategies that circumvent, forestall, or resist the
replication of authoritarian or proto-violent modes of control" (307).
Such a subjectivity, he maintained, is conducive to a "post-pedagogy
of the 'act'," demanding "the new, the unthought, the un-accomodat-
able" (313), decentering stable subjects and allowing a subject to trans-
gress social norms (313-14). This pedagogy, he claimed, is an "exhor-
tation to dare, to invent, to create, to risk" (314), not a set of codifiable
strategies but a valuing of unorthodox work.

   In 2002, Debra Jacobs responded to postmodern critiques of the
writing process. She argued that "dismissing process theories and
pedagogies by conflating all of them with expressivism, or by pointing
out limitations of other strands of process as they were conceptualized
during, say, the 1970s or mid-1980s [. . .] can limit instructional practices aimed at intervening in students' ethical development" (664). She
claimed that teaching writing as a process helps teachers to engage students in critical inquiry. In(ter)ventional acts of critical inquiry "foster
affective engagement, challenge existing *doxa,* and contribute to new
understanding" (670). They entail "interventions over time that disrupt the quotidian stream of consciousness, [including] inquiry into
ways of reading processes and products (and their means of production)" (670). She further maintained that "deliberate discursive action
will not occur if there are no inventional practices to help students
align their lived experiences with what they read" (672). She concluded by saying that "in(ter)ventional practices foreground writing as a
process and disrupt the 'flows' of power and control in the writing
classroom" (673). See also Helen Foster's response to postmodern critiques of the writing process.

Evaluations of Inventional Pedagogies

Chapter 4 discussed various criteria for evaluating theories of heuristics. This chapter presents other criteria for assessing the pedagogical merits of inventional practices.

In 1984, George Hillocks published the first meta-analysis of experimental studies of writing pedagogy. This new statistical method enabled researchers to calculate the effectiveness of different pedagogies as tested in many studies and thus draw broader conclusions. Hillocks analyzed the relative effects of three "focuses" related to teaching invention: the use of models, writing as inquiry, and freewriting. He also assessed the effectiveness of three "modes" of instruction in composition classes: presentational (lecturing), natural process (using no guiding strategies), and environmental (using strategies in context). His results showed that each of these focuses and modes had some positive impact on students' writing as judged by holistic evaluations, but their *levels* of effectiveness (effect size) differed. (An effect size can range from −3.00 to 0 to +3.00. An effect size of about .20 to .50 is important; anything above .50 is a major difference.) Teaching writing as inquiry had the greatest impact (effect size: .57). The other two had some impact: the use of models (effect size: .21) and freewriting (effect size: .16). All three modes of writing also had some beneficial influence: the environmental mode (effect size: .44), the natural process mode (effect size .18), and the presentational mode (effect size: .02).

In *Research on Written Composition*, Hillocks elaborated on this research, reviewing a number of studies on different aspects of invention: the assignment conditions, freewriting, heuristics, and inquiry. In the first group, two studies (Kock, 1972, and Anderson, Bereiter, and Smart, 1980) demonstrated that students who did free associating before writing wrote better essays than those who did not (174-75). He cited six studies of freewriting in which the experimental group achieved significant gains: Alloway, et al., (1979); Olson and DiStefano (1980); Wagner, Zemelman, and Malone-Trout (1981); Hilgers (1981); and Cummings (1981). Thirteen studies of freewriting showed no significant difference between experimental and control groups (178). For teaching heuristics, Hillocks cited four studies in which students using the tagmemic heuristic had a range of gains in investigative acts and abilities: Young and Koen (1973), Odell (1974), Lamberg (1974), and Burns and Culp (1980).

In 1985, Lester Faigley, Roger Cherry, David Jolliffe, and Anna Skinner, in *Assessing Writers' Knowledge and Processes of Composing*, compiled an account of research on aspects of invention that included 1) the time spent on planning; 2) the strategies involved in planning (e.g., creating goals, generating content, organizing, analyzing the rhetorical situation); and 3) instruction on planning. They argued for the importance of descriptive writing assessment, outlining the steps involved in the development of Performative Assessment writing tasks and scoring rubrics. They also reviewed methodologies for assessing these processes of composing, including observation and microethnography, verbal reports in cognitive research, and text analysis. Discussing how process instruments show changes in students' composing strategies, they examined a close-reading approach and a continuum approach. Other evaluation instruments for invention include Mary Murray's "Insight Scale and Questionnaire," Judith Langer's ""Measure of Topic-Specific Knowledge," and Judith Bechtel's "Verbal Reasoning Subtest of the DAT."

David Perkins, in *The Mind's Best Work*, provided suggestions for the effective use of heuristics. He suggested that they should be employed along with field knowledge and taught, illustrated, practiced, and individually adapted. In 1985, Nickerson, Perkins, and Smith in *The Teaching of Thinking* reviewed the current literature on instruction in improving various kinds of thinking using conceptual models and understanding, such as learning, classifying, and deductive and inductive reasoning. They evaluated pedagogies in the areas of problem-solving, creativity, and metacognition, assessed the effectiveness of instruction in heuristics in different fields, and described language and symbol-manipulation approaches to teaching thinking. Jeanne Simpson narrated her efforts to develop an evolving set of criteria for heuristic procedures and argued for the importance of a meta-theory for introducing students to invention strategies. In 1990, Richard Fulkerson elaborated a set of questions to be asked when adopting an approach to teaching writing, including invention: What axiology does the approach adhere to (i.e., what does it consider good writing)? What procedural view does it hold (i.e., how do or should writers write)? What pedagogical practices does it advocate (e.g., workshops, models, rhetorical, strategies)? What epistemological position does the approach maintain (i.e., the relationship between writing and knowledge)? (410-11).

In 1994, Young and Yameng Liu edited a collection of landmark essays on rhetorical invention in writing

Chapter Synopsis

This chapter's initial section described five broad issues about teaching invention. The first revolved around the relative merits of four pedagogies in developing inventional powers: reliance on a person's natural abilities, teaching strategies for invention and guiding their use, engaging students in practicing invention, or offering students models and examples for imitation. The second issue centered on the relative effectiveness of different heuristics from structured to somewhat unstructured heuristic procedures. The third issue concerned whether invention was considered as individual or social. The fourth issue stemmed from whether invention was a hermeneutical or heuristic act. The fifth issue dealt with whether or not inventional strategies had an epistemic purpose.

The chapter then presented a chronological account of the following inventional strategies or practices: prewriting and journals, classical rhetoric; tagmemic rhetoric; Burkean invention; the double-entry notebook; freewriting; Larson's heuristic; inquiry strategies; problem-solving heuristics; strategies for writing across the curriculum, computers and composition, and visual rhetoric; and strategies based on deconstruction, cultural studies, postmodernism, and feminist studies. As the pedagogies were characterized, they were examined in the light of the above issues. The chapter closed with a discussion of evaluative studies and essays suggesting criteria for inventional pedagogies.

6

Glossary

Kelly Pender

Agency—Controlling forces in discourse production and subjectivity formation. Agency is a key issue for composition theorists who try to determine how much and what kind of control writers have in the composing process.

Aleatory Procedure—A trial-and-error or chance-based approach to problem solving.

Algorithm—An unchanging rule for solving a problem (i.e., a mathematical formula).

Antifoundationalism—Philosophical position that there is no absolute, immutable truth grounding reality. Antifoundationalists believe that truth is relative to specific situations.

Art—The use of principles and strategies to guide a complex process like composing. Art is often contrasted to *knack*, a habit acquired through repeated practice, and *magic*, a mysterious natural ability or talent. Those who consider rhetoric an art believe that while not all of the writer's composing processes are subject to conscious direction, many are and can be improved by learning heuristics.

Backing—Proof that supports the warrant of an argument. According to Stephen Toulmin, when an audience does not accept the warranting principles of an argument, a speaker must support these principles with another argument, or backing.

Circumference—In Burkean theory, the overall scene against which human relations, behavior, and conduct are examined in a pentadic analysis.

Collaborative Planning—Model of planning in which co-authors begin, explore, and position a project together. A collaborative plan functions as a contract, schedule, and possibly as an evaluative tool for a group.

Commonplaces—A rhetorical *techne* or art. The commonplaces are often thought of as regions, storehouses, or locations since arguments are "housed" there. The term *commonplaces* was used historically to mean both the common topics like cause and effect and also in the Renaissance to mean "apt sayings." In the first sense, they assisted rhetors in discovering, arranging, and delivering culturally relevant and audience specific arguments. In contemporary usage, the term often refers to lines of argument.

Cultural Codes—Historically and socially specific semiotic practices, usually constituted by a set of opposing terms, that work like terministic screens, influencing or constructing particular interpretations of reality, as well as forms of subjectivity.

Current-Traditional Rhetoric—Refers to the predominant composition theory and pedagogy of the late nineteenth and twentieth centuries. Based on redactions of eighteenth-century rhetorical theory, current-traditional rhetoric is formalistic and rule-governed. In accordance with its belief that invention cannot be taught, it emphasizes the arrangement and superficial correctness of discourse. This emphasis can be seen in its "four modes" theory of discourse (exposition, description, narration, and argument) and in its part-to-whole approach to writing, especially the five-paragraph essay assignment.

Deconstruction—Strategy of reading associated primarily with French philosopher Jacques Derrida that seeks to show how textual meanings are unstable and multiple. By isolating and rearranging key hierarchies and binaries in texts, deconstruction attempts to reveal that what is present in a text depends upon what is absent in it. In America, deconstruction is most frequently associated with the rhetorical analysis of Yale theorist Paul de Man, who tried to show that the rhetorical figures upon which philosophical texts depend continuously destabilize the texts' meaning.

Deliberative Discourse—One of the three genres of rhetoric classified by Aristotle. Deliberative or political discourse is concerned with counseling an audience of judges about a future course of action. Examples of deliberative topics include advantage and disadvantage, expedience and inexpedience, war and peace, and finances.

Dialectic—The counterpart of rhetoric, dialectic is an art of inquiry and argumentation in which two opponents debate an issue. While both rhetoric and dialectic begin with probable premises, the latter, according to Aristotle, is more concerned with testing truths than with persuading an audience. Dialectic, therefore, usually involves expert interlocutors while rhetoric usually involves a speaker and a popular audience.

Dianoetic—Pertaining to reasoning, intellectual activity, processes of thinking.

Discourse Community—Related to the linguistic concept *speech community* and the literary concept *interpretive community*, a discourse community is a group of individuals who share ways of understanding and communicating. Discourse communities usually have a regulatory function, determining what objects and methods are suitable for examination, as well as what conventions are appropriate for communication. Social and social-epistemic theories of composition emphasize the role that discourse communities play in writing.

Dissoi Logoi—An anonymous fifth-century BCE. sophistic text that examines the relationship between culture and nature, epistemological relativism, and the art of rhetoric. In Greek, the phrase means "different words" and refers to the rhetorical epistemology of arguing both sides of an issue.

Dissonance—A tension or puzzlement which occurs when experience differs from values and expectations or when a writer's conceptual systems clash. Dissonance often provides a starting place for inquiry.

Dramatism—Kenneth Burke's theory that language is primarily a form of action rather than knowledge. Dramatism looks at the ways in which humans use symbols and how motives are represented in and created by such usage. Burke's pentad provides a vocabulary and methodology for analyzing motives in language.

Enthymeme—Defined by Aristotle as a form of rhetorical reasoning, the enthymeme is one of the two modes of rhetorical proof (the other being example). Enthymemes are claims supported by probable premises that the speaker assumes the audience will accept. As such, they form the basis of arguments.

Epicheireme—A more complex form of rhetorical reasoning used to structure proofs according to five parts: the proposition, the reason, the proof of the reason, the embellishment, and the resume.

Epideictic discourse—One of the three genres of rhetoric first classified by Aristotle. Epideictic or demonstrative discourse tries to entertain, inspire, or impress the audience, which is composed of spectators rather than judges or political assemblies. Examples of epideictic discourses include funeral orations (eulogies), festival orations (panegyric speeches), ceremonial addresses, and encomia. Such speeches commonly address topics such as virtues, vices, condemnable acts, and praiseworthy acts.

Epistemic—Refers to the ability to generate or create knowledge. *Epistemic rhetoric* refers to the use of discourse to construct knowledge or to the processes of rhetoric as knowledge-making. Although there are several variations of this position, it is opposed to the view that rhetoric merely communicates pre-given knowledge. Rhetoric as epistemic positions often facilitate or lead to an inquiry-based approach to teaching composition since they maintain that rhetorical acts begin with questions, exploration and possibilities rather than with certainties.

Epistemology—Derived from the Greek word, *episteme* (knowledge), epistemology is the branch of philosophy that studies the nature and origin of knowledge. Epistemologists ask what counts as knowledge, how it is created or obtained, who can create knowledge, and what its conditions are. Debates about the epistemic status of rhetoric are epistemological debates.

Ethos—One of the three means of persuasion identified and systematically studied by Aristotle. *Ethos* refers to persuasion through the text's construction of the character or virtue of the rhetor. When using *ethos* as an appeal to the audience, rhetors attempt to show that they possess traits such as credibility, fairness, modesty, and intelligence. Throughout history rhetoricians have debated the nature of *ethos*, some maintaining that it is the actual character of the speaker, others arguing that it is more of an image the speaker creates in rhetorical situations.

Field-dependent—A term Stephen Toulmin used to refer to and describe the elements of arguments that change from context to context. The criteria used to evaluate arguments, for instance, are field-dependent elements, while the force of qualifying terms is field-invariant. The notion of field-dependence supports Toulmin's claim that no particular field of arguments is inherently more logical than another.

Focus—The statement of the insight gained from inquiry that sets the stage for a text and contains two parts: the subject and the point of significance for the writer. The subject names the situation investigated by the writer and the point of significance presents the writer's new understanding.

Freewriting—Invention strategy in which writers write quickly and without stopping for ten to twenty minutes in order to generate as many ideas as possible without editing their text. Freewriting can also be seen as a strategy for helping writers develop voice.

Freirean—Term used to describe pedagogies influenced by the work of Brazilian educator and scholar Paulo Freire. Among other things, Freire advocated a form of pedagogy based on dialogue between students and teachers that proceeds from and always takes into account the material conditions of students' lives. As a Christian Marxist, Freire also believed that consciousness raising was a primary educational aim that required a commitment to teaching literacy skills.

Hermeneutic—A theory of interpretation. Hermeneutics began as theories of scriptural interpretation and was developed in philosophy by scholars such as Friedrich Schleiermacher,

Hans-Georg Gadamer, and Paul Ricoeur, and in literary and rhetorical studies, by scholars like Stanley Fish and Steven Mailloux. Hermeneutics is a prominent component of rhetorical studies, especially in rhetorical criticism, a sub-field of rhetoric that uses rhetorical theory to interpret texts. Scholars such as Michael McGee, Wayne Booth, Edwin Black, Michael Leff, Carolyn Miller, Charles Bazerman, and Alan Gross—among many others—have used rhetorical theory to interpret texts from popular culture, professional environments, and academic disciplines. Some rhetoric and composition theorists argue that hermeneutics ought to be the only inventional act.

Heuristics—Modifiable strategies or plans that serve as guides in creative processes. Writing heuristics try to prompt thinking, intuition, memory, inquiry, and imagination without controlling the writer's writing process. Heuristics are based on expert writers' strategies, which can be taught.

Imitation—Method of rhetorical training in which students try to emulate the styles, voices, conventions, and themes of master texts. In addition to learning the art of rhetoric, natural talent, and practice, classical rhetoricians believed that imitation was a key element of the rhetor's development. The use of readings and models in composition classes demonstrates the role that imitation continues to play in composition pedagogy.

Inquiry—Pedagogical approach to writing in which students begin with questions rather than a thesis or a focus. Based on the idea that writing creates new knowledge, inquiry-based pedagogies believe that by starting a writing project with questions, curiosities, or puzzlements, students will be more invested in their work, more likely to go beyond what they already know, more likely to explore, and therefore more likely to learn something new. In short, writing to inquire is writing to investigate, gain insight and communicate that insight.

Insight—The outcome of inquiry. Insight refers to the new understanding, perspective, or knowledge that results from the exploratory and creative processes of writing to inquire.

Intertextuality—Refers to the ways in which texts refer to and depend upon other texts for their meaning. First used by French psychoanalyst and linguist Julia Kristeva, the concept of intertextuality turns critical attention from a text's author to the social conditions of its production (i.e., the discourse community to which it belongs). Composition theorist James Porter identifies two types of intertextuality: iterability (the repetition of certain parts of a text in another text, i.e., citation) and presupposition (assumptions a text makes about its referent, readers, or context).

Issue—A point of discussion, debate, or dispute. Issues in the field of Rhetoric and Composition arise from disagreements over theoretical and pedagogical aspects of written discourse.

Judicial discourse—One of the three genres of rhetoric first classified by Aristotle. Also called forensic discourse, judicial speeches are usually about the past and concerned with issues of guilt, innocence, justice, and injustice. Audiences for judicial discourse are judges and jurors.

Kairos—Rhetorical principle of discoursing at the appropriate time and in due measure. For the Sophists, particularly the Pythagoreans, *kairos* was the rhetorical principle of determining which truth to argue according to the specifics of time, place, and audience. As such, it was a generative principle, a way of initiating discourse by considering the conflicting elements (or truths) in light of a particular rhetorical situation.

Logocentrism—Central term in Derrida's critique of metaphysics. Logocentrism refers to the belief that words and truth correspond, thereby making language a truth-conveying medium. Derrida argues that the Western metaphysical tradition is characterized by logocentrism, or philosophy's desire to make true statements about the world.

Logos—One of the three means of persuasion identified and systematically studied by Aristotle. *Logos* refers to artistic appeals made to reason or the validity of arguments. These appeals involve the use of enthymemes or examples. Unlike analytic logic, rhetorical reasoning entails probabilities, presumptions, and values.

Master Narratives—Teleological narratives that structure societies or communities by requiring that all parts of life relate to an overarching whole. French philosopher Jean-Francois Lyotard introduced the virtually synonymous term, grand narratives, in his treatise on postmodernity, *The Postmodern Condition*. There Lyotard argues that the two grand narratives of modernity are political liberty and complete philosophic knowledge or totality. Lyotard also argues that postmodernity is characterized by incredulity toward these master narratives.

Ontology—The branch of philosophy that examines being. Ontologists are concerned with what exists. Ontology is closely related to and often confused with metaphysics, the branch of philosophy concerned with the nature or essence of what exists. The work of philosophers such as Jean-Paul Sartre and Martin Heidegger investigates ontological questions.

Paralogy—Term used by Jean-Francois Lyotard in *The Postmodern Condition* to refer to the method by which players in postmodern language games create new rules for the language games. According to Lyotard, postmodernity, with its *petit recits* (or small narratives) depends on performativity rather than consensus as its mode of knowledge legitimation. The rules of language of postmodern language games, then, cannot depend on consensus; they must be local, agreed upon by their present players, and subject to cancellation. Paralogy seeks to produce these new rules by questioning consensus, which is to say, by creating dissensus.

Pathos—One of the three means of persuasion identified and systematically studied by Aristotle. *Pathos* refers to rhetorical appeals made to the audience's emotions. Aristotle establishes the relationship between emotions and persuasion in *Rhetoric* when he defines emotions as "those things through which, by undergoing change, people come to differ in their judgments, and which are accompanied by pain and pleasure (2.1.8). In order to move the audience through *pathos*, Aristotle says that a rhetor must understand what the emotions are, the states of mind caused by particular emotions, and the kinds of people toward whom one feels particular emotions. In addition, the art of pathos requires that speakers understand the attitudes, beliefs, and experiences of their audience. Many classical rhetoricians warn that the use of emotion in speeches must be proportionate to the subject at hand.

Pedagogy—The art of teaching. Concerned with teaching students how to analyze and produce discourse, composition pedagogy encompasses many philosophic, political, and theoretical positions, and has a long history. Because citizens in ancient Greece had to advocate for themselves, rhetorical training was a key component of classical rhetorical treatises. Classical as well as contemporary debates about pedagogy often deal with the relationships among art, natural talent, practice, and imitation. While most classical rhetoricians defined rhetoric as an art, and taught it as such, subsequent rhetoricians and pedagogues, for instance the current-traditionalists, considered it a mere skill or an unteachable natural talent. During these periods, composition pedagogy became formalistic, rule-governed, and product-focused, if not nonexistent. Renewed interest in rhetoric as the art of persuasion in the mid-twentieth century led to major pedagogical changes, such as the process movement, inquiry-based writing, critical pedagogies, and cultural studies pedagogies.

Pentad—Analytical tool associated with dramatism, Kenneth Burke's theory of language as symbolic action. The pentad allows one to analyze motive in terms of five elements: scene (where something happened), act (what happened), agent (who acted), purpose (why something happened), and agency (the power used to make something happen). According to Burke, any complete statement of motive will incorporate all five terms, showing how they interact with each other in relationships he calls ratios. Burke also maintained that philosophies can be distinguished from each other on the basis of which pentadic term they privilege. For instance, materialist philosophies privilege scene, while idealist philosophies privilege the agent.

Phenomenology—Branch of philosophy initiated by Edmund Husserl that attempts to study the nature and structure of human consciousness by analyzing mental acts such as perception. Key to phenomenological analysis is Husserl's notion of "phenomenological reduction," or isolation of the phenomena to be studied. Although many of Husserl's followers questioned the possibility of exclusive focus on the "thing itself," his ideas were developed by other philosophers such as Maurice Merleau-Ponty. Phenomenology has influenced a number of other areas of inquiry, including existentialism, reader-response theory, discourse theory, and rhetoric.

Pragmatism—Type of philosophy that measures the truth-value of an action or idea in terms of its consequences. Pragmatism originated in America with the work of Charles Sanders Pierce and is also associated with American philosophers William James and John Dewey. Although it does not focus on discourse in the same ways that poststructuralist theory does, pragmatism shares poststructuralism's critique of metaphysics or any kind fixed, essential value.

Prewriting—The stage in writing when a writer assimilates the subject to himself or herself. First used by composition scholar Gordon Rohman, *prewriting* refers to the "groping" processes through which writers try to conceptualize or personalize the subjects about which they wish to write. Examples of prewriting include journaling, meditating, and creating analogies.

Probability—A statement whose truth is contingent rather than certain. Probability is the cornerstone of rhetoric, distinguishing it from analytic logic as well as propaganda. Beginning with uncertain premises that audience is likely to accept, rhetorical proofs seek to establish probable, yet ethical, forms of knowledge that are responsive to the particularities of situation, time, and place.

Postmodernism—Highly contested term referring to modes of cultural production, phenomena, and thought seen in tension with various aspects of humanism, the Enlightenment, and modernism. Jean-Francois Lyotard defines postmodernism in two ways: first, in terms of knowledge legitimation, as incredulity toward grand narratives; and second, in terms of avant-garde aesthetics, as that which puts forward the unpresentable in presentation itself. Fredric Jameson elaborates the concept of the postmodern in terms of capital and space, arguing that postmodernism corresponds to a third stage of capitalism (global capitalism) in which the market has become a substitute for itself. The result of this substitution is that everything is commodified, producing "barrages of immediacy" that destroy spatial coordinates and make it impossible for an individual to map his or her location in postmodern space. Jean Baudrillard combines economic and semiotic approaches in his analysis of postmodernism, arguing that signs, no longer valued in terms of use, exchange, or reference to models, have moved into a fractal stage of existence in which they have no referents or determining principles. This loss of reference through the increasingly accelerated production of signs results in the loss of the real, or what Baudrillard calls the creation of the hyperreal. Importantly, these brief descriptions by no means represent all of the theories that fall under the rubric of postmodernism. A fuller account would include theories of subjectivity, epistemology, feminism, post-colonialism, literary production, and aesthetic production, just to name a few.

Poststructuralism—Term referring to theories from a number of disciplines that problematized structuralism's attempt to show that all aspects of human culture can be accounted for systematically through a science of signs. Although there is no unified poststructuralist position, poststructuralists generally reject the determinate view of meaning yielded by structuralist analysis in favor of an unstable or indeterminate view of meaning. For instance, poststructuralism is often associated with deconstruction and its aim to show that a text's meanings are multiple and ultimately undecidable. Influenced greatly by Friedrich Nietzsche, Michel Foucault's genealogical approach to history is poststructuralist insofar as it tries to understand truth not in terms of origins or essences but rather in terms of chance events, personal conflicts, errors, and discontinuity. Many theorists, including Foucault, Jacques Lacan, Roland Barthes, and Julia Kristeva, have extended structuralist theory into a poststructuralist critique of subjectivity. Foucault and Barthes, for example, argue that traditional notions of the author as the unique, individual, creative force behind a text are no longer viable and that authorship should be seen as a product or function of the text. Jacques Lacan and Julia Kristeva bring psychoanalytic theory to bear on poststructuralism, both providing accounts of subjectivity that challenge Freudian theories by focusing on discontinuity and language.

Ratios—Formal relationships among the five terms of Burke's pentad. Ratios describe motives for action and are analyzed in order to determine how one term affects the other. For instance, a scene-act ratio encourages the analyst to look at how a person's actions could be the result of his or her environment, while an agent-act ratio asks the analyst to understand the action in terms of the characteristics, beliefs, and practices of the person who performed it.

Signifying Practices—The historically and socially specific ways in which particular groups of people create and interpret meaning (i.e., essay writing, scholarly debate, film-making, conference presentations, sculpture, quilting, etc.) In addition, poststructuralists argue that material conditions and subjectivity are meditated, if not constructed, by signifying practices, which always bear the mark of the dominant ideology.

Social Construction—A group of epistemological theories maintaining that knowledge cannot be understood as the product of ideal forms (metaphysics), unmediated experience with the world (empiricism), or the logical workings of the mind (rationalism) but rather as the product of the interaction of a group of people in a specific context at a specific time. Social constructionists argue that these interactions are mediated if not constructed by language and that the conditions of knowledge vary from situation to situation. Arguments for rhetoric as epistemic, for intertextual interpretations of texts, and for inquiry-based pedagogies are examples of social constructionist arguments in Rhetoric and Composition.

Sophists—Traveling teachers in fifth-century BCE. Greece who taught politics, philosophy, and rhetoric for a fee. In addition to their rhetorical and poetical skills, the Sophists are known for believing that knowledge was relative to specific situations and that only probable knowledge was available to humans. Because of their epistemological beliefs, *kairos* (the situational appropriateness of speech) and *dissoi logoi* (arguing both sides of an issue) were key elements in sophistic rhetoric. Protagoras and Gorgias are two of the most well known Sophists.

Stasis, status—technique of rhetorical invention in which discourse is initiated by determining the issue at hand or the point of contention in an argument. The key treatise on *stasis* is Hermogenes of Tarsus's *On Status*. Written in approximately 176 CE and based on Hermagoras of Temnos's earlier text, *On Status*, prescribes a set of questions for helping rhetors determine which of thirteen stases (literally, "stopping places") is at issue in their dispute. Example stases include conjecture, definition, quality, and justification. Identifying issues through this stasiastic procedure provides a first step toward finding appropriate topics and creating an argument.

Subjectivity—A broad term referring to theories about the nature of the self, the ways in which individuals come to know themselves as selves, as well as the kinds of agency or control individuals have over the formation of their selves. Initially a phenomenological or psychoanalytic concern, subjectivity has become a highly debated issue since the advent of structuralist, poststructuralist, and postmodern theory. Generally speaking, contemporary theories of subjectivity replace the term *self* with the term *subject*, which is often opposed to the Freudian ego and the Cartesian *cogito*, or any model of the subject as a present, unified, rational entity. The psychoanalytic theory of Jacques Lacan represents perhaps the most radical break from the notion of a present self, arguing that the subject is a decentered, divided entity created by a failed attempt to represent the Real. Other theorists, such as Louis Althusser, have taken a Marxist approach to subjectivity, maintaining that it is constituted by dominant ideologies. Still others, such as Gilles Deleuze and Felix Guattari, argue that the subject is a collection of many relationships, connections, and assemblages that constantly change according to new desires.

Tagmemics—A modern theory of linguistics initiated by Kenneth L. Pike and developed into a method of rhetorical invention by Pike, Richard Young, and Alton Becker. Tagmemics is based on the ideas that sentences and whole discourses have to be interpreted in the light of larger contexts, that understanding cultural differences is important, and that any unit of behavior can be identified, classed, differentiated, and employed in itself (particle), in a system (wave), or as a system within a particular discourse or context (field). Tagmemics is also based on the idea that disagreements happen because different groups of people can view units from these different perspectives. One way to begin inquiry, then, is to locate possible disagreements or dissonances by exploring units as particles, waves, and fields and to examine their distinctive features, range of variation, and distribution. Young, Becker, and Pike formalized these assumptions into a nine-cell heuristic in their textbook, *Rhetoric: Discovery and Change.*

Terministic Screen—Kenneth Burke's idea that the qualities of a person's terminology affect the nature of his or her observations. According to Burke, terministic screens are verbal filters through which reality is reflected, selected, and deflected and by which an individual's attention is directed to one set of concerns, issues, or ideas rather than another.

Topics—Resources for inventing arguments that include lines of reasoning, types of evidence, and appeals to audiences. Aristotle divided the topics into two kinds: common and special. The twenty-eight common topics could be used across subjects in deliberative, judicial, and epideictic speeches. Examples include arguments based on opposites, definition, cause and effect, and contrast. The special topics served as guides to finding subject matter or content (although they were not considered subject matter themselves) for the three types of discourse. Special topics for deliberative discourse include finance and defense; injustice and justice are special topics for judicial rhetoric; and courage and prudence are special topics for epideictic discourse. Rhetoricians throughout history have debated the epistemic status of the topics, some maintaining that they are non-epistemic storehouses or checklists, others arguing that they function epistemically as socially shared instruments for creating new knowledge.

Tropes—Rhetorical figures of thought that change meaning by changing the way something is named or identified. Opposed to schemes, which rearrange the order of words, tropes change the meaning of words, often creating new meanings. Metaphor, the trope in which one thing is substituted for another, is considered the master trope. Other tropes include hyperbole (exaggeration), synecdoche (substituting the part for the whole or the whole for the part), metonymy (replacing an object with one of its attributes), and periphrasis (circumlocution).

Warrants—General hypothetical statements or lines of argument that allow movement from the grounds to the claim of an argument. Stephen Toulmin described warrants as registers of the legitimacy of the bridge between claims and grounds and said that they are usually appealed to implicitly.

7

Annotated Bibliography

Kelly Pender

Arranged chronologically, these annotated bibliographic entries seek to provide readers with summaries of key texts on rhetorical invention and with a sense of the many ways in which invention can be conceived, investigated, and applied. For instance, while some texts describe specific heuristics for teaching invention (e.g., Young, Becker, and Pike and Berlin and Vivion), others are theoretical inquiries into the processes of invention (e.g., Flower, LeFevre, and Perkins). Whereas many of the earlier texts are primarily concerned with revitalizing interest in invention and demonstrating its importance to modern classrooms (e.g., Corbett, Lauer), as well as to modern politics and public discourse (e.g., Booth), a number of the later texts extend theories of rhetorical invention into other fields in order to understand how those fields produce knowledge (e.g., Simons and Gross and Keith). Much of this later work, often referred to as "the rhetoric of inquiry" or "the rhetoric of science," was enabled by the earlier "rhetoric-as-epistemic" movement, which is represented here by the scholarship of Robert Scott, Michael Leff, Richard Cherwitz, and James Hikins. A number of the texts included are historical investigations of invention, some focusing on its classical roots (e.g., Atwill, Carter), and others its demise during the Enlightenment (e.g., Crowley, Berlin and Inkster). In addition to these kinds of texts, this annotated bibliography includes philosophical investigations of invention, meta-theories of invention, and several bibliographic essays.

Burke, Kenneth. "The Five Master Terms." *View* 2 (1943): 50-52.

"The Five Master Terms" is a helpful introduction to Burke's thought, particularly to the relationship between his new epistemological system of investigation, the pentad, and philosophy. Burke devotes the bulk of the essay to explaining his understanding of statements of motive—particularly their ubiquity in all systems of belief and fields of study—and how the five terms of the pentad provide "a general method that would enable [a reader] in a sense to 'anticipate' any specific notions about motives" (50). The pentad, according to Burke, anticipates the various philosophies, which is to say that philosophic systems take their form from the logic of the interrelationships between the terms of the pentad. Key to Burke's understanding of this relationship between the pentad and different philosophies is the idea that even when one term is ostensibly absent, it is still present, merely looming in the background. This presence is possible because the boundaries between the terms are fluid. Any rounded statement of motive, then, will include all of the terms.

Such rounded statements of motive, however, are rare. In fact, what distinguishes one philosophy from another is, according to Burke, the term that it privileges at the expense of the others. Materialism, for instance, privileges scene since it holds the environment—the material surrounding conditions—as the primary motivating factor of behavior. Burke continues this demonstration, discussing the featured terms for idealism (agent), pragmatism (agency), mysticism (purpose), and realism (act). He then stresses the overlap among the terms, particularly in the two pairings that have dominated modern thought: the agent-scene dialectic (idealism vs. materialism) and agency-purpose (pragmatism vs. mysticism). Burke concludes his explanation of the pentad by discussing the modern philosophies that oppose dramatism (i.e., behaviorism and logical empiricism) and the four ways in which he sees drama dissolved by philosophies.

Corbett, Edward P. J. *Classical Rhetoric for the Modern Student*. New York: Oxford UP, 1965.

Classical Rhetoric for the Modern Student helped rekindle interest in invention by making classical inventional strategies relevant to modern writers and modern writing situations. As Corbett explains in the preface, the foundation of the book is his belief that classical rhetoric provides students with a useful and effective system for inventing, arranging, and phrasing arguments. After providing a brief overview of the classical tradition, Corbett focuses on what he considers to be the three most vital canons of classical rhetoric: invention, arrangement, and style. Invention receives the most extended treatment of the three since, according to Corbett, most writing problems stem from the absence of a viable thesis and useful strategies for discovering one. In his chapter on invention, Corbett explains how the concept of *status* can help writers state a thesis; he covers Aristotle's three modes of persuasion (the logical, ethical, and emotional); and he discusses the common topics and the special topics of each of the three kinds of discourse in classical rhetoric: deliberative, judicial, and ceremonial. For each idea or principle that he presents, Corbett provides illustrations and suggestions for its implementation.

Rohman, Gordon, D. "Pre-Writing: The Stage of Discovery in the Writing Process." *College Composition and Communication* 16 (1965): 106-12.

In this 1965 essay, Rohman defines prewriting as "the stage in the writing process when a person assimilates his subject to himself." In order to bring more attention to this inventional stage of writing, Rohman tries to isolate and describe the principle of pre-writing and devise ways for students to imitate its dynamic. He first establishes the relationship between thinking and writing, maintaining that "students must learn the structure of thinking that leads to writing since there is no other 'content' to writing apart from the dynamic of conceptualizing" (107). Rohman then characterizes prewriting as a kind of "groping for" the discovery of conceptualizations, combinations, or arrangements that will allow writers to fit their subject to themselves. Good writing, he continues, is produced when writers make such a discovery about their subjects within the context of their personal lives. It is in this regard that Rohman considers prewriting a form of self-actualizing and recommends three methods for imitating its principle: journal-keeping, meditation, and analogy. By emphasizing the importance of thinking and writing done before drafting, Rohman's work on prewriting helped initiate interest in invention among composition teachers and scholars.

Perelman, Chaim, and Lucie Olbrechts-Tyteca. *The New Rhetoric: A Treatise on Argumentation*. Trans. John Wilkinson and Purcell Weaver. Notre Dame: U of Notre Dame P, 1969.

Originally published in 1958, Perelman and Olbrects-Tyteca's study of argumentation represents a significant break from the work of most early to mid-twentieth-century philosophers and logicians. The authors argue that because formal logic neglects anything (such as emotions or values) that cannot be demonstrated as self-evident through mathematical proof, it cannot account for the reasoning processes by which moral, judicial, political, and philosophical decisions are made. The goal of *The New Rhetoric*, then, is to provide the theory of demonstration (formal logic) with a theory of argumentation that explains how speakers and writers achieve or increase audiences' adherence to particular theses in these realms. Perelman and Olbrects-Tyteca call this theory the "new rhetoric" because they see it as an attempt to reinvigorate the ancient art of persuasion long-neglected by logic and philosophy. Key to this reinvigoration of rhetoric is the authors' study of audience. Argumentation differs greatly from demonstration in that its audiences are particular, not universal. In fact, for Perelman and Olbrechts-Tyteca, the most important rule of rhetoric is to adapt the discourse to the audience.

Also like many classical rhetoricians Perelman and Olbrechts-Tyteca place a great deal of emphasis on the initiation and invention of arguments. In addition to covering possible premises or starting points of arguments (such as facts, values, and presumptions), Perelman and Olbrechts-Tyteca discuss at length the loci or topics that speakers can use to build arguments. Like Aristotle, the authors define loci as the headings under which arguments fall, separating them into common loci (loci that can be used in many situations) and special loci (loci that are situation or discipline-specific). The largest part of *The New Rhetoric* looks in depth at two major loci or argumentative schemes: association and dissociation. Associative schemes, which attempt to bring separate elements together, include three kinds of arguments: (1) quasi-logical arguments (arguments that claim similarity to formal logic); (2) arguments based upon the structure of the real (arguments that attempt to link unaccepted judgments about reality to accepted judgments); and (3) arguments which aim at establishing the structure of the real (arguments which seek to establish reality through the use of example or analogy). Dissociative schemes are the schemes by which speakers dissociate elements united within a single conception and designated by a single notion. Perelman and Olbrechts-Tyteca distinguish dissociation from simply breaking the links between independent elements.

In addition to their focus on audience and invention, Perelman and Olbrechts-Tyteca devote considerable attention to the selection, interpretation, and presentation of data. Essential to this discussion is the authors' concept of presence. Perelman and Olbrechts-Tyteca argue that by simply selecting certain data and presenting them to the audience, speakers endow them with a special importance or presence. In addition to providing advice for creating presence, the authors cover techniques for strengthening, amplifying, and judging arguments in specific rhetorical situations.

Toulmin, Stephen. *The Uses of Argument.* Cambridge: Cambridge UP, 1969.

Although *The Uses of Argument* is not about rhetoric per se, this 1958 book played an important role in the revitalization of the discipline by showing that argument in all fields is contextualized and practical, which is to say, rhetorical. In order to make this point, Toulmin challenges the authority and applicability of analytic or syllogistic logic as the "paradigm" case of logical reasoning to which all other forms of reasoning should be compared. Specifically he argues that the three-part structure of the syllogism is too simplistic to represent and evaluate what he calls substantial arguments—the arguments that people use all the time in all fields in order to justify claims.

In order to develop a scheme for analyzing and assessing substantial arguments, Toulmin then looks at the ways in which arguments remain the same and change from one field to another. He finds that the force of modal terms such as *probably* and *certainly* do not vary across fields, but the criteria used to determine probability or certainty change from one field of arguments to another. As a result, he argues that validity can only be determined by studying the structure of arguments in a specific field or context. To facilitate this kind of analysis, Toulmin provides a six-part layout of arguments. The first three parts—claim, grounds, and warrant—do not differentiate substantial arguments from analytic arguments. The second three elements—backing, modal qualifier, and rebuttal—however, do distinguish substantial arguments from analytic arguments. The backing of a warrant, for instance, reveals the set of beliefs or the body of knowledge from which the warrant derives its authority. Such backing is absent in syllogistic logic since it is assumed that the major premise is an a priori truth. Toulmin's layout, then, distinguishes substantial arguments from analytic arguments by illuminating their contextualized nature. Moreover, by allowing readers and writers to map out that contextualization, it provides a scheme for recognizing the merits and defects of each type of argument. Teachers in composition and speech communication have found this aspect of Toulmin's work helpful for both analyzing and inventing arguments.

Young, Richard E., Alton L. Becker, and Kenneth L. Pike. *Rhetoric: Discovery and Change.* New York: Harcourt, Brace, Jovanovich, 1970.

Based on tagmemic linguistics and Rogerian psychology, this text sought to break with the current-traditional paradigm of composition pedagogy by providing students with systematic, yet rich and flexible strategies for initiating inquiry and communicating discoveries. Specifically, the text replaced the current-traditional emphasis on style and arrangement (a non-epistemic view of rhetoric) with an emphasis on invention (an epistemic view of rhetoric). Young, Becker, and Pike explain the theoretical foundation of this shift in the first part of the book by reviewing the history of rhetoric, explaining Rogerian rhetoric, and by describing tagmemic linguistics, which is a branch of linguistics that maintains that people understand the world in terms of repeatable units that are organized hierarchically. Young, Becker, and Pike develop this tagmemic view of language and understanding into a method for discovering multiple perspectives on a subject and for identifying and stating problems. For instance, to provide students with a heuristic for exploring a problem, the authors suggest that writers explore problems from three different perspectives: the particle perspective, which looks at a problem as a static entity; the wave perspective, which looks at it as a dynamic object or event; and the field perspective, which looks at it as an abstract, multidimensional field. In addition to providing inventional strategies, Young, Becker, and Pike offer writers strategies for verifying and evaluating hypotheses, discovering audiences' beliefs, establishing the importance of subjects, and for editing.

Lauer, Janice. "Heuristics and Composition." *College Composition and Communication* 21 (1972): 396-404.

Based on her 1967 dissertation, "Invention in Contemporary Rhetoric: Heuristic Procedures," which argued that interdisciplinary research on heuristics offered a new way of understanding invention as more flexible and open-ended than logic and as a guide to creative acts and complex arts, this bibliographic essay on heuristics and composition provoked an exchange with Ann Berthoff who disagreed with Lauer's recommendation that composition theorists use work in psychology to study invention. Their exchange foregrounded several issues, including: 1) the use of material from another field, especially the social sciences, in English Studies, 2) the humanities/ science divide, 3) the conception of "problem-solving," 4) an understanding of invention that includes the notion of strategy or art.

Booth, Wayne. *Modern Dogma and the Rhetoric of Assent*. Chicago, IL: U of Chicago P, 1973.

By arguing that the chief purpose of persuasion is to engage in mutual inquiry, Wayne Booth's *Modern Dogma and the Rhetoric of Assent* helped illuminate the importance of invention not only for the composition classroom, but also for understanding public discourse and debate. Booth's central claim in the book is that rhetoric in the modern era has become overwhelmingly dogmatic, which is to say that people very rarely believe in or offer good reasons as a means of persuasion. Focused exclusively on predetermined ends, they instead reduce rhetoric to trickery or manipulation in order to further one agenda while completely invalidating others. In Booth's words, rhetorical probability has become propagandistic plausibility (89). For the author this means that the difference between good and bad persuasion is not a matter of knowledge or wisdom, but rather simply a matter of skill (87). The cornerstone of this dogmatic view and use of rhetoric is the radical split modernism has induced between fact and value, between the objective and the subjective. On the objectivist side of this split are those whom Booth describes as "scientismic," and on the subjective side are the "irrationalists." Booth illustrates the differences between these two positions through his discussion of five kinds of dogma (i.e., dogma about the methods or means of producing change, dogma about the nature of the thing changed—the mind—and dogma about the scene of change—the world). Booth illustrates these dogmas in the work of twentieth-century philosopher, Bertrand Russell, a man in whom Booth is able to locate both the scientismic and irrationalist sides.

In order to move beyond these modern dogmas, Booth proposes what he calls "a rhetoric of assent"—an epistemic rhetoric in which there are grounds for mutually discovering knowledge through argument and for seeing language as more than a vehicle for communication. According to Booth, this rhetoric of assent would be characterized by the command to "assent pending disproof" rather than the dogmatic command to "doubt pending proof" (101). Moreover, it would be characterized by a pluralistic approach to knowledge and truth. That is, it would not assert, as objectivism does, that all reasonable minds will agree on what is truth, but rather that minds will disagree. This disagreement, however, does not lead to complete relativism or the impossibility of consensus but, in fact, creates the need and the possibility of real rhetorical inquiry and argument.

Elbow, Peter. *Writing Without Teachers*. New York: Oxford UP, 1973.

Elbow's objectives in this book are to assist writers in learning ways of generating ideas and words better and in improving their ability to judge their writing. Elbow proposes freewriting (writing quickly and without stopping for ten to twenty minutes) because it prevents writers from generating text and editing it at the same time. Often writers fail, Elbow maintains, because they attempt to get it right the first time by editing every bit of writing they produce. As a result of this premature editing, writers become frustrated, the writing process difficult, and the writing voiceless. By regularly freewriting or keeping a freewriting journal, Elbow believes that writers can develop a voice that will work its way into regular writing. In addition, freewriting provides a method of discovering subjects. After freewriting, Elbow recommends that writers look back over their text, determine what passages seem significant or strong, and continue writing about those passages. Freewriting also helps writers find topics through digressions. By straying from the subject in a freewrite, Elbow believes that writers can discover a new perspective or direction for their writing. Elbow also explains his developmental approach to writing through two metaphors: writing as growing and writing as cooking, while providing advice for setting up a teacherless classroom.

Winterowd, Ross W. "'Topics' and Levels in the Composing Process."
   College English 34 (1973): 701-9.

Winterowd argues in this essay that the importance of the topics (or
places of invention) has been overlooked in both composition theory
and pedagogy. In order to revitalize the topics, Winterowd provides a
method of categorizing them according to their nature and operation.
First, topics may be finite or non-finite. Methods of paragraph development and Aristotle's topics are examples of non-finite lists. Burke's
pentad provides an example of a finite set of topics. In order for a set
of topics to be finite, Winterowd explains, it must not allow one to
generate a question that cannot be classed under an item in the set
of topics. Winterowd argues that in order for rhetorical theory to be
logical and consistent, rhetoricians must understand not only the difference between finite and non-finite sets of topics, but also the difference between form-oriented and content-oriented sets of topics. Form-
oriented topics, he explains, generate paragraph and sentence structures (e.g., Winterowd's "The Grammar of Coherence" and Francis
Christensen's "free modifiers"). Young, Becker, and Pike's tagmemic
heuristic is an example of a content-oriented set of topics.

   Winterowd also proposes a three-level conceptualization of the
composing process: the first level is the level of the proposition—a
sentence made up of a modality plus a proposition. The teacher cannot intervene at this level of generation. The second level is that of
inter-propositional connections—syntax. While the teacher can help
students at this second level, Winterowd maintains that it is at the
third level—the level of transition—that attention to invention is
most helpful. At this level students are dealing with paragraphs and
essays, and therefore need topics to generate ideas and solve problems
concerning their subject.

Young, Richard. "Invention: A Topographical Survey." *Teaching
   Composition: Ten Bibliographic Essays*. Ed. Gary Tate. Fort Worth,
   TX: Texas Christian UP, 1976.1-44

In this 1976 essay, Young reviews three areas of scholarship on invention: 1) historical studies; 2) the four major methods of invention; and
3) the contexts necessary for understanding and teaching invention.
Young begins each section of the essay by defining terms, providing
historical background, and illuminating central issues or controver-
sies.

In his review of historical studies of invention, Young finds that there is a lack of histories of invention per se. Young also reviews current attempts to incorporate classical rhetoric and invention into modern rhetoric and into composition courses. He then reviews the literature on the four major methods of invention: 1) Neo-Classical; 2) Dramatistic; 3) Pre-Writing; and (4)Tagmemic. Finally, he reviews the scholarship on four contexts necessary for understanding and teaching invention: 1) problem-solving; 2) criteria for determining the adequacy of methods of invention; 3) the relationships between methods of invention and conceptions of the composing process; and 4) teaching invention.

Scott, Robert. "On Viewing Rhetoric as Epistemic." *Central States Speech Journal* 27 (1976): 9-17.

Scott shows how the belief in *a priori* truth has allowed only marginal roles for rhetoric throughout history. Specifically, he argues that when one believes in the existence of a priori truths, rhetoric can only serve as either a neutral presentation of data or as a way to persuade inferior hearers of the truth they are incapable of seeing and grasping. In order to cultivate a new, epistemic understanding of rhetoric, Scott argues, using Toulmin's distinction between analytic and substantial arguments, that such a priori truths do not exist. Scott then explores the philosophic, epistemological, and ethical implications of his argument. For instance, he borrows (and extends) Douglas Ehninger and Wayne Brockriede's conception of "cooperative critical inquiry" to argue that truth is created in time, rhetorically, and through inquiry. Relying on sophistic rhetorical theory, particularly Gorgias's "On Being," Scott then argues that because truths are contingent rather than certain, men have to act in dissonant circumstances. In order to do so, he offers three ethical guidelines: toleration, will, and responsibility.

Emig, Janet. "Writing as a Mode of Learning." *College Composition and Communication* 28 (1977):122-28.

Emig's main contention in this essay is that writing, compared to the other three languaging processes (reading, listening, talking), corresponds uniquely to important learning strategies. Emig first reviews the criteria that have been used to distinguish writing from the other three processes. Most important among these is the creating/originating distinction. While talking, listening, and reading create verbal constructs, they do not originate a verbal construct that is graphically recorded. Hence Emig establishes an important connection between the act of writing and rhetorical invention. Using the work of psychologists and linguists such as Lev Vygotsky and Dell Hymes, Emig continues to identify eleven additional ways in which writing is further distinguished from speaking.

Next she explains some ways in which writing uniquely corresponds to important learning strategies. For instance, she maintains that writing almost simultaneously deploys the three main modes of learning: the enactive (learning by doing), the iconic (learning through depiction in an image), and symbolic (learning by restatement in words). In addition, because writing is epigenetic, it provides immediately accessible and long-term feedback for students. Also based on Bruner's work, as well as Lev Vygotsky's, Emig argues that writing requires students to structure their inner thought through the establishment of connections and relationships, making writing a more self-rythmed, self-reliant, and engaged activity than talking.

Leff, Michael C. "In Search of Ariadne's Thread: A Review of the Recent Literature on Rhetorical Theory." *Central States Speech Journal* 29 (1978): 73-91.

In this essay, Leff isolates leading tendencies in meta-rhetorical theories, the most prominent of which is the idea that rhetoric is epistemic or knowledge-making. As the author explains, much of the meta-rhetorical work asserts that this conception of rhetoric is a major break from the modern rhetorical tradition. In order to test this assertion, Leff reviews three historical/textual studies, finding that, with the exception of figures such as Vico, all modern rhetorics examined present a view of rhetoric as non-epistemic. Leff then presents and explains four ways in which rhetoric can be seen as epistemic. The first claim that rhetoric has to epistemic status is the idea that rhetoric brings about new knowledge by altering our perception of an object within a fixed scheme of general standards. The second is that rhetoric is epistemic because it creates social knowledge through intersubjective agreement. Rhetoric can also be considered epistemic in a third sense in that it can act as a method for deciding between two paradigms that present different though internally consistent views of reality. Finally, the fourth and most radical conception of rhetoric as epistemic is the claim that epistemology is rhetorical, or that all knowledge is a rhetorical construct. Although Leff does not directly connect epistemic rhetoric and invention, the idea that rhetoric (or rhetorical inquiry) creates knowledge has helped to illuminate the importance of invention in both teaching and studying writing.

Harrington, David, et al. "A Critical Survey of Resources for Teaching Rhetorical Invention: A Review Essay." *College English* 40 (1979): 641-61.

Written in order to complement Richard Young's 1976 survey of scholarship on invention, this essay reviews composition textbooks that incorporate or emphasize invention. The authors use Young's four kinds of heuristic procedures (neoclassical, dramatistic, prewriting, and tagmemic) as a way to categorize textbooks. In addition, they review Speech Communications textbooks that deal with invention.

The authors note three kinds of neoclassical textbooks: 1) discussions of classical rhetorical theory; 2) adaptations of classical rhetoric for the purpose of teaching writing; and 3) composition texts in which features of classical rhetoric are assimilated but still recognizable. Next they review a number of prewriting centered texts. In addition to a thorough review of the tagmemic texts, Harrington et al. provide a discussion of tagmemic invention and its role in the larger process of inquiry. Also they explain Kenneth Burke's work and how it has been used in composition studies. In order to review textbooks influenced by Burke, Harrington et al. make the distinction between the sophistic understanding of the pentad (the idea that the pentad is a generalizable tool that can be used no matter the situation) and the dialectic understanding of the pentad (the idea that the pentad is simply part of a dialectic that allows writers to broaden their perspectives). Finally, Harrington et al. categorize the Speech Communications texts into four kinds, reviewing each based on its treatment of invention. The four categories are: 1) Public Speaking; 2) Argumentation and Debate; 3) Persuasion; and 4) Rhetorical Theory and Criticism.

Burke, Kenneth. "Questions and Answers about the Pentad." *College Composition and Communication* 29 (1978): 330-35.

In this essay Burke compares his conceptualization and use of the pentad as an interpretive tool to William Irmscher's conceptualization and use of it as an inventional tool in his 1976 textbook, *The Holt Guide to English*. In order to make the comparison, Burke first synopsizes his work, explaining how he developed the pentad. He explains, for instance, its relationship to his theory of literary forms and to his use of dramatism, which is the notion that language is primarily a mode of action rather than a mode of knowledge. By way of this short history, Burke also explains how symbolism and nonsymbolic motion are related in his work.

Burke begins his comparison of Irmscher's work to his own by problematizing the parallel that Irmscher draws between the pentad and Aristotle's topics. According to Burke, the topics help the writer discover something to say, while the pentad is designed to help him discover what to ask. He continues to explain that his intention was not to provide writers with a means of producing text, but rather to provide critics with a means of interpreting what was already written. Burke also stresses that in his work the ratios (the way two terms of the pentad are related in an interpretation of motive, e.g., scene-act) and their circumference (the overall scene of the human behavior being interpreted) receive much more attention than the terms of the pentad themselves. Burke then returns to a review of his work, focusing on how the pentad has changed, in order to explain how Irmscher's use could differ so significantly from his own.

Berlin, James, and Robert Inkster. "Current-Traditional Rhetoric: Paradigm and Practice." *Freshman English News* 8 (1980): 1-4, 13-14.

In this essay, Berlin and Inkster maintain that while the traits of current-traditional rhetoric are easily discernible, its underlying epistemological assumptions are elusive, accounting for the paradigm's longevity and strength. In order to identify and evaluate its epistemological tenets, Berlin and Inkster examine how four current-traditional textbooks conceptualize and treat reality, the writer, the audience, and the discourse. First, though, they briefly trace the historical origins of current-traditional rhetoric, focusing on the ideas and traditions it inherited from the work of George Campbell, Hugh Blair, and Richard Whately. Among these ideas, one of the most prominent—and most devastating for composition—was the notion that invention fell outside the domain of rhetoric. In Campbell, for instance, invention was a logical or scientific matter; for Blair, it was a matter of genius and mystery—something that could not be taught because it was different for each rhetor. And from Whatley's rhetoric, Berlin and Inkster explain, the current-traditional paradigm received its mistrust of persuasion, an attitude that helped to keep invention outside the boundaries of rhetoric.

Through their analysis of the four textbooks, Berlin and Inkster find that the current-traditional paradigm understands reality as fixed, knowable, observable, and rational. As a result of this view, there was no need for persuasion, instead just reporting. This premium placed on reality put constraints on the writer. For instance, it eliminated the need for heuristic procedures, reduced the role of the writers, and limited the ways in which writers could interact with their audience. In conclusion, they urge scholars and teachers to scrutinize the epistemology guiding their beliefs and practices.

Perkins, David. *The Mind's Best Work*. Cambridge: Harvard UP, 1981.

By examining common assumptions about invention, the work of famous inventors, and some of the literature on invention in the arts and sciences, Perkins argues that creating is better understood in terms of the "commonplace resources" of the mind than in terms of natural talent, sudden insight, mental leaps, and other "special accounts" that do not respect the reality of invention. He argues that reasoning, remembering, searching, noticing, and selecting are the real boundary-breaking ways of thinking involved in creation. Perkins also maintains that the essence of invention should not be understood as a process but instead as product. Creativity also requires standards and criteria according to Perkins. When searching for answers and ideas, what matters are the standards guiding the search, not the length of the search. Having good standards, though, can help a searcher sustain a search longer, preventing premature closure.

Perkins also assesses the role that plans play in invention. He first looks at the question of "plans down deep," or the underlying mechanisms (such as scientific paradigms) that guide invention. Although many people see such plans as an encumbrance, Perkins argues that prefabricated units, plans, and schemata are necessary for the kinds of creation that require improvisation. Moreover, Perkins maintains that new skills are acquired through a mix of learning new schemata and adapting old ones. Despite the necessity of underlying plans in learning and creating, the author does acknowledge how new or anomalous observations are often subsumed into the dominant schemata or paradigm. Perkins then looks at "plans up front," or heuristics, which he defines as rules of thumb that often help in solving certain kinds of problems without providing guarantees (192). Although heuristics are not problem-solving formulas (like algorithms), Perkins believes that they are ways of preventing premature closing, redirecting thinking, and making creators more aware of their thinking processes. Because many heuristics are general, Perkins explains, people must modify them to fit particular situations and needs. This process of modification itself, he argues, can lead to increased awareness of thinking and creating processes. Perkins also discusses the role of heuristics in solving discipline or genre-specific problems. He argues that even though general heuristics cannot replace field-specific knowledge, they can provide strategies for developing such knowledge. In addition to assessing their value, Perkins makes recommendations for teaching heuristics.

Cherwitz, Richard, and James W. Hikins. "Toward a Rhetorical Epistemology." *Southern States Speech Journal* 47 (1982): 135-62.

Continuing the rhetoric-as-epistemic discussion, Cherwitz and Hikins introduce a systematic theory of rhetorical epistemology in this essay. In order to make clear the epistemological, metaphysical, and rhetorical assumptions upon which their theory rests, the authors define rhetorical discourse and knowledge. Rhetorical discourse, they maintain, is the "description of reality through language" (136). In other words, a writer uses rhetorical discourse when he/she makes a statement about the world in an attempt to establish belief in the minds of a particular audience. While such statements may be true or false, Cherwitz and Hikins contend that in order for statements to attain the status of knowledge, they must be true. In addition, in order for a statement to be considered knowledge it must be believed in, and it must be justified through evidence. Based on these three criteria, they define knowledge as "justified true belief" (147). In addition, the authors argue that because all knowledge is inherently linguistic (or propositional), rhetoric is epistemic. Finally, Cherwitz and Hilkins present the central features of their theory of rhetorical epistemology by analyzing the ways in which rhetorical discourse provides the basis for knowledge. Specifically, they maintain that rhetorical discourse is differentiative (it allows one to distinguish objects of knowledge); associative (it allows for the combination of descriptions of reality); preservative (it ensures that epistemic judgments are maintained); evaluative (it allows for critique); and perspectival (it illustrates that disagreement in human discourse over the same object of knowledge results from rhetors perceiving different aspects of that object).

Burns, Hugh. "A Writer's Tool: Computing as a Mode of Inventing." *The Writer's Mind: Writing as a Mode of Thinking*. Ed. Janice N. Hays, et al. Urbana, IL: NCTE, 1983. 87-94.

Burns describes his attempt to provide his students with practical, computer-assisted instruction for rhetorical invention through a program that generated specific heuristic questions. More specifically, this computer program determined the direction and motivational sequence of a line of inquiry, while the writer was responsible for providing the content of the inquiry. According to Burns, this program created a dialogue between the computer and the writer that encouraged the writer to recognize dissonance or articulate problems. Burns describes programs based on tagmemics, Aristotle's topics, and Burke's pentad. In conclusion, he argues that combining heuristic procedures and computer media is a viable way to improve methods of inquiry.

Lauer, Janice. "Issues in Rhetorical Invention." *Essays on Classical Rhetoric and Modern Discourse*. Ed. Robert J. Connors, Lisa S. Ede, and Andrea A. Lunsford. Carbondale, IL: Southern Illinois UP, 1984. 127-39.

In this essay Lauer identifies and historicizes the three main differences in textbook treatments of invention by tracing them back to their roots in classical rhetoric. The first salient difference is the genesis of writing—the question of how best to stimulate or generate discourse. A number of texts suggest that students select a topic and narrow it. Other texts, however, ask students to pose questions in order to resolve a problem or dissonance. Lauer traces this difference back to the classical doctrine of *status*, the earliest art governing the genesis of discourse. The second difference is the purpose of exploration, or the relationship between exploratory acts and judgment. One group of texts gives exploration a support role, while the other gives exploration an epistemic or investigative role. Lauer locates this difference in the long-standing disagreement over the roles and purposes of rhetoric and the topics. The final difference centers on these questions: Can rhetorical invention generate material for any kind of discourse, or is it limited to certain kinds? How are we to understand certainty and probability in terms of rhetorical invention? Contemporary textbooks, she observes, offer different kinds of *topoi* for the generation of different kinds of discourse. These discrepancies guide students to different kinds of material and lead them to draw conclusions with varying levels of probability. In order to locate this issue in historical debate, Lauer reviews a number of both primary and secondary sources.

Kinneavy, James. "*Kairos*: A Neglected Concept in Classical Rhetoric." *Rhetoric and Praxis: The Contribution of Classical Rhetoric to Practical Reasoning.* Washington DC: Catholic UP, 1986. 79-105.

Kinneavy's objective in this essay is to demonstrate the relevance and applicability of *kairos*, a principle of discourse initiation, to composition studies and programs. While scholars in fields such as speech communications, anthropology, theology, and philosophy have realized and written about the importance of concepts such as *kairos*, rhetoricians and compositionists, Kinneavy maintains, have not given it serious attention. In order to revitalize the concept, then, Kinneavy first traces its history, focusing on its role in the work of figures such as Hesiod, Pythagoras, Gorgias, Plato, and Cicero. He then reviews the work of three important scholars—Rostagni, Untersteiner, and Tillich—in order to show how the concept has been investigated and conceptualized in other fields.

Next Kinneavy considers the two fundamental elements of *kairos*—right timing and proper measure—as they are embodied in five dimensions: ethics, epistemology, rhetoric, aesthetics, and civic education. Through this analysis Kinneavy is able to demonstrate both the pervasiveness of *kairos* in the ancient world, as well as its relevance to the modern (or postmodern) world. In addition, he proposes a composition program based on the five dimensions of *kairos*, exploring how each dimension could change and enhance a writing program. Key among these changes would be increased attention to 1) the situational contexts of writing; 2) the value systems of particular contexts; 3) persuasive discourse; and 4) finding realistic audiences for writing. Although Kinneavy does not address invention directly, it follows that a *kairos*-based program—a program that emphasizes situational context and persuasion—would also be an invention-based program.

Miller, Carolyn. "Invention in Scientific and Technical Discourse: A Prospective Survey." *Research in Technical Communication: A Bibliographic Sourcebook.* Ed. Michael G. Moran and Debra Journet. Westport, CT: Greenwood Press, 1985. 117-62.

Miller's review begins with a discussion of the conditions—the requisite conceptions of rhetoric, science, and technology—that are necessary for even considering the role of invention in scientific and technical discourse. In addition to providing a brief history of these conditions and conceptions, Miller reviews the work of scholars (e.g., Charles Kneupper, Floyd Anderson, Michael Halloran, James Kinneavy) who have tried to understand (or re-understand) the relationships among rhetoric, science, and technology. With these preconditions and issues established, Miller turns to the history of invention in terms of the rhetoric/dialectic split (a split articulated most clearly by Peter Ramus) that removed invention from rhetoric. According to Miller, and to the scholarship she reviews, this split led to two conceptions of invention: a broad conception which considers the processes of scientific inquiry and technological problem-solving to be part of invention, and a narrow conception which considers these processes to be antecedent to discourse.

While this broad view legitimizes inquiry into invention in scientific and technical discourse, it does not provide a single or clear direction for that inquiry. Therefore, Miller qualifies the scholarship included in the remainder of the survey, explaining that it is only potentially relevant to invention. Miller divides this material into three major areas: 1) a broad view of invention that deals with the process of inquiry and the creation of ideas; 2) a narrower view of invention that concerns the persuasiveness of expression and presentation; and 3) scholarship on the application and teaching of invention in scientific and technical discourse. Among the many issues that Miller looks at in the first area of literature is the question of how scientific knowledge is created. Under this rubric, she reviews the work of rhetoricians and philosophers of science, such as Hans Reichenbach, Aristotle, Francis Bacon, Michael Polanyi, and Bruno Latour. Miller also reviews work of the "Weltanschauung philosophers of science"—philosophers such as Steven Toulmin, Thomas Kuhn, and Walter Weimer, who "understand science as a thoroughly rhetorical enterprise" (129). Also in this area Miller reviews relevant literature on problem-solving, dividing it into two categories: that which approaches problem-solving as a psychological process, and that which approaches it as a social phenomenon. Miller's survey of the second area of scholarship focuses on the contexts, constraints, and forms of presentation in scientific and technical discourse. Here she reviews scholarship such as Charles Bazerman's that analyzes the kinds of arguments made in scientific and technical documents, scholarship such as Robert Merton's, Jacques Ellul's, and Daniel Bell's that deals with scientific and technical ethos, and scholarship such as James March's that looks at the social and institutional frameworks that effect the production and presentation of scientific and technical discourse.

Miller begins her review of the final category of literature by reporting that there are few sources for teaching and applying invention in scientific and technical discourse. She divides the few sources that do exist into two groups: those that try to improve technical and scientific productivity, and those that address the writing problems of professionals and students in scientific and technical fields. Among the sources in the second group that deal with invention, Miller points out J. W. Allen's "Introducing Invention to Technical Students" and Michael Moran's "A Problem-Solving Heuristic." Miller concludes her review of these sources by illuminating the few writing texts (e.g., John C. Mathes and Dwight Stevenson's *Designing Technical Reports*) that provide more than a superficial treatment of invention for scientific and technical discourse. In conclusion to the review, Miller remarks on the ability of theory to bring together disparate research on invention in scientific and technical discourse, the dangers and benefits of drawing on scholarship from other fields, and the importance of examining the rhetorical tradition for continuing this line of inquiry.

LeFevre Burke, Karen. *Invention As a Social Act*. Carbondale, IL: Southern Illinois UP, 1986.

LeFevre's book draws on scholarship in linguistics, psychology, rhetoric, and philosophy to offer a theory of invention as a social and dialectical act. Opposed to this theory, LeFevre explains, is the traditional, Platonic view of invention that has dominated composition. According to LeFevre, this view is atomistic and asocial, assuming that individuals are capable of generating subject matter or ideas privately through means such as introspection and self-examination.

LeFevre explains the social act theory of invention as an alternative to this Platonic view, arguing that there are at least seven ways in which invention is a social act. She maintains, for instance, that invention is social because the self is socially constituted, because inventive acts build on a social legacy of ideas, and because they are influenced by social collectives, such as institutions, bureaucracies, and governments. In order to explain her claim that invention is dialectical, LeFevre argues there is a dialectical partnership between human agents and the contexts in which they exist and act. In order to explain why she considers invention an act, LeFevre borrows from the work of Hannah Arendt and Michel Foucault. From Arendt she borrows the idea that while an inventive act is initiated by a rhetor, it requires an audience to be completed. From Foucault she borrows the idea that inventive acts are constant potentialities that extend over time through a series of social transactions and texts. LeFevre also proposes a four-part continuum to study the "socialness" of invention, explains the linguistic, psychological, and philosophical foundations of her theory, and explores its implications.

Young, Richard. "Recent Developments in Rhetorical Invention."
      Teaching Composition: Twelve Bibliographic Essays. Ed. Gary Tate.
      Fort Worth, TX: Texas Christian UP, 1987. 1-38.

This essay examines six developing areas of scholarship on invention. In his discussion of the first area, The Composing Process, Young argues that all methods of invention either directly or indirectly present a conception of the composing process. He then reviews scholarship on these conceptions, illuminating some of the major debates about the composing process. Next Young reviews recent scholarship about Rhetoric as an Epistemic Activity, and surveys the body of literature about writing as a mode of learning. He also explores how the idea that rhetoric is epistemic could affect other disciplines, the WAC movement, and technical writing. In the third area, Situational Context, Young discusses studies of *kairos*, audience, discourse community theory, and the ethos of the writer. In Heuristics, the fourth area, Young reviews new scholarship about heuristics, dividing it into two categories: The Nature of Heuristic Procedures and The Utility of Heuristic Procedures. In his review of the fifth area, Pedagogy and Methods of Invention, Young surveys new scholarship on the four methods of invention presented in his 1976 essay: classical, Romantic (formerly pre-writing), dramatistic, and tagmemic. Young warns that since each method implies a different conception of the composing process, and is embedded in a different set of theories, teachers should not assume that they are necessarily compatible or interchangeable with one another. Finally in the fifth area, the History of Invention, he reviews bibliographic studies of rhetoric from both English and Speech Communications departments.

Carter, Michael. "*Stasis* and *Kairos:* Principles of Social Construction in Classical Rhetoric." *Rhetoric Review* 7 (1988): 97-112.

Carter examines two concepts of classical rhetoric—*stasis* and *kairos*—in order to demonstrate that rhetoric and composition has roots in social theories of knowledge. Both of these concepts, according to Carter, were central to the generation or invention discourse. Carter explains the role of *stasis* in the classical tradition (particularly in the work of Cicero, Quintilian, and Hermegenes) as a method for identifying the issue at hand and also for leading the rhetors to the *topoi* appropriate to it. Based on this understanding, Carter provides five identifying features of *stasis* (e.g., that stasis grows out of the conflict of opposing forces, that the stasiastic conflict is generative, creating an impetus for rhetorical action, and that it is a doctrine of inquiry associated with asking questions).

In order to map out some of the ways in which *kairos* has been used and conceptualized, Carter provides a helpful history of the concept, concentrating on its role in the Pythagorean understanding of the universe and in sophistic rhetorics such as Gorgias's. Also in this discussion of *kairos*, Carter explores its ethical dimensions, arguing that it was through *kairos*, a principle of situational appropriateness, that the Sophists acted despite their belief that all truths are in some way false. Carter then explores the possibility of a historical relationship between the two principles that could cast doubt on the split between the sophistic tradition and the Aristotelian-Ciceronian tradition, and strengthen the case for the social constructionist roots of classical rhetoric. He concludes the essay by discussing the ways in which composition has suffered due to the loss of the *stasis-kairos* principle.

Crowley, Sharon. *The Methodical Memory: Invention in Current-Traditional Rhetoric.* Carbondale: Southern Illinois UP, 1990.

Using a deconstructive approach, Crowley examines the history and nature of current-traditional rhetoric, focusing on its theory of invention. Among Crowley's objectives is to show that current-traditional rhetoric is a reduction of the eighteenth-century rhetorical theory upon which it is based. Her examination begins with eighteenth-century rhetorical theory and its break from classical rhetorical theory, particularly the classical emphasis on communal knowledge and the rhetorical situation. As Crowley explains, eighteenth-century rhetoric reflected the values of the Enlightenment, especially its faith in science and reason. Rather than positing an epistemic view of language or rhetoric, rhetoricians like George Campbell, Hugh Blair, and Adam Smith advocated an understanding of language as the representation or vehicle of thought and knowledge. Influenced by movements such as faculty psychology, these British rhetoricians believed that all minds worked in linear ways that could be investigated through self-reflection. Rhetorical success, then, meant understanding the universal principles of human nature rather than the particularities of the rhetorical situation. As a result, invention during this time became an individualistic process of introspection.

According to Crowley, these eighteenth-century rhetorical theories had developed into current-traditional rhetoric in America by the nineteenth century thanks to the work of writers such as Samuel Newman and Richard Green Parker. These writers, and others like them, she explains, turned the principles of eighteenth-century rhetoric into formulas for producing texts. The introspective theory of invention, for example, was reduced to a prescription to simply "select" an object from memory and transform it into a subject for writing. Expressing these subjects in discourse became an issue of method: writers were instructed to arrange their ideas in ways that accurately reflected mental processes or movements. As attention to invention continued to diminish, this emphasis on method and arrangement overtook current-traditional rhetoric, giving rise to the modes of discourse: exposition, description, narration, and argumentation, or EDNA. Eventually EDNA became for the current-traditionalists an arrangement-based genre theory in which the formal features of texts represented and distinguished different rhetorical aims or objectives. In addition, the emphasis on arrangement and formal features encouraged a unit-based approach to discourse in which the current-traditionalists looked at texts as collections of words, sentences, and paragraphs. Thanks to this unit-based approach, the five-paragraph essay soon dominated composition, making it an increasingly methodical and less rhetorical enterprise. Crowley also explores the ethical and epistemological limitations imposed on current-traditional rhetoric by its adherence to rigid conceptions of accuracy, reason, propriety, and universality.

Simons, Herbert W., ed. *The Rhetorical Turn: Invention and Persuasion in the Conduct of Inquiry.* Chicago: U of Chicago P, 1990.

Herbert W. Simons's "The Rhetoric of Inquiry as an Intellectual Movement" introduces *The Rhetorical Turn* by exploring the motivations, scope, and implications of the rhetoric of inquiry movement. In general, Simons explains, this movement argues that the process of inquiry can be understood more usefully in rhetorical terms, according to the idea that all stages of the inquiry process depend upon communal and individual judgments. While there are several rhetorics of inquiry, Simons suggests that as a whole, this movement is built around conceptions of rhetoric as "the study of how one ought to argue and use language in situations and on issues for which there can be no proof in the strict sense of that term" (6). A major consequence of this conception, Simons explains, has been the effort to rethink and revise the intellectual history of rhetoric. Another key consequence has been an alliance between rhetoric and social constructionism. Part of the rhetorical analyst's job, he maintains, is to determine how discursive constructions of the real are made persuasive. While some rhetoricians believe that this task applies only to the extra-logical, extra-factual aspects of a text (i.e., style), others argue that fact, logic, and reason are themselves rhetorical. This difference constitutes a pivotal distinction between approaches to the rhetoric of inquiry. While Simons does not directly argue for one approach over the other, he does believe that rhetoric provides the means to evaluate and choose among competing rationalities. This ability, however, will never be fully developed unless rhetoricians begin to study "the arts of the sayable," or invention. Such a study, he concludes, might include formalistic theories of conceptual development, lines of argument, methods of arrangements, and stylistic choices.

In "Scientific Discovery and Rhetorical Invention: the Path to Darwin's *Origin*" John Angus Campbell studies Charles Darwin's process of invention in order to provide a new perspective on the development of the theory of natural selection. Drawing from Darwin's notebooks, Campbell argues that his work follows an informal logic of rhetorical invention rather than a formal, scientific logic. In other words, Campbell argues that Darwin's work was guided primarily by the inventional task of convincingly presenting his findings to an audience of skeptical colleagues. To this end, Darwin grounded each of his theories in a trope, or central metaphor. Campbell's analysis of these metaphors, as well as analogies, images, and lines of argument, begins with Darwin's conversion to transmutation following his return from the Beagle voyage. Campbell then sketches key moments in the strategic logic by which Darwin arranged his images and arguments into distinct narratives. In conclusion he suggests that by taking the facts and interpretations of his colleagues for granted, and by arguing that his new version of natural selection best explained them, Darwin formed his mature theory of natural selection. Campbell's main point about this process of formation is that in it discovery and justification were not separates procedures but rather two aspects of "a single logic of inquiry and presentation" (86).

Like Campbell, Alan G. Gross uses rhetorical theory to understand the production of scientific knowledge. In "The Origin of the Species: Evolutionary Taxonomy as an Example of the Rhetoric of Science" Gross argues that a complete rhetoric of science should be able to reconstruct the natural sciences without remainder, that is, without any idea or feature left unaccounted for. Gross tests this hypothesis of completeness against evolutionary taxonomy, the science of classifying plants and animals as species in accordance with evolutionary theory. Specifically, he attempts to translate the analytical categories of evolutionary taxonomy (the stages at which species are identified, defined, or redefined) into rhetorical terms. For instance, drawing on concepts such as Perelman and Olbrects-Tyteca's universal audience and presence, Gross shows how evolutionary taxonomists placed plants and animals in taxonomic groups in a way that made such placement seem natural and inevitable, as if the species ontologically belonged there. These placements, in turn, worked to demonstrate and justify evolutionary theory, which, according to Gross signals the end of the species as a natural kind and its beginning as a rhetorical construction. Gross then considers the implication of this rhetorical construction without remainder, arguing that the rhetoric of science demonstrates that there is "no theoretical or empirical core, no essential science that reveals itself all the more clearly after the rhetorically analyzed parts have been set aside" (107). While this demonstration does not mean that rational reconstructions are wrong, for Gross it does eliminate any sharp distinction between rationality and rhetoric. In conclusion he discusses the implications of this position for the disciplinary status of rhetoric.

In "The Rhetoric of Decision Science, or Herbert W. Simons Says" Carolyn R. Miller argues that decision science, a theory for generating procedures that will guarantee best decisions, attempts to reverse the rhetorical turn. To support this claim Miller compares decision science to the art of deliberative rhetoric, citing three main differences: 1) the treatment of uncertainty; 2) the treatment of audience; and 3) conceptions of human rationality. Based on this comparison, Miller argues that decision science exhibits what Wayne Booth called motivism, the inability to reason about values, and scientism, the belief that there is a dichotomy between fact and reason. As a body of theory predicated on the superiority of procedures, she argues, decision science is unable to deal with the problem of choice about human action, the very choices that are the focus of Aristotelian deliberative rhetoric. Because of this inability to deal with choice, as well as the inability to account for the importance of symbolic interchange, the same problems appear and reappear in decision no matter how it is reconceived. Importantly, Miller continues, the points at which these problems reappear have direct analogues to concepts of rhetorical theory, particularly invention. In sum, she suggests that because decision science is too narrow and authoritarian to be of use in real conflicts, rhetoric as a deliberative art is a much better model for how to exercise reason and make choices in real conflicts.

Dilip Parameshwar Gaonkar's contribution to *The Rhetorical Turn*, "Rhetoric and Its Double: Reflections on the Rhetorical Turn in the Human Sciences," marks a departure from the position expressed in most of the collection's essays. Generally speaking, Gaonkar questions the legitimacy of the turn by looking at its implications for rhetoric's self-understanding. He argues, for instance, that the rhetorical turn is actually a "flight from mere rhetoric," or from rhetoric as an empty, supplemental discipline. Fueled by its epistemic anxiety and its hunger for disciplinary legitimacy rhetoric has executed this flight through two moves: a diachronic move which tries to create an appropriate intellectual history for the field, and a synchronic move which tries to find a subject matter. According to Gaonkar, recent attempts to uncover the hidden history of rhetoric (i.e., attempts to rediscover sophistic rhetoric) are the product of the diachronic move. He associates the synchronic move with the rhetorical turn, arguing that there are actually two turns: the implicit and the explicit. While the explicit turn still conceives rhetoric as a supplement, the implicit turn conceives it as a theoretical and epistemological enterprise that has been suppressed by philosophy throughout history. Gaonkar argues that rhetoricians are lured by the implicit turn because it provides them with more disciplinary legitimacy than the explicit turn. However, once the internal crisis in philosophy that has caused the rhetorical turn is over, he believes that rhetorical consciousness will fade and rhetoric will be forced to deal with its role as a supplement.

Berlin, James A., and Michael J. Vivion, eds. *Cultural Studies in the English Classroom*. Portsmouth, NH: Boynton/Cook Heinemann, 1992.

Authors in this collection describe the effects that Cultural Studies has had on English programs and classes and suggest heuristics for writing cultural critiques. In the introduction to the collection, Berlin and Vivion describe the rise of cultural studies in America, explaining many of the conflicts surrounding it, particularly its clash with traditional, canonical literature-based English curricula. In addition, the editors offer a broad definition of cultural studies as the study of the ways social formations, practices, and discourses are involved in the shaping of subjectivity. Most program and classroom descriptions in the collection evidence a similar definition of cultural studies, as well as corresponding writing pedagogies, practices, and heuristics. In his report on Carnegie-Mellon's shift to a cultural studies-based English program, for instance, Alan Kennedy describes the "teaching the conflicts" pedagogy used by many of his colleagues. In order to help students write about scholarly arguments, teachers at Carnegie-Mellon ask them to create "issue trees." The purpose of this heuristic, Kennedy explains, is to show students that the world is multi-positioned and that by taking a position on one particular aspect of an issue, scholars necessarily remain silent on other issues. According to Kennedy, this strategy prepares students for writing by allowing them to determine what positions they are invested in and by teaching them that their own writing does not have to offer a definitive answer or solution.

Phillip Smith II describes similar practices at the University of Pittsburgh, where some teachers adopted a Freirean "problem-posing" pedagogy. Specifically, Smith reports on Mariolina Salvatori's attempt to redefine critical reading and writing through two techniques: self-reflexive hermeneutical critique and deconstructive critique. The goal of this heuristic, Smith explains, is to help students write about literature and literary scholarship by asking them first to locate their own position and investments in the act of interpretation (self-reflexive hermeneutics) and second to expose and explore the fissures or gaps in the text (deconstruction). Like many cultural studies heuristics, the advantage of problem-posing is that it makes students active creators of knowledge rather than passive receivers.

Several contributors in the collection describe heuristics that ask students to answer questions in order to generate analysis. In order to help students decode the meaning of visual texts, for example, Joel Foreman and David R. Shumway have them answer seven questions about the conditions of production, key features, and ideological structures represented in visual texts. As a way to encourage students to inquire into the cultural construction of gender, Alan W. France asks them to answer nine questions about gender representation. For instance, in any given object (e.g., a film or advertisement) students must figure out who is looking at whom, what physical contacts are made, who refers to the body, who takes off clothing, and who is good at what task. Other heuristics discussed in the collection ask students to examine and deconstruct the binary oppositions they find in texts. Generally speaking, all of these cultural studies heuristics aim to prepare students for writing by teaching them to recognize and analyze the meaning, values, and assumptions of both canonical and marginalized texts.

Flower, Linda. *The Construction of Negotiated Meaning: A Social Cognitive Theory of Writing.* Carbondale: Southern Illinois UP, 1994.

In this book Flower argues for a social cognitive theory of literacy as the construction of negotiated meaning. Unlike limited definitions of literacy, which substitute specific parts of literacy for the whole, and general definitions, which see literacy as a generalized capacity of thought, Flower's social cognitive theory claims literate action is a socially situated problem-solving process. As such it recognizes the importance of rhetorical situation as well as the problem-solving skills a learner uses to interpret the situation. Such skills, Flower maintains, are the intellectual moves which allow people to construct meaning by reorganizing problems, recalling information, recognizing patterns, setting goals, making inferences, and responding to prior texts and other voices.

Looking more closely at this social cognitive theory of literacy, Flower examines its two most important metaphors: negotiation and construction. She compares negotiation to other common literacy metaphors, arguing that negotiation gets at the interactive as well as the internal aspects of literacy. In other words, it focuses attention on individual thinking processes, but places those processes within the circle of socially structured, purposeful discourse, thereby illuminating the goal-driven or dilemma-driven aspects of meaning making. Asking what it means to say that meaning making is a constructive process, Flower then looks at the specific interpretive and inventive acts by which individual writers create personal meaning. For instance, she examines theories of how writers represent and network information; how they develop and use schemas; and how they rely on contexts and prior knowledge. She then compares this social cognitive understanding of construction to social construction and to social interaction, emphasizing its distinct goal of creating observation-based literacy theory.

Flower turns next to questions of application, looking specifically at how a social-cognitive theory of literacy can be implemented or supported in education. She argues that by bringing the goals, dilemmas, and interpretive processes of meaning making to the table, collaborative planning increases the chances that learners will become aware of their "strategic knowledge," or understanding in action. In addition to collaboration, Flower suggests cognitive apprenticeship as a way to increase learners' metacognitive awareness. Building on strategies such as modeling, scaffolding, and fading, cognitive apprenticeship uses expert/novice distinctions to teach rhetorical awareness and the conscious control of one's options through problem-solving heuristics. Finally, because these kinds of metacognitive skills are central to Flower's theory of literacy, she offers a theory of reflection (a method through which students can reconstruct their literate acts), which she illustrates through actual episodes of collaborative planning taken from in-depth studies of two college writers. Although invention is not a key term for Flower in this book, her investigations of problem-solving and meaning-construction make it an important text for understanding the intersection of social and cognitive forces in rhetorical invention.

Couture, Barbara. *Toward a Phenomenological Rhetoric: Writing,*
    Profession, and Altruism. Carbondale, IL: Southern Illinois UP,
    1995.

In *Toward a Phenomenological Rhetoric*, Barbara Couture investigates
connections between rhetorical invention and phenomenology in order to restore truth to rhetorical practice. She begins by arguing that
current critical and rhetorical theories exclude truth from writing by
accepting philosophical relativism and by proffering resistance as the
primary method of creating and maintaining identity. As a way to
make rhetoric a truth seeking activity, Couture proposes a phenomenological rhetoric. Before delineating this alternative rhetoric, Couture
examines the premises of philosophical relativism as well as the ways
in which critical theory associates self-identity and representation with
forms of resistance, namely narcissism and fetishism.

   In the heart of her argument, Couture provides a broad outline of
phenomenology, focusing on the work of Edmund Husserl and Maurice Merleau-Ponty. After reviewing some critiques of phenomenology
(e.g., Derrida's), Couture presents three criteria phenomenology develops for truth and explores the ways in which these three criteria apply
to rhetorical practice and, in particular, to methods of discovering
truth. She maintains that a phenomenological rhetoric engages us with
the world and moves us from alienating resistance toward open collaboration. Couture discusses two specific ways in which individuals can
engage in this process of truth-seeking through rhetoric—profession
and altruism. Finally, Couture reviews the work of Jürgen Habermas,
Charles Altieri, and Thomas Kent in order to discern three standards
for evaluating the truth and rightness of discourse: congruence, consensus, and commensurability. She argues that in order to meet these
standards, each discursive act must be founded on an a priori commitment to maintain goodwill and to respect each participant's intrinsic
worth as a person (203).

Gross, Alan, and William Keith, eds. *Rhetorical Hermeneutics:*
    Invention and Interpretation in the Age of Science. Albany: SUNY
    Press, 1997.

Essays in this collection respond to questions Dilip Parameshwar
Gaonkar raises about rhetorical criticism in his essay, "The Idea of
Rhetoric in the Rhetoric of Science." Based on his analysis of the rhe-
torical criticism of scholars such as Alan Gross and John Campbell,

Gaonkar argues that classical rhetoric (Aristotelian rhetoric) is a productive rather than hermeneutic or interpretive enterprise. As such, it cannot provide rhetorical critics with the tools necessary for profitably interpreting scientific texts. In other words, because doctrines such as topical theory and stasis theory are "rules of thumb" meant to generate speeches, Gaonkar finds rhetoric a "thin" interpretive theory, lacking the hermeneutic constraints necessary for fruitful interpretation. Gaonkar attributes the current "globalization" of rhetoric to this thinness rather than to actual knowledge-making merits of rhetorical theory. In addition, Gaonkar argues that classical rhetoric is unsuitable as a hermeneutic theory because it presents an agent-centered model of invention incommensurate with the insights of structuralist and poststructuralist theories of subjectivity.

Michael Leff responds to Gaonkar'a assessment of rhetorical theory by arguing that in the classical tradition, production and interpretation were not discrete activities but rather two parts of a fluid, dialectical relationship. An example of this dialectical relationship, he maintains, is the doctrine of imitation. According to Leff, ancient rhetors had to interpret speeches in order to imitate them; this act of interpretation then served as a method for invention since it not only familiarized rhetors with historical texts but also inculcated rhetorical judgment in them (97). Alan Gross also defends the value of rhetorical criticism, arguing that rhetorical criticism in fact does generate knowledge. Key to Gaonkar's argument against the knowledge-making status of rhetorical criticism is his claim that such knowledge is not vulnerable to falsification. Gross counters this claim by recounting scholars' attempts to falsify particular textual interpretations yielded by rhetorical criticism. Gross also shows how case studies of the rhetoric of scientific discourse (e.g., his own rhetorical criticism of Copernicus's *Narratio Prima*) have become starting-points for theories of discourse. Like Leff and Gross, Carolyn Miller takes issue with the claims that classical rhetoric is productionist and agent-centered, arguing that such perceptions are more attributable to modern (and for Leff, foundationalist) interpretations of the classical tradition than to the tradition itself. According to Miller, the doctrines of classical rhetoric are far too diverse and even conflicted to be seen as offering a dominant ideology. Miller also problematizes Gaonkar's use of the metaphor "translation" to describe the task of creating a rhetorical hermeneutic. Gaonkar's choice of the term "translation," Miller argues, ignores the role of interpretation in this task; that is, it ignores the "dialectical tacking" between part and whole, new and familiar, and taking and giving that generates incremental understanding (165). For Miller, the metaphor "dialogue" more accurately describes the movement between production and interpretation necessary for a rhetorical hermeneutic. Rhetorical hermeneutics, she maintains, is doubly hermeneutic since it is an interpretive device based on the act of interpretation itself.

William Keith and David Kaufer respond to Gaonkar by arguing that rhetorical theory is thin only because rhetoric has been misclassified as a practical art rather than as a design art. For Keith, rhetoric, like engineering and architecture, is a techne (a productive art) which fulfills its purpose by responding to its exigencies. Also like other design arts, the success of rhetoric depends upon the artist's ability to hide its design or strategy. Keith points out that this feature puts rhetoric in a strange situation: its subject matter (strategy) is never present in its products. Given this aspect of a design art, Keith asks what kind of interpretive theory is suitable for rhetoric? Borrowing from the art of engineering, Keith proposes that rhetorical critics follow the interpretive model of "reverse engineering," a process of reconstruction that tries to relate the features of the product to the constraints of ends and means (237). In other words, reverse engineering is a critical approach to rhetorical designs as the products of "sets of strategic responses to the constraints that obtain for them" rather than the intentions of the rhetor. For Kaufer, classifying rhetoric as a design art means understanding it as a theory of reception monitored and informed by a theory of production. While other design arts such as engineering immediately seem to fit this bill, rhetoric has been less frequently defined in these terms because historically rhetoricians have had little awareness of what they do, of their art. For example, Kaufer argues that the topics have been understood as either a plan for building arguments or a tactic for creating leverage with an audience. In actuality, however, the topics function for rhetors simultaneously as plans and tactics (as well as language events, memory stimulants, etc.); as such they attend to reception and production. Like Keith, Kaufer believes that a theory of rhetorical hermeneutics must account for rhetoric's status as a design art. He suggests that rhetorical critics adopt an interpretation-by-design approach which attempts to interpret the utterances of an rhetorical artifact against their alternatives—against what could have been said but wasn't. Unlike general hermeneutics, Kaufer writes, interpretation-by-design constrains critics by limiting possible interpretations to what can be "rescinded through an alternative rendering of the speaker's productive choice" (257).

Atwill, Janet M. *Rhetoric Reclaimed.* Ithaca, NY: Cornell UP, 1998.

Atwill examines Aristotle's concept of productive knowledge (techne), contrasting it to both practical and theoretical knowledge, in order to challenge the "normalizing tendencies" of the Western humanist tradition. According to Atwill, these tendencies have been made possible, in part, by the neglect of the techne tradition, a tradition that was far less concerned with establishing models of subjectivity, value, and knowledge than it was with inventing and intervening within the productive forces of time and circumstance. Atwill illustrates this concern by examining ancient Greek medical, technical and rhetorical treatises, as well as mythical accounts, such as the Prometheus narratives depicted by Hesiod, Aeschylus, Protagoras, and Isocrates. While she admits that techne is not necessarily linked to democratic movements in these texts and by these figures, Atwill does argue that because productive knowledge is markedly different from other kinds of knowledge, especially theoretical, it provides a method for re-understanding difference not as an anomaly or problem but rather as a condition and opportunity.

Atwill illustrates some of these major differences in the book by explaining techne's relationship to *kairos* (opportune or appropriate timing) and *metis* (cunning or resourcefulness). Unlike philosophical knowledge or reasoning, which must be timeless to be true, techne involves knowledge and reasoning that is explicitly temporal and contextual. As Atwill puts it, the aim of techne is "neither to formalize a rigorous method nor to secure and define an object of study but rather to reach an end by way of a path that can be retraced, modified, adapted, and 'shared'" (69). The purpose of such a path, she continues, is not to discern or study a "thing" but rather to invent—to deform limits so that alternative destinations can be reached. Atwill continues the discussion of techne and invention, looking closely at how forces such as nature, spontaneity, and chance both enable and constrain productive knowledge. She then examines techne's roles in social, political, and economic orders, arguing that as techne came to be associated with individual ability and economic capital, its potential to disrupt and re-create social boundaries diminished. Atwill also explains how this potential was further diminished, if not stifled, by Plato's separation of logos and techne. Next she explores the role of techne in Aristotle's work, arguing that although it is clearly part of Aristotle's epistemological taxonomy, productive knowledge has been neglected due to the theory/practice binary. She then criticizes the idea that rhetoric can be contained within or understood by this binary, citing in particular its failure to account for rhetoric's implication in exchange, its resistance to epistemological and axiological ends, and its dependence on time and circumstance. In conclusion Atwill argues that by extricating rhetoric from this binary, that is by re-understanding it as a form of productive knowledge, scholars might move beyond some of the impasses and violence of the humanistic tradition.

Vitanza, Victor. "From Heuristic to Aleatory Procedures; or, Toward 'Writing the Accident.'" *Inventing a Discipline*. Ed. Maureen Daly Goggin. Urbana, IL; NCTE, 2000. 185-206.

In this essay Vitanza explores the theoretical and practical possibilities of adopting aleatory procedures as an alternative to heuristics. For Vitanza, heuristics represent the "old economy" of writing—an economy based on definition or restriction, binary logic, and the law of noncontradiction. As a result of this economy, heuristics exclude the third term, the possible, or the compossible. Aleatory procedures, which represent the new economy, however, seek to include this excluded third term through excess, chance, and accident. By including the third term and thus destroying binary logic, aleatory procedures would, according to Vitanza, change the foundation of rhetorical invention, moving it from stasis to metastasis. In addition, aleatory procedures would not use *topoi* as arguments, but instead as tropes. For Vitanza, changes such as these could alter writing in the disciplines and initiate positive political, ethical, and social action.

As examples of aleatory procedures, Vitanza discusses Greg Ulmer's *heuretics* and anagrammatic writing. The heart of Ulmer's heuretics is his CATTt heuristic, which is an acronym that stands for Contrast, Analogy, Theory, Target, and tale. It replaces argumentative writing with associational networks, the logic of cyberspace, or what Ulmer calls electracy. Vitanza's second example of aleatory procedures, anagrammatic writing, is the idea that language can think, or more precisely, that too much mastery of the object by the subject has resulted in the object's accidental ability to make meaning.

Bawarshi, Anis. *Genre and the Invention of the Writer: Reconsidering the Place of Invention in Composition.* Logan, UT: Utah State UP, 2003.

Anis Bawarshi's *Genre and the Invention of the Writer* examines how what she calls "the synchronic relationship between writers and genres" gets enacted in rhetorical invention (10). Specifically Bawarshi is interested in using recent genre theory to provide an account of invention that challenges discussions which understand invention as a pre-social process of introspection. Building on the work of scholars such as Karen Burke LeFevre, Carolyn Miller, Anthony Giddens, and Charles Bazerman, Bawarshi argues that genres are constitutive of social and rhetorical actions, relations, and subjectivities. As such, she believes that they help maintain the desires they are designed to fulfill. In other words, genres are sites of both the articulation and acquisition of desire. It is here at this intersection between articulation and acquisition that Bawarshi locates rhetorical invention, arguing that writers invent by "locating themselves within genres, which function as habits or habitats for acting in language" (110). "Rather than being identified as the agency of the writer," she continues, "invention is more a way that writers locate themselves, via genre, within various positions and activities. Invention is thus a process in which writers act as they are acted upon" (143).

In order to make this process of invention more accessible to students, Bawarshi advocates and describes a genre-based pedagogy in which teachers teach students "how to identify and analyze genred positions so that they can locate themselves and begin to participate within these positions more meaningfully, critically, and dexterously" (146).

Carter, Michael. *Where Writing Begins: A Postmodern Reconstruction.* Carbondale, IL: Southern Illinois UP, 2003.

Michael Carter's *Where Writing Begins: A Postmodern Reconstruction* begins, appropriately enough, with the question: where does writing begin? This question, though, quickly morphs into another: what is writing? Carter tries to answer this colossal question against the backdrop of charges that writing teachers, in their effort to make writing definable and teachable, have made it servile or instrumental, that is, a means to some other, more worthy end, such as self-expression, the creation of knowledge, the critique of ideology, etc.

In part, Cater agrees with these charges—he agrees that by locating the value of writing outside of the event of writing, we've ignored what's intrinsically valuable about it. Importantly, though, Carter does not stop here, at critique. Instead he uses his search for writing's beginnings as an opportunity to reconstruct an understanding of writing as both teachable and intrinsically valuable.

One of Carter's first reconstructive moves is to dismiss the notion of a temporal beginning for writing, seeking instead an ontological conception of beginning, which he finds in the Greek term *arche*. As Carter explains, *arche* as beginning represents a threshold point where the infinite enters the finite, the divine enters the human, and the spiritual enters the material. Characterized by the interpenetration of contradictory forces, *arche* evokes a kind of Janusian thinking that Carter describes as state of "doubleness and betweenness"—being neither in nor out but at once in and out; at once facing the past and future, the known and the unknown (25).

In order to develop this alternative understanding of beginnings, Carter turns to modern dialectical theory and Alfred North Whitehead's process philosophy, both of which help him distinguish the kind of creativity associated with archeological beginnings from the kind associated with temporal beginnings. Unlike most Western notions of creativity, which tend to be monolithic and unilateral, positing a subject-creator who produces a created object in a singular, identifiable event, archeological creativity is ongoing or continuous, each moment understood as a threshold between the past and future that represents an opportunity for newness, change, and disruption. Moreover, as Carter explains, this conception of creativity is also "utterly collaborative" in that it views all things, biotic and abiotic, as creative. Instead of unilateral, then, creativity in this *arche*ological model is multilateral, flowing in all directions, erasing the division between creator-subject and derivative, commodified object (206).

For Carter it is here, in the multilateral, ongoing, and (dis)continuous creativity associated with *arche*ological beginnings, that we can find the intrinsic value of writing. As he points out, many scholars in Rhetoric and Composition have defined good writing as the juxtaposition of opposing forces, but none have argued, as he does, that its intrinsic value lies in such juxtaposition. And none have so explicitly argued that these are the terms through which we should understand invention. "Invention," Carter writes, "is not about finding answers, figuring out what to write, or supporting a thesis. Rather it is about placing everything into question, the threshold event between the unknown and known, the familiar and unfamiliar." As such, he continues, it "is essential to the creative experience of writing as beginnings. [. . . It] is how we conceive of creativity as utterly intrinsic to writing" (223-24). Offering a radically new perspective on writing's beginnings, Carter argues that "invention is not focused on making writing good, but rather "on the good of writing, the destabilizing experience of participating in beginnings" (225). It is from this new perspective, and with the help of reconstructive postmodern theory and theology, that Carter offers a re-understanding of both the meaning and the ethicality of teaching writing in late postmodernism.

Bibliography and Works Cited

Abbott, Don. "Mayans' *Rhetorica* and the Search for a Spanish Rhetoric." *Rhetorica* 11 (1993): 157-80.

—. "Rhetoric and Writing in Renaissance Europe and England." *A Short History of Writing Instruction From Ancient Greece to Twentieth-Century America.* Davis, CA: Hermagoras, 1990. 95-120.

Agnew, Lois. "Rhetorical Style and the Formation of Character: Ciceronian *Ethos* in Thomas Wilson's *Arte of Rhetorique.*" *Rhetoric Review* 17 (1998): 93-106.

Allen, Virginia. "A Survey of Some Rhetorical Heuristics and Their Implications for the Teaching of Composition." Diss. Florida State University, 1980.

Alloway, E., J. Carroll, J. Emig, B. King, I. Marcotrigiano, J. Smith, and W. Spicer. *The New Jersey Writing Project.* New Brunswick, NJ: Rutgers University, The Educational Testing Service, and Nineteen New Jersey Public School Districts, 1979.

Althusser, Louis. "Ideology and Ideological State Apparatuses." *Mapping Ideologies.* Ed. Slavoj Žižek. London: Verso, 1994. 100-39.

Andersen, Wallis May. "Computerized Invention for Composing: An Update and Review." *Computers and Composition* 9 (1991): 25-38.

Anderson, Bonnie, and Judith Zinsser. *A History of Their Own: Women in Europe from Prehistory to the Present.* New York: Harper and Row, 1988.

Anderson, V., Carl Bereiter, and D. Smart. "Activation of Semantic Networks in Writing: Teaching Students How to Do It Themselves." Paper, Annual Meeting of AERA, 1980.

Anonymous of Bologna. *The Principles of Letter-Writing (Rationes dictandi). Three Medieval Arts.* Ed. James J. Murphy. Berkeley, CA: U of California P. 1971.

Aphthonius of Antioch. "Progymnasmata." Trans. Ray Nadeau. *Speech Monographs* 19 (1952): 264-85.

Applebee, Arthur N. *Tradition and Reform in the Teaching of English: A History.* Urbana, IL: NCTE, 1974.

Aristotle. *On Rhetoric: A Theory of Civic Discourse.* Trans. George A. Kennedy. New York: Oxford UP, 1991.

Ashton-Jones, Evelyn. "Conversation, Collaboration, and the Politics of
Gender." *Feminine Principles and Women's Experience in American Com-
position and Rhetoric.* Ed. Janet Emig and Louise Phelps. Pittsburgh: U of
Pittsburgh P, 1995. 5-26.

Astell, Mary. *A Serious Proposal to the Ladies for the Advancement of Their
True and Greatest Interest.* PTS. 1-2. 4th ed. London, 1701. *Rhetorical The-
ory by Women before 1900.* Ed. Jane Donawerth. New York: Rowan and
Littlefield, 2002.

Atwill, Janet. *Rhetoric Reclaimed: Aristotle and the Liberal Tradition.* Ithaca,
NY: Cornell UP, 1998.

Atwill, Janet, and Janice M. Lauer, eds. *New Perspectives on Rhetorical Invention.* Knoxville, TN: U of Tennessee P, 2002.

Augustine. *De Doctrina Christiana.* Trans. D. W. Robertson. Indianapolis:
Liberal Arts Press, 1958.

Axelrod, Rise B., and Charles R. Cooper. *The St. Martin's Guide to Writing.*
New York: St. Martin's, 1988.

Backes, J. "Aristotle's Theory of *Stasis* in Forensic and Deliberative Speech in
the *Rhetoric.*" *Central States Speech Journal* 12 (1960): 6-8.

Bacon, Francis. *The Advancement of Learning* and *Novum Organum. Great
Books of the Western World.* Ed. Mortimer Adler. Chicago: Encyclopedia
Britannica, 1952.

Bailey, Dudley. "A Plea for a Modern Set of *Topoi.*" *College English* 26 (1964):
111-17.

Barilli, Renato. *Rhetoric.* Trans. Giuliana Menozzi. Minneapolis: U of Minneapolis P, 1989.

Barker, Thomas. "Word Processors and Invention in Technical Writing."
The Technical Writing Teacher 16 (1989): 126-35.

Barlow, Jamie. "Daring to Dialogue: May Wollstonecraft's Rhetoric of Feminist Dialogics." *Reclaiming Rhetorica.* Ed. Andrea Lunsford. Pittsburgh,
PA: U of Pittsburgh P, 1995. 117-36.

Barnes, Jonathan. "Is Rhetoric an Art?" *DARG Newsletter* 2 (1986): 2-22.

Barratt, Alexandra, ed. *Women's Writing in Middle English.* London: Longman Annotated Texts, 1992.

Barthes, Roland. "The Death of the Author." *Image, Music, Text.* Trans. Stephen Heath. New York: Hill and Wang, 1977. 142-48.

Barton, B. F., and M. S. Barton "Toward a Rhetoric of Visuals for the Computer Era." *The Technical Writing Teacher* 12 (1985): 126-45.

Baudrillard, Jean. *Simulations.* Trans. Paul Foss, Paul Patton, and Philip Be-
itchman. New York: Semiotext[e], 1983.

Bawarshi, Anis. *Genre and the Invention of the Writer: Reconsidering the Place
of Invention in Composition.* Logan, UT: Utah State UP, 2003.

Bazerman, Charles. "From Cultural Criticism to Disciplinary Participation:
Living with Powerful Words." *Writing, Teaching and Learning in the Dis-*

ciplines, Ed. Anne Herrington and Charles Moran. New York, NY: MLA, 1992.

—. *Shaping Written Knowledge: The Genre and Activity of the Experimental Article in Science.*" Madison: U of Wisconsin P, 1988.

Bechtel, Judith. "The Composing Processes of Six Male College Freshman Enrolled in Technical Programs." Diss. U of Cincinnati, 1978.

Beers, Terry. "The Knack for Art: The Why and the Wherefore of Combining Strategies of Invention." *Freshman English News* 17 (1989): 25-29.

Belanoff, Pat, Peter Elbow, and Sheryl Fontaine, eds. *Nothing Begins with N: New Investigations of Freewriting.* Carbondale, IL: Southern Illinois UP, 1991.

Benoit, William. "Isocrates and Plato on Rhetoric and Rhetorical Education." *Rhetoric Society Quarterly* 21 (1991): 60-71.

Berlin, James. "Composition and Cultural Studies." *Composition and Resistance.* Ed. C. Mark Hurlbert and Michael Blitz. Portsmouth, NH: Boynton/Cook , 1991. 47-55.

—. "Poststructuralism, Cultural Studies, and the Composition Classroom: Postmodern Theory in Practice." *Rhetoric Review* 11 (1992): 16-33.

—. "Rhetoric and Ideology in the Writing Class." *College English* 50 (1988): 477-94.

—. "Richard Whately and Current-Traditional Rhetoric." *College English* 42 (1980): 10-17.

—. "The Transformation of Invention in Nineteenth Century American Rhetoric." *Southern Speech Communication Journal* 46 (1981): 292-304.

—. *Writing Instruction in Nineteenth-Century American Colleges.* Carbondale, IL: Southern Illinois UP, 1984.

Berlin, James, and Michael Vivion, eds. *Cultural Studies in the English Classroom.* Portsmouth, NH: Boynton/Cook Heinemann, 1992.

Berlin, James, and Robert Inkster. "Current-Traditional Rhetoric: Paradigm and Practice." *Freshman English News* 8 (1980): 1-4, 13-14.

Bernard-Donals, Michael. "Composition in an Anti-Foundational World: A Critique and Proposal." *Rhetoric in an Antifoundational World: Language, Culture, and Pedagogy.* Ed. Michael Bernard-Donals and Richard R. Glejzer. New Haven: Yale UP, 1998. 436-53.

Bernhardt, Stephen. "Seeing the Text." *College Composition and Communication* 37 (1986): 66-78.

Berthoff, Ann. "Abstraction as a Speculative Instrument." *The Territory of Language: Linguistics, Stylistics, and the Teaching of Composition.* Ed. Donald McQuade. Carbondale, IL: Southern Illinois UP, 1987. 227-39.

—. "Dialectical Notebooks and the Audit of Meaning." *The Journal Book.* Ed. Toby Fulwiler. Portsmouth, NH: Boynton/Cook. 1987. 11-18.

—. *forming, thinking, writing: The Composing Imagination.* Rochelle Park, NJ: Hayden Book Co., 1978.

—. "From Dialogue to Dialectic to Dialogue." *Reclaiming the Classroom: Teacher Research as an Agency of Change*. Ed. Dixie Goswami and Peter R. Stillman. Portsmouth, NH: Boynton/Cook, 1987. 75-86.

—. "From Problem Solving to a Theory of Imagination." *College English* 33 (1972): 636-51.

—. " Learning the Uses of Chaos." *Reinventing the Rhetorical Tradition*. Conway, AR: L&S Books, 1980. 75-78.

—. *The Making of Meaning: Metaphors, Models, and Maxims for Writing Teachers*. Portsmouth, NH: Boynton/Cook Publishers, 1981.

—."The Problem of Problem Solving." *College Composition and Communication* 22 (1971): 237-42.

—. "Response to Janice Lauer." *College Composition and Communication* 23 (1972): 414-15.

Berthoff, Ann E., and Louise Smith, eds. *Audits of Meaning: A Festschrift in Honor of Ann E. Berthoff.* Portsmouth, NH: Boynton/Cook, 1988.

Bevilacqua, Vincent. "Adam Smith and Some Philosophical Origins of Eighteenth-Century Rhetorical Theory." *Modern Language Review* 63 (1968): 559-68.

—. "Philosophical Assumptions Underlying Hugh Blair's *Lectures.*" *Western Speech* 31 (1967): 150-64.

Biesecker, Barbara. "Coming to Terms with Recent Attempts to Write Women into the History of Rhetoric." *Rethinking the History of Rhetoric*. Ed. Takis Poulakos. Boulder, CO: Westview Press 1993. 169-71.

Bilsky, Manuel, et al. "Looking for an Argument." *Teaching Freshman Composition*. Ed. Gary Tate and Edward Corbett. New York: Oxford UP, 1967. 217-224.

Bitzer, Lloyd. "Aristotle's Enthymeme Revisited." *Quarterly Journal of Speech* 45 (1959): 399-408.

—. "Hume's Philosophy in George Campbell's *Philosophy of Rhetoric.*" *Philosophy and Rhetoric* 2 (1969): 139-66.

—. "The Rhetorical Situation." *Philosophy and Rhetoric* 1 (1968): 1-14.

Bitzer, Lloyd, and Edwin Black, eds. *The Prospect of Rhetoric*. New York: Prentice-Hall, 1971.

Bizzell, Patricia. "Cognition, Convention, and Certainty: What We Need to Know." *PRE/TEXT* 3 (1982): 213-45.

—. "Marxist Ideas in Composition Studies." *Contending with Words*. Ed. Patricia Harkin and John Schilb. New York: MLA, 1991. 52-68.

Black, Edwin. *Rhetorical Criticism: A Study in Method*. New York: Macmillian, 1978.

Blair, Carole. "Contested Theories of Rhetoric: The Politics of Preservation, Progress, and Change." *Quarterly Journal of Speech* 78 (1992): 404-28.

Blair, Carole, and Mary Kahl. "Introduction: Revising the History of Rhetorical Theory." *Western Journal of Speech Communication* 54 (1990): 148-59.

Blair, Kristine, and Pamela Takayoshi, eds. *Mapping the Terrain of Feminist Cyberspace.* Stamford, CT: Ablex, 1999.

Blair, Hugh. *Lectures on Rhetoric and Belles Lettres.* In *The Rhetoric of Blair, Campbell, and Whatley.* Ed. James L. Golden and Edward P. J. Corbett. New York: Holt, Rinehart and Winston, 1968.

Blakesley, David. *The Elements of Dramatism.* New York: Longman, 2002.

Boethius, Anicius Manlius Severinus. "An Overview of the Structure of Rhetoric." Trans. Joseph Miller. *Readings in Medieval Rhetoric.* Ed. Joseph Miller, Michael Prossner, and Thomas Benson. Bloomington, IN: Indiana UP, 1973. 69-76.

—. *De topicis differentiis.* Ed. and trans. Eleanore Stump. Ithaca, NY: Cornell UP, 1978.

Bolter, Jay, Michael Joyce, and John Smith. *STORYSPACE.* Software. Cambridge, MA: Eastgate Systems, 1991.

Booth, Wayne C. *Modern Dogma and the Rhetoric of Assent.* Chicago: U of Chicago P, 1973.

Bordelon, Suzanne. "Resisting Decline Stories: Gertrude Buck's Democratic Theory of Rhetoric." *The Changing Tradition: Women in the History of Rhetoric.* Ed. Christine Sutherland and Rebecca Sutcliffe. Calgary, Alberta: U of Calgary P, 1999. 183-98.

Braddock, Richard. "Crucial Issues." *College Composition and Communication* 16 (1965): 165-69.

Brereton, John, ed. *Traditions of Inquiry.* New York: Oxford UP, 1985.

Bridwell-Bowles, Lillian. "Discourse and Diversity: Experimental Writing Within the Academy." *Feminine Principles and Women's Experience in American Composition and Rhetoric.* Ed. Janet Emig and Louise Phelps. Pittsburgh: U of Pittsburgh P. 1995. 43-66.

Bridwell-Bowles, Lillian, Paula Reed Nancarrow, and Donald Ross. "The Writing Process and the Writing Machine: Current Research on Word Processors Relevant to the Teaching of Composition." *New Directions in Composition Reearch.* Ed. Richard Beach and Lillian Bridwell-Bowles. New York: The Guilford Press, 1984. 381-98.

Britton, James. "Shaping at the Point of Utterance." *Reinventing the Rhetorical Tradition.* Ed. Ian Pringle and Aviva Freedman. Conway, AK: L and S Books, 1980. 61-66.

Brockriede, Wayne. "Toward a Contemporary Aristotelian Theory of Rhetoric." *Quarterly Journal of Speech* 46 (1960): 44-53.

Broderick, James. " A Study of the Freshman Composition Course at Amherst: Action, Orders, and Language." *Harvard Education Review* 28 (1958): 44-57.

Brody, Miriam. *Manly Writing: Gender, Rhetoric, and the Rise of Composition.* Carbondale, IL: Southern Illinois UP, 1993.

Brown, James. "Freshman English and General Education." *The Journal of Higher Education* 21 (1950): 17-20.

Brown, Joseph S., et al. *Free Writing!: A Group Approach. Toward a New and Simple Method of Learning and Teaching Writing: Exercises, Examples, Fourteen Points of View, a Poem, and Footnotes.* Rochelle Park, NJ: Hayden Book Co., 1977.

Brown, Richard. "Logics of Discovery as Narratives of Conversion: Rhetorics of Invention in Ethnography, Philosophy, and Astronomy. *Philosophy and Rhetoric* 27 (1994): 1-34.

Bruffee, Kenneth. "Social Construction, Language, and the Authority of Knowledge: A Bibliographic Essay." *College English* 48 (1986): 773-90.

—. "Writing and Reading as Collaborative Social Acts." *The Writer's Mind: Writing as a Mode of Thinking.* Ed. Janice N. Hays, et al. Urbana, IL: NCTE, 1983. 159-70.

Brummett, Barry. "The Reported Demise of Epistemic Rhetoric." *Quarterly Journal of Speech* 9 (1990): 69-72.

—. "Some Implications of 'Process' or 'Intersubjectivity': Postmodern Rhetoric," *Philosophy and Rhetoric* 9 (1976): 21-51.

Bruner, Jerome. *On Knowing: Essays for the Left Hand.* Cambridge: Belknap-Harvard UP, 1966.

—. *The Process of Education.* Cambridge: Harvard UP, 1960.

Bryant, Donald. "The Most Significant Passage (for the moment) in Plato's *Phaedrus.*" *Rhetoric Society Quarterly* 11 (1981): 9-11.

—. "Rhetoric: Its Function and Scope." *Philosophy, Rhetoric, and Argumentation.* Es. Maurice Natanson and Henry Johnstone. University Park, PA: Penn State UP, 1965. 32-62.

Buck, Gertrude. *A Course in Argumentative Writing.* New York: Henry Holt, 1899.

—. *Figures of Rhetoric.* Contributions to Rhetorical Theory, No. 1 Ed. Fred Newton Scott. Ann Arbor, MI: Inland Press, 1895.

—. *The Metaphor—A Study in the Psychology of Rhetoric.* Contributions to Rhetorical Theory, No. 5 Ed. Fred Newton Scott. Ann Arbor, MI: Inland Press, 1899.

—. " The Study of English." *Vassar Miscellany Weekly* 2 (1917): 6.

Bullock, Richard H., John Trimbur, and Charles Schuster, eds. *The Politics of Writing Instruction: Postsecondary.* Portsmouth, NH: Boynton/Cook, 1991.

Burger, Ronna. *Plato's Phaedrus: A Defense of the Philosophical Act of Writing.* Birmingham, AL: The U of Alabama P, 1980.

Burhan, Clifton. *The Would-Be Writer.* 3rd ed. Waltham, MA: Xerox, 1971.

Burke, Kenneth. "The Five Master Terms." *View* 2 (1943): 50-52.

—. *Language as Symbolic Action*. Berkeley: U of California P, 1966.

—. "Questions and Answers about the Pentad." *College Composition and Communication* 29 (1978): 330-35.

—. *A Rhetoric of Motives*. Berkeley: U of California P, 1950.

Burke, Rebecca. *Gertrude Buck's Rhetorical Theory*. Occasional Papers in Composition History and Theory. Ed. Donald Stewart. Kansas State University, 1978. 1-26.

Burke, Virginia. "The Composition-Rhetoric Pyramid." *College Composition and Communication* 16 (1965): 3-7.

Burns, Hugh. "Computers and Composition." *Teaching Composition: Twelve Bibliographic Essays*." Ed. Gary Tate. Fort Worth: Texas Christian UP, 1987. 378-400.

—. "Recollections of First-Generation Computer-Assisted Prewriting." *The Computer in Composition Instruction*. Ed. William Wresch. Urbana, IL: NCTE, 1984. 15-33.

—. *DAEDALUS INVENT*. Software. Austin, TX: The Daedalus Group, 1979.

—. "Stimulating Rhetorical Invention in English Composition through Computer-Assisted Instruction." Diss., University of Texas, Austin, 1979.

—. "A Writer's Tool: Computing as a Mode of Inventing." *The Writer's Mind: Writing as a Mode of Thinking*. Ed. Janice N. Hays, et al. Urbana IL: NCTE, 1983. 87-94.

Burns, Hugh, and G. Culp. "Stimulating Invention in English Composition through Computer-Assisted Instruction." *Educational Technology* 20 (1980): 5-10.

Butler, Marilyn, and Janet Todd. "General Introduction." *The Works of Mary Wollstonecraft*. 7 vols. Washington Square: New York UP, 1989.

Byard, Vicki. "Considering Heuristics as Symbolic Acts: Their Relevance to Epistemic Rhetoric, Social Invention, and Cultural Studies." Diss., Purdue U., 1993.

Camargo, Martin. "Toward a Comprehensive Art of Written Discourse: Geoffrey of Vinsauf and The *Ars Dictiminis*." *Rhetorica* 6 (1988): 167-94.

Campbell, George. *The Philosophy of Rhetoric. The Rhetoric of Blair, Campbell, and Whatley*. Ed. James L. Golden and Edward P. J. Corbett. New York: Holt, Rinehart and Winston, 1968.

Campbell, JoAnne. *Toward a Feminist Rhetoric: The Writing of Gertrude Buck*. Pittsburgh, PA: U of Pittsburgh P, 1996.

—. "Women's Work, Worthy Work: Composition Instruction at Vassar." *Constructing Rhetorical Education*. Ed. Marie Secor and Davida Charney. Carbondale, IL: Southern Illinois UP, 1992. 26-42.

Campbell, John Angus. "Scientific Discovery and Rhetorical Invention: The Path to Darwin's *Origin*." *The Rhetorical Turn: Invention and Persuasion in the Conduct of Inquiry*. Ed. Herbert W. Simons. Chicago: U of Chicago P, 1990. 58-90.

Campbell, Karlyn Kohrs. "Consciousness Raising: Linking Theory, Criticism, and Practice " *Rhetoric Society Quarterly* 32 (2002): 45-64.

—. *Man Cannot Speak for Her: Vol 1: A Critical Study of Early Feminist Rhetoric, 1830-1925;* Vol. 2. *Key Texts of Early Feminism, 19830-1925*. Westport, CT:Greenwood, 1989.

Caplan, Harry. "The Decay of Eloquence at Rome in the First Century." *Studies in Speech and Drama in Honor of Alexander M. Drummond*. Ed. Herbert A. Wichlens. Ithaca, NY: Cornell UP, 1944. 295-325.

Carter, Michael. "Problem-Solving Reconsidered: A Pluralistic Theory of Problems." *College English* 50 (1988): 551-65.

—. "*Stasis* and *Kairos:* Principles of Social Construction in Classical Rhetoric." *Rhetoric Review* 7 (1988): 97-112.

—. *Where Writing Begins: A Postmodern Reconstruction*. Carbondale, IL: Southern Illinois UP, 2003.

Caywood Cynthia, and Gillian Overing, eds. *Teaching Writing: Pedagogy, Gender, and Equity*. New York: State U of New York, 1987.

Cherwitz, Richard, and James W. Hikins. "Burying the Undertaker: A Eulogy for the Eulogists of Rhetorical Epistemology." *Quarterly Journal of Speech* 9 (1990): 73-77.

—. *Communication and Knowledge: An Investigation in Rhetorical Epistemology*. Columbia, SC: The U of South Carolina P, 1986.

—. "Toward a Rhetorical Epistemology." *Southern Speech Communication Journal* 47 (1982): 135-62.

Church, D., and R. Cathcart. "Some Concepts of the Epicheireme in Greek and Roman Rhetoric." *Western Speech* 29 (1965): 140-147.

Cicero. *De Inventione*. Trans. H. M. Hubbell. Cambridge, Mass.: Harvard UP, 1949.

—. *De Oratore*. Trans. J. S. Watson. Carbondale, IL: Southern Illinois UP, 1970.

Clark, Gregory, and Michael Halloran, eds. *Oratorical Culture in Nineteenth-Century America*. Carbondale, IL: Southern Illinois UP, 1993.

Clifford, John. "'Ideology into Discourse': A Historical Perspective." *Journal of Advanced Composition* 7 (1987): 121-30.

Clifford, John, and John Schilb, eds. *Writing Theory and Critical Theory*. New York: MLA, 1994.

Cole, A. T., *The Origins of Rhetoric in Ancient Greece*. Baltimore, MD: Johns Hopkins, 1991.

Collins, Paul. *Community Writing: Researching Social Issues Through Composition*. Mahwah, NJ: Erlbaum, 2001.

Comprone, Joseph. "Burke's Dramatism as a Means of Using Literature to Teach Writing." *Rhetoric Society Quarterly* 9 (1979): 142-55.

—. "Kenneth Burke and the Teaching of Writing." *College Composition and Communication* 29 (1978): 336-40.

Conley, Thomas. "'Logical Hylomorphism' and Aristotle's *Konoi Topoi.*" *Central States Speech Journal* 29 (1978): 92-97.

Connelly, Francis. *A Rhetoric Case Book.* New York: Harcourt, 1959.

Connors, Robert J. *Composition-Rhetoric: Backgrounds, Theory, and Pedagogy.* Pittsburgh, PA: U of Pittsburgh P, 1997.

—. "Greek Rhetoric and the Transition from Orality." *Philosophy and Rhetoric* 19 (1986): 38-65.

—. "Women's Reclamation of Rhetoric in Nineteenth-Century America." *Feminine Principles and Women's Experience in American Composition and Rhetoric.* Ed. Louise Phelps and Janet Emig. Pittsburgh: U of Pittsburgh P, 1995. 67-90.

Connors, Robert J., Lisa S. Ede, and Andrea A. Lunsford, eds. *Essays on Classical Rhetoric and Modern Discourse.* Carbondale, IL: Southern Illinois UP, 1984.

Consigny, Scott. "Rhetoric and Its Situations." *Philosophy and Rhetoric* 7 (1974): 175-86.

Conway, Kathyrn. "Woman Suffrage and the History of Rhetoric at the Seven Sisters Colleges, 1865-1919." *Reclaiming Rhetorica.* Ed. Andrea Lunsford. Pittsburgh, PA: U of Pittsburgh P, 1995. 203-26.

Cooper, Charles R., Lee Odell, and Cynthia Courts."Discourse Theory: Implications for Research in Composing." *Research on Composing: Points of Departure.* Ed. Charles R. Cooper and Lee Odell. Urbana, IL: NCTE, 1978. 1-12.

Cooper, Charles R., and Lee Odell, eds. *Research on Composing: Points of Departure.* Urbana, IL: NCTE, 1978.

Cooper, Martha. *Analyzing Public Discourse.* Prospect Heights, IL: Waveland Press, 1989.

Cope, E. M. *The Rhetoric of Aristotle with a Commentary.* 3 vols. Ed. John E. Sandys. Cambridge: Cambridge UP, 1877.

Corbett, Edward P. J. *Classical Rhetoric for the Modern Student.* New York: Oxford UP, 1965.

—. "A Look at the Old Rhetoric." *Rhetoric: Theories for Application.* Ed. Robert M. Gorrell. Urbana, IL: NCTE, 1967. 16-22.

—. "Rhetoric and Teachers of English." *Quarterly Journal of Speech* 51 (1965): 375-81.

—. "The Usefulness of Classical Rhetoric." *College Composition and Communication* 14 (1963): 102-4.

Couture, Barbara. *Toward a Phenomenological Rhetoric: Writing, Profession, and Altruism.* Carbondale, IL: Southern Illinois UP, 1998.

Covino, William. *The Art of Wondering: A Revisionist Return to the History of Rhetoric*. Portsmouth, NH: Boynton/Cook, 1988.

Crowley, Sharon. "Invention in the Nineteenth Century." *College Composition and Communication* 36 (1985): 51-60.

—. *Methodical Memory: Invention in Current Traditional Rhetoric*. Carbondale, IL: Southern Illinois UP, 1990.

—. *A Teacher's Guide to Deconstruction*. Urbana, IL: NCTE, 1989.

Crowley, Sharon, and Debra Hawhee. *Ancient Rhetorics for Contemporary Students*. New York: Macmillan, 1994.

Csikszentmihalyi, Mihaly. *Creativity: The Flow and Psychology of Discovery and Invention*. New York: Harper Collins, 1996.

Cummings, B. "Pre-writing, Writing, Rewriting: Teaching the Composing Process to Basic Writers at the College Level." *DAI* 42 (1981); 2465-A.

Cyganowski, Carol. "The Computer Classroom and Collaborative Learning: The Impact on Student Writers." *Computers and Community: Teaching Composition in the Twenty-First Century*. Ed. Carolyn Handa. Portsmouth, NH: Boynton/Cook, 1990. 68-88.

D'Angelo, Frank. *Composition in the Classical Tradition*. Boston, MA: Allyn & Bacon, 1999.

—. *A Conceptual Theory of Rhetoric*. Englewood Cliffs, NJ: Winthrop Press, 1975.

Daumer, Elizabeth, and Sandra Runzo. "Transforming the Composition Classroom." *Teaching Writing: Pedagogy, Gender, and Equity*. Ed. Cynthia Caywood & Gillian Overing. Albany, NY: SUNY Press, 1987. 45-62.

Dean, Harold H. "The Communication Course: A Ten-Year Perspective." *College Composition and Communication* 10 (1959): 80-84.

Dearin, Roy. "Persuasion and the Concept of Identification." *Central States Speech Journal* 17 (1966): 277-82.

DeBono, Edward. *Lateral Thinking: Creativity Step by Step*. New York: Harper and Row, 1970.

de Lauretis, Teresa. "The Essence of the Triangle or, Taking the Risk of Essentialism Seriously: Feminist Theory in Italy, the U. S., and Britain." *The Essential Difference*. Ed. Naomi Schor and Elizabeth Weed. Bloomington, IN: Indiana UP, 1994. 1-39.

Dieter, Otto. "Stasis." *Speech Monographs* 17 (1950): 345-69.

Deleuze, Gilles, and Felix Guattari. *Anti-Oedipus: Capitalism and Schizophrenia*. Trans. Robert Hurley, Mark Seem, and Helen R. Lane. Minneapolis: U of Minnesota P, 1983.

De Man, Paul. *Allegories of Reading: Figural Language in Rousseau, Nietzsche, Rilke, and Proust*. New Haven: Yale UP, 1985.

Derrida, Jacques. *Of Grammatology*. Trans. Gayatri Chakravorty Spivak. Baltimore: Johns Hopkins UP, 1976.

—. *Positions*. Trans. Alan Bass. Chicago: U of Chicago P, 1982.

Detienne, Marcel, and Jean-Pierre Vernant. *Cunning Intelligence in Greek Culture and Society*. Trans. Janet Lloyd. Atlantic Highlands, NJ: Humanities Press, 1978.

Dewey, John. *Nature and Experience*. New York: Dover, 1958.

Dick, Robert. "*Topoi*: An Appeal to Inventing Arguments." *The Speech Teacher* 13 (1964): 313-19.

Dillon, Ronna F., and Robert J. Sternberg, eds. *Cognition and Instruction*. Orlando, FL: Academic Press, 1986.

Dillon, Ronna F. "Issues in Cognitive Psychology and Instruction." *Cognition and Instruction*. Ed. Ronna F. Dillon and Robert J. Sternberg. Orlando, FL: Academic Press, 1986. 1-12.

Dissoi Logoi or Dialexeis. Trans. Rosamund Kent Sprague. *The Older Sophists: A Complete Translation by Many Hands of the Fragments in Die Fragmente der Vorsokratiker*. Ed. Rosamund Sprague. Columbia, South Carolina UP, 1972. 279-93.

Dobrin, D. "What's Technical About Technical Writing?" *New Essays in Technical and Scientific Communication, Theory and Research*. Ed. Paul Anderson, R Brockmann, and Carolyn Miller. Farmingdale, NY: Baywood, 1983.

Donawerth, Jane. "Bibliography of Women and the History of Rhetoric. *Rhetoric Society Quarterly* 20 (1990): 403-14.

—. "Conversation and the Boundaries of Public Discourse in Rhetorical Theory by Renaissance Women." *Rhetorica* 16 (1998): 181-99.

—. *Rhetorical Theory by Women before 1900*. New York: Rowan and Littlefield, 2002.

duBois, Page. *Sowing the Body: Psychoanalysis and the Ancient Representations of Women*. Chicago: U of Chicago P, 1988.

Duhamel, Albert. "The Function of Rhetoric as Effective Expression." *The Journal of the History of Ideas* 10 (1949): 344-56.

—. The Logic and Rhetoric of Peter Ramus." *Modern Philology* 46 (1949): 163-71.

Dunne, J. *Back to the Rough Ground: 'Phronesis' and 'Techne' in Modern Philosophy and in Aristotle*. South Bend, IN: U of Notre Dame P, 1993.

Dwyer, Karen. "A Cultural and Rhetorical Analysis of Internationalized Human Rights Discourse." Diss., Purdue University, 1997.

Ede, Lisa S., and Andrea A. Lunsford. *Singular Texts, Plural Authors: Perspectives on Collaborative Writing*. Carbondale, IL: Southern Illinois UP, 1990.

Ede, Lisa, Cheryl Glenn, and Andrea Lunsford. "Border Crossings: Intersections of Rhetoric and Feminism," *Rhetorica* 13 (1995): 401-41.

Eden, Kathy. "The Rhetorical Tradition and Augustinian Hermeneutics in *De Doctrina Christiana*." *Rhetorica* 8 (1990): 45-64.

Edwards, Bruce. *The Tagmemic Contribution to Composition Teaching.* Occasional Papers in Composition History and Theory. Ed. Donald Stewart. Manhattan, KS: Kansas State University, 1979.

Einhorn, Lois. "Richard Whately's Public Persuasion: The Relationship between His Rhetorical Theory and His Rhetorical Practice." *Rhetorica* 4 (1986): 47-65.

Elbow, Peter. *Embracing Contraries: Explorations in Learning and Teaching.* New York: Oxford UP, 1986.

—. "In Defense of Private Writing: Consequences for Theory and Research." *Written Communication* 16 (1999): 139-70.

—. "Toward a Phenomenology of Freewriting." *Nothing Begins with N: New Investigations of Freewriting.* Ed. Pat Belanoff, Peter Elbow, and Sheryl I. Fontaine. Carbondale, IL: Southern Illinois UP, 1991. 189-213.

—. *Writing Without Teachers.* New York: Oxford UP, 1973.

—. *Writing With Power: Techniques for Mastering the Writing Process.* New York: Oxford UP, 1981.

Emig, Janet. *The Composing Process of Twelfth Graders.* Urbana, IL: NCTE, 1971.

—. "Writing as a Mode of Learning." *College Composition and Communication* 28 (1977): 122-28.

Emmel, Barbara A. "Toward a Pedagogy of the Enthymeme: The Roles of Dialogue, Intention, and Function in Shaping Argument." *Rhetoric Review* 13 (1994): 132-49.

Enos, Richard L., and Janice M. Lauer. "The Meaning of 'Heuristic' in Aristotle's *Rhetoric* and Its Implications for Contemporary Rhetorical Theory." *A Rhetoric of Doing.* Ed. Stephen Witte, Roger Cherry, and Neil Nakadate. Carbondale, IL: Southern Illinois UP, 1991. 37-44.

Enos, Richard L. "The Epistemology of Gorgias' Rhetoric: A Re-Examination." *Southern States Speech Communication Journal* 42 (1976): 25-51.

—. "The Effects of Imperial Patronage on the Rhetorical Tradition of the Athenian Second Sophistic." *Communication Quarterly* 25 (1977): 3-9.

—. *Greek Rhetoric before Aristotle.* Prospect Heights, IL: Waveland Press, 1993.

—. *The Literate Mode of Cicero's Legal Rhetoric.* Carbondale, IL: Southern Illinois UP, 1988.

—. Literacy in Athens During the Archaic Period: A Prolegomenon to Rhetorical Invention." *New Perspectives on Rhetorical Invention.* Ed. Janet Atwill and Janice M. Lauer. Knoxville, TN: U of Tennessee P, 2002.

—. "The Most Significant Passage in Plato's *Phaedrus*: A Personal Nomination." *Rhetoric Society Quarterly* 11 (1981): 15-18.

Faigley, Lester, Roger Cherry, David Jolliffe, and Anna Skinner. *Assessing Writers' Knowledge and Processes of Composing.* Norwood, NJ: Ablex, 1985.

Faigley, Lester. "Competing Theories of Process: A Critique and a Proposal." *College English* 48 (1986): 527-41.

—. *Fragments of Rationality: Postmodernity and the Subject of Composition.* Pittsburgh: U of Pittsburgh P, 1992.

Fantham, Elaine, et al. *Women in the Classical World: Image and Text.* New York: Oxford UP, 1994.

Fantham, Elaine. "The Concept of Nature and Human Nature in Quintilian's Psychology and Theory of Instruction." *Rhetorica* 13 (1995): 125-136.

Farnsworth, Rodney, and Avon Crismore. "On the Reefs: The Verbal and Visual Rhetoric of Darwin's Other Big Theory." *Rhetoric Society Quarterly* 21 (1991): 11-25.

Farrell, Thomas B. "From the Parthenon to the Bassinet: Death and Rebirth Along the Epistemic Trail." *Quarterly Journal of Speech* 9 (1990): 78-84.

—. *Norms of Rhetorical Culture.* New Haven, London: Yale UP, 1993.

—. "Practicing the Arts of Rhetoric: Tradition and Invention." *Philosophy and Rhetoric* 24 (1991): 183-212.

—. "Social Knowledge II." *Quarterly Journal of Speech* 64 (1978): 329-34.

Fenner, Dudley. *The Artes of Logike and Rhetorike, plainelie set foorth in the Englishe tounge.* 1584. Ed. Robert Pepper. Gainesville, FL: Scholars' Facsimiles and Reprints, 1966. 143-180.

Ferguson, Charles. *Say It With Words.* New York: Alfred Knopf, 1959.

Ferguson, Moira, and Janet Todd. *Mary Wollstonecraft.* Boston: Twayne, 1984.

Ferrante, Joan. "The Education of Women in the Middle Ages in Theory, Fact, and Fantasy." *Beyond Their Sex: Learned Women of the European Past.* Ed. Patricia Labalme. New York: New York UP, 1980. 9-42.

Festinger, Leon. *A Theory of Cognitive Dissonance.* San Francisco: Stanford UP, 1965.

Fish, Stanley. *Doing What Comes Naturally: Change, Rhetoric, and the Practice of Theory in Literary and Legal Studies.* Durham: Duke UP, 1989.

Florescu, Vasile. "Rhetoric and Its Rehabilitation in Contemporary Philosophy." *Philosophy and Rhetoric* 3 (1970): 193-224.

Flower, Linda S. "Cognition, Context, and Theory Building." *College Composition and Communication* 40 (1989): 282-311.

—. "Cognitive Rhetoric: Inquiry into the Art of Inquiry." *Defining the New Rhetorics.* Ed. Theresa Enos and Stuart C. Brown. Newbury Park, CA: Sage, 1993. 171-90.

—. *The Construction of Negotiated Meaning: A Social Cognitive Theory of Writing.* Carbondale: IL: Southern Illinois UP, 1994.

—. *Problem-Solving Strategies for Writing.* San Diego: Harcourt Brace Jovanovich, 1984.

Flower, Linda S., and Julia Deems. "Conflict in Community Collaboration." *New Perspectives on Rhetorical Invention*. Ed. Janet Atwill and Janice M. Lauer. Knoxville, TN: U of Tennessee P, 2002. 96-130.

Flower, Linda S., and John R. Hayes. "The Cognition of Discovery: Defining a Rhetorical Problem." *College Composition and Communication* 31 (1980): 21-32.

—. "A Cognitive Process Theory of Writing." *College Composition and Communication* 32 (1981): 365-87.

—. "The Dynamics of Composing: Making Plans and Judging Constraints." *Cognitive Processes in Writing: An Interdisciplinary Approach*. Ed. Lee Gregg and Erwin Steinburg. Hillsdale, NJ: Erlbaum, 1980. 31-50.

—. "Images, Plans, and Prose." *Written Communication* 1 (1984): 120-60.

—. "Plans that Guide the Composing Process." *Writing: Process, Development and Communication*. Ed. Carl Frederickson and Joseph Dominic. Hillside, NJ: Erlbaum, 1981. 39-58.

—. "The Pregnant Pause: An Inquiry into the Nature of Planning." *Research in the Teaching of English* 15 (1981): 229244.

—."Problem-Solving Strategies and the Writing Process." *College English* 39 (1977): 449-61.

Flower, Linda, Elenore Long, and Lorraine Higgins. *Learning to Rival: A Literate Practice for Intercultural Inquiry*. Mahwah, NJ: Erlbaum, 2000.

Flynn, Elizabeth. "Composing as a Woman." *College Composition and Communication* 39 (1988): 423-35.

—. "Composing 'Composing as a Woman': A Perspective on Research." *College Composition and Communication* 41 (1990): 83-89.

Flynn, Elizabeth, and Patracinio Schweickart, eds. *Gender and Reading: Essays on Readers: Texts, and Contexts*. Baltimore: Johns Hopkins UP , 1986.

Fogarty, Daniel J. *Roots for a New Rhetoric*. New York: Columbia UP, 1959.

Fortune, Ron. "Visual and Verbal Thinking: Drawing and Word Processing Software in Writing Instruction." *Critical Perspectives On Computers and Composition Instruction*. Ed. Gail Hawisher and Cindy Selfe. New York: Teachers College Press, Teachers College, Columbia U, 1989. 145-16.

Foster, Helen. "An Institutional Critique of Writing Process." Diss., Purdue University, 2001.

Foucault, Michel. "What Is an Author?" Trans. Josue V. Harari. *Textual Strategies: Perspectives in Post-Structuralist Criticism*. Ed. Josue V. Harari. Ithaca: Cornell UP, 1979. Rpt. *The Foucault Reader*. Ed. Paul Rabinow. New York: Pantheon Books, 1984. 101-20.

Francesconi, Robert, and Charles Kneupper. "Invention and Epistemic Rhetoric: The Knowing/Knowledge Interaction." *Visions of Rhetoric: History, Theory, and Criticism*. Ed. Charles Kneupper. Arlington, TX: Rhetoric Society of America, 1987. 106-18.

Frank, Francine, and Paula Treichler, eds. *Language, Gender, and Professional Writing*. New York, MLA, 1989.

Fraunce, Abraham. *The Arcadian Rhetorike*. London, 1588.

Freeman, Kathleen. *Ancilla to the Pre-Socratic Philosophers*. Cambridge, MA: Harvard UP, 1948.

—. *The Pre-Socratic Philosophers: A Companion to Diels Fragments der Voraskratiker*. 2nd. Ed. Oxford: Basil Blackwell, 1966.

Freire, Paulo. *Pedagogy of the Oppressed*. Trans. Myra Bergman Ramos. New York: Continuum, 1989.

Fulkerson, Richard. "Composition Theory in the 1980s: Axiological Consensus and Paradigmatic Diversity." *College Composition and Communication* 41 (1990): 409-29.

Fuller, Margaret. *Woman in the Nineteenth Century*. 1895. New York: Norton, 1971.

Fulwiler, Toby, ed. *The Journal Book*. Portsmouth, NH: Boynton/Cook, 1987.

—. "The Personal Connection: Journal Writing Across the Curriculum." *Language Connections: Writing and Reading Across the Curriculum*. Ed. Toby Fulwiler and Art Young. Urbana, IL: NCTE, 1982.

Fulwiler, Toby, and Bruce Petersen. "Toward Irrational Heuristics: Freeing the Tacit Mode." *College English* 43 (1981): 621-29.

Fulwiler, Toby and Art Young, eds. *Language Connections: Writing and Reading across the Curriculum*. Urbana IL: NCTE, 1982.

Fuss, Diana. *Essentially Speaking: Feminism, Nature, and Difference*. New York: Routledge, 1989.

Gabin, Rosalind, ed. *Discourse Studies in Honor of James Kinneavy*. Potomac, MD: Scripta Humanistica, 1995.

Gadamer, Hans-Georg. *Philosophical Hermeneutics*. Trans. and ed. David E. Linge. Berkeley: U of California P, 1976.

Gage, John. "An Adequate Epistemology for Composition: Classical and Modern Perspectives." *Essays on Classical Rhetoric and Modern Discourse*. Ed. Robert Connors, Lisa Ede, and Andrea Lunsford. Carbondale, IL: Southern Illinois UP, 1984. 152-73.

—. "A General Theory of the Enthymeme for Advanced Composition." *Teaching Advanced Composition*. Ed. Katherine H. Adams and John Adams. Portsmouth, NH: Boynton/Cook-Heinemann, 1991. 161-78.

Gannett, Cinthia. *Gender and Journal: Diaries and Academic Discourse*. New York: SUNY P, 1992. 19-42.

Gaonkar, Dilip Parameshwar. "The Idea of Rhetoric in the Rhetoric of Science." *Rhetorical Hermeneutics: Invention and Interpretation in the Age of Science*. Ed. Alan Gross and William Keith. Albany, NY: SUNY P, 1997. 60-102.

—. "Object and Method in Rhetorical Criticism: From Wichelns to Leff and McGee." *Western Journal of Speech Communication* 54 (1990): 290-316.

Gardner, Howard. *Frames of Mind: The Theory of Multiple Intelligences.* New York: Basic Books, 1983.

Garver, Eugene. "The Modesty of Aristotle's Rhetoric." *Inventing a Discipline: Rhetoric Scholarship in Honor of Richard E. Young.* Ed. Maureen Goggin. Urbana,. IL: NCTE, 2000. 123-45.

Gates, Jr., Henry Louis. "The Signifying Monkey and the Language of Signifyin[g]: Rhetorical Difference and the Orders of Meaning." *Signifying Monkey: A Theory of Afro-American Literary Criticism.* New York: Oxford UP, 1988.

Geisler, Cheryl. *Academic Literacy and the Nature of Expertise: Reading, Writing, and Knowing in Academic Philosophy.* Hillsdale, NJ: Erlbaum, 1994.

Genung, John. *Practical Elements of Rhetoric.* Boston: Ginn & Company, 1916.

George, Diana, and Diana Shoos. "Issues of Subjectivity and Resistance." *Cultural Studies in the English Classroom.* Ed. James Berlin and Michael Vivion. Portsmouth, NH: Boynton/Cook, 1992. 200-10.

Gere, Anne. *Roots in the Sawdust: Writing to Learn Across the Disciplines.* Urbana, IL: NCTE, 1985.

Gilleland, Brady B. "The Development of Cicero's Ideal Orator." *Classical, Medieval, and Renaissance Studies in Honor of Berthold Louis Ullman.* Ed. Charles Henderson, Jr. Rome: Edixioni D. Storia E. Letteratura, 1964. 91-98.

Gilligan, Carol. "In a Different Voice: Women's Conceptions of Self and Morality." *Harvard Educational Review* 47 (1977): 481-517.

Glenn, Cheryl. "Locating Aspasia on the Rhetorical Map." *Listening to their Voices: The Rhetorical Activities of Rhetorical Women."* Ed. Molly Wertheimer. Columbia, SC: U of South Carolina P, 1997. 19-41

—. "Reexamining *The Book of Margery Kempe:* A Rhetoric of Autobiography." *Reclaiming Rhetorica.* Ed. Andrea Lunsford. Pittsburgh, PA: U of Pittsburgh P, 1995. 53-72.

—, *Rhetoric Retold: Rendering the Tradition From Antiquity through the Renaissance.* Carbondale, IL: Southern Illinois UP, 1997

Goggin, Maureen Daly. "Composing a Discipline: The Role of Scholarly Journals in the Disciplinary Emergence of Rhetoric and Composition Since 1950." *Rhetoric Review* 15 (1997): 322-48.

Goody, Jack, and Ian Watt. "The Consequences of Literacy." *Literacy in Traditional Societies.* Ed. Jack Goody. Cambridge, MA: Cambridge UP, 1968. 27-68

Gordon, William J. J. *Synectics: The Development of Creative Capacity.* New York: Harper, 1961.

Gorrell, Robert M., "Freshman Composition." *Teaching Freshman Composition*. Ed. Gary Tate and Edward Corbett. New York: Oxford UP, 1967. 25-43.

—, ed. *Rhetoric: Theories of Application*. Urbana, IL: NCTE, 1967.

—. "Very Like a Whale—A Report on Rhetoric." *College Composition and Communication* 16 (1965): 138-43.

Gregg, Lee, and Erwin Steinberg. *Cognitive Processes in Writing*. Hillsdale, NJ: Erlbaum, 1980.

Gregg, Richard. "Rhetoric and Knowing: The Search for Perspective." *Central States Speech Journal* 32 (1981): 133-44.

Griggs, Karen. "Audience Complexities in Administrative Law: An Historical Case Study of an Environmental Policy," Diss. Purdue University, 1994.

Grimaldi, William. *Aristotle: A Commentary*. 2 vols. New York: Fordham UP, 1980-1988.

—. *Studies in the Philosophy of Aristotle's Rhetoric*. Wiesbaden: Franz Steiner Verlag GMBH, 1972.

Griswold, Charles. *Self-Knowledge in Plato's Phaedrus*. New Haven: Yale UP, 1986.

Gross, Alan. ""The Origin of Species: Evolutionary Taxonomy as an Example of the Rhetoric of Science." *The Rhetorical Turn: Invention and Persuasion in the Conduct of Inquiry*. Ed. Herbert W. Simons. Chicago: U of Chicago P, 1990. 91-115.

—. "What if We're Not Producing Knowledge? Critical Reflections on the Rhetorical Criticism of Science." *Rhetorical Hermeneutics: Invention and Interpretation in the Age of Science*. Ed. Alan Gross and William Keith. Albany: SUNY P, 1997. 138-55.

Gross, Alan, and William M. Keith, eds. *Rhetorical Hermeneutics: Invention and Interpretation in the Age of Science*. Albany, MD: SUNY P, 1997.

Hagaman, John. "Modern Use of the *Progymnasmata* in the Teaching of Rhetorical Invention." *Rhetoric Review* 5 (1986): 22-29.

—. "On Campbell's Philosophy of Rhetoric and Its Relevance to Contemporary Invention." *Rhetoric Society Quarterly* 21 (1981): 145-55.

Halloran, Michael. "The Birth of Molecular Biology: An Essay in the Rhetorical Criticism of Scientific Discourse." *Rhetoric Review* 3 (1984): 70-83.

—. "From Rhetoric to Composition: The Teaching of Writing in America to 1900." *A Short History of Writing Instruction: From Ancient Greece to Twentieth-Century America*. Davis, CA: Hermagoras Press, 1990. 151-82.

—. "Rhetoric in the American College Curriculum: The Decline of Public Discourse." *PRE/TEXT* 3 (1982): 245-65.

Hariman, Robert. "Critical Rhetoric and Postmodern Theory." *Quarterly Journal of Speech* 77 (1991): 67-70.

Harkin, Patricia, and John Schilb, eds. *Contending with Words*. New York: MLA, 1991. 173-88.

Harmon, Sandra. "'The Voice, Pen, and Influence of Our Women Are Abroad in the Land': Women and The Illinois State University, 1857-1899." *Nineteenth-Century Women Learn To Write*. Ed. Catherine Hobbs. Charlottesville, VA: UP of Virginia, 1995. 84-102.

Harrington, David, et al. "A Critical Survey of Resources for Teaching Rhetorical Invention: A Review Essay." *College English* 40 (1979): 641-61.

Harrington, Elbert. "A Modern Approach to Invention." *Quarterly Journal of Speech* 48 (1962): 373-78.

Harris, Jeanette. "Rethinking Invention." *Freshman English News* 17 (1988): 13-16.

Hauser, Gerard. "The Most Significant Passage in Aristotle's *Rhetoric*, or How Function May Make Moral Philosophers of Us All." *Rhetoric Society Quarterly* 12 (1982): 13-16.

—. *The Rhetoric of Publics and Public Spheres*. Columbia, SC: U of South Carolina P, 1999.

Havelock, Eric. *Preface to Plato*. Cambridge, MA: Belknap Press, Harvard UP, 1963.

Hawhee, Debra. "Kairotic Encounters." *New Perspectives on Rhetorical Invention*. Ed. Janet Atwill and Janice M. Lauer. Knoxville, TN: U of Tennessee P, 2002. 16-35.

Hays, Janice, et al., eds. *The Writer's Mind: Writing as a Mode of Thinking*. Urbana, IL: NCTE, 1983.

Hays, Janice. "The Development of Discursive Maturity in College Writers." *The Writers Mind: Writing as A Mode of Thinking*. Ed. Janice Hays, et al. Urbana, IL: NCTE, 1983. 127-44.

—. "Intellectual Parenting and a Developmental Feminist Writing Pedagogy." *Feminist Principles and Women's Experience in American Composition and Rhetoric*. Ed. Janet Emig and Louise Phelps. Pittsburgh, PA: U of Pittsburgh P, 1995. 153-90.

Heffernan, James, John Lincoln, and Janet Atwill. *Writing: A College Handbook*. 5th ed. New York: Norton, 2001.

Heidegger, Martin. *Being and Time*. Trans. John Macquarrie and Edward Robinson. New York: Harper, 1962.

Herberg, Erin. "Mary Astell's Rhetorical Theory: A Woman's Viewpoint." *The Changing Tradition: Women in the History of Rhetoric*. Ed. Christine Sutherland and Rebecca Sutcliffe. Calgary, Alberta: U of Calgary P, 1999. 147-60.

Hermogenes of Tarsus. "Progymnasmata." Trans. Charles Baldwin. *Medieval Rhetoric and Poetic*. New York: Macmillan, 1928. 23-38.

Hilgers, Thomas. "Training College Composition Students In the Use of Freewriting and Problem-Solving Heuristics for Rhetorical Invention." *Research in the Teaching of English* 14 (1980): 293-307.

Hillocks, George. "Inquiry and the Composing Process: Theory and Research." *College English* 44 (1982): 659-73.

—. *Research on Written Composition: New Directions for Teaching.* Urbana, IL: National Conference on Research in English, 1986.

—. "What Works in Teaching Composition: A Meta-Analysis of Experimental Treatment Studies." *American Journal of Education* 93 (1984): 133-70.

Hobbs, Catherine, ed. *Nineteenth-Century Women Learn to Write.* Charlottesville, VA: UP of Virginia, 1995.

—. *Rhetoric on the Margins of Modernity: Vico, Condillac, Monboddo.* Carbondale, IL: Southern Illinois UP, 2002.

Hoffman, Charles. "Tradition and Revolt in Freshman English." *College Composition and Communication* 11 (1960): 97-99.

Holbrook, Sue Ellen. "Women's Work: The Feminizing of Composition." *Rhetoric Review* 9 (1991): 201-29.

Hollis, Karyn. "Feminism in Writing Workshops: A New Pedagogy." *College Composition and Communication* 43 (1992): 340-48

—. "Liberating Voices: Autobiographical Writing at the Bryn Mawr Summer School for Women Workers, 1921-1938." *College Composition and Communication* 45 (1994): 31-60.

Hope, M. B. *The Princeton Textbook in Rhetoric.* New Jersey: Princeton, 1895.

Horner, Winifred. *Rhetoric in the Classical Tradition.* Boston, MA: St. Martin's, 1983.

House, Elizabeth, and William House. "Problem-Solving: The Debates in Composition and Psychology." *Journal of Advanced Composition* 7 (1987): 62-75.

Howell, Wilbur Samuel. "Adam Smith's Lectures on Rhetoric." *Speech Monographs* 36 (1960): 393-418.

Hudson, Hoyt. "The Field of Rhetoric." *Philosophy, Rhetoric, and Argumentation.* Ed. Maurice Natason and Henry Johnstone. University Park, PA: Penn State UP, 1965. 20-31.

Hughes, Richard. "The Contemporaneity of Classical Rhetoric." *College Composition and Communication* 16 (1965): 157-64.

Hult, Christine. *Researching and Writing Across the Curriculum.* Boston, MA: Allyn and Bacon, 1996.

Hurlbert, C. Mark, and Michael Blitz, eds. *Composition and Resistance.* Portsmouth, NH: Boynton/Cook, 1991.

Husserl, Edmund. *The Essential Husserl: Basic Writings in Transcendental Phenomenology.* Ed. Donn Welton. Bloomington: Indiana UP, 1999.

Irmscher, William. *The Holt Guide to English: A Contemporary Handbook of Rhetoric, Language, and Literature*. New York: Holt, Rinehart, and Winston, 1972.

Isidore of Seville. "The Etymologies, II.1-15: Concerning Rhetoric." Trans. Dorothy V. Cerino. *Readings in Medieval Rhetoric*. Ed. Joseph M. Miller, Michael H. Prosser, and Thomas W. Benson. Bloomington, IN: Indiana UP, 1974. 79-95.

Jacobs, Debra. "Disrupting Understanding: The Critique of Writing as a Process." *Journal of Advanced Composition* 21 (2001): 662-74.

James, William. *Pragmatism*. New York: Meridian, 1955.

Jameson, Fredric. *Postmodernism, Or the Cultural Logic of Late Capitalism*. Durham, NC: Duke UP, 1991.

Jamieson, Kathleen. "Generic Constraints and the Rhetorical Situation." *Philosophy and Rhetoric* 7 (1974): 162-70.

Janack, Marianne, and John Adams. "Feminist Epistemologies: Rhetorical Traditons and the *Ad Hominem*." *The Changing Tradition: Women in the History of Rhetoric*. Ed. Christine Sutherland and Rebecca Sutcliffe. Calgary, Alberta: U of Calgary P, 1999. 213-24.

Jarratt, Susan. "Feminism and Composition: The Case for Conflict." *Contending with Words*. Ed. Patricia Harkin and John Schilb. New York: MLA, 1991. 105-23.

—. "The First Sophists and the Uses of History." *Rhetoric Review* 6 (1987): 67-77.

—. "Performing Histories, Rhetorics." *Rhetoric Society Quarterly* 22 (1992): 1-6.

—. *Rereading the Sophists: Classical Rhetoric Refigured*. Carbondale, IL: Southern Illinois UP, 1991.

—. "Sappho's Memory." *Rhetoric Society Quarterly* 32 (2002): 11-44.

Jarratt, Susan, and Rory Ong. " Aspasia: Rhetoric, Gender, and Colonial Ideology." *Reclaiming Rhetorica*. Pittsburgh, PA: U of Pittsburgh P, 1995. 9-24.

Johnson, Nan. *Nineteen-Century Rhetoric in North America*. Carbondale, IL: Southern Illinois UP, 1991.

Johnstone, Henry. "A New Theory of Philosophical Argumentation." *Philosophy, Rhetoric, and Argumentation*. Ed. Maurice Natanson and Henry Johnstone. University Park, PA: Penn State UP, 1965. 126-134.

—. *Validity and Rhetoric in Philosophical Argument: An Outlook in Transition*. University Park, PA: Dialogue Press of Man and World, 1978.

Jordan, Mary Augusta. *Correct Writing and Speaking*. The Woman's Home Library. New York: A. S. Barnes, 1904. *Rhetorical Theory by Women before 1900*. Ed. Jane Donawerth. New York: Rowan and Littlefield, 2002. 300-16.

Joseph, Sister Miriam. *Rhetoric in Shakespeare's Time: Literary Theory of Renaissance Europe*. New York: Harcourt, Brace and World, 1962.

Jost, Walter. "Teaching the Topics: Character, Rhetoric, and Liberal Education." *Rhetoric Society Quarterly* 21 (1991): 1-16.

Katz, Sandra. "Teaching the Discovery Procedure: A Case Study of a Writing Course." Diss. Carnegie-Mellon University, 1983.

Kaufer, David, and Cheryl Geisler. "Structuring Argumentation in a Social Constructivist Framework: A Pedagogy with Computer Support." *Argumentation* 4 (1990): 379-96.

Keith, Philip. "Burke for the Composition Class." *College Composition and Communication* 28 (1977): 348-51.

—. "Burkeian Invention, from Pentad to Dialectic." *Rhetoric Society Quarterly* 9 (1979): 137-41.

Kemp, Fred. "Getting Smart with Computers: Computer-Aided Heuristics for Student Writers." *Writing Center Journal* 8 (1987): 3-11.

—. *MINDWRITER*. Software. Austin, TX: The Daedalus Group, 1988.

Kennedy, George. *The Art of Rhetoric in the Roman World: 300 B.C.—A.D. 300*. Princeton, NJ: Princeton UP, 1977.

—. *Classical Rhetoric in Its Christian and Secular Tradition from Ancient to Modern Times*. Chapel Hill, NC: U of North Carolina P, 1999.

—. *Greek Rhetoric under the Christian Emperors*. Princeton, NJ: Princeton UP, 1983.

Kent, Thomas. "Paralogic Hermeneutics and the Possibilities of Rhetoric." *Rhetoric Review* 8 (1989): 24-42.

—. *Paralogic Rhetoric: A Theory of Communicative Interaction*. Lewisburg, PA: Bucknell UP, 1993.

—, ed. *Post-Process Theory: Beyond the Writing-Process Paradigm*. Carbondale, IL: Southern Illinois UP, 1999.

Kindrick, Robert. *Henryson and the Medieval Arts of Rhetoric*. New York: Garland Publishing, 1993.

King, Margaret, and Albert Rabil, eds. *Her Immaculate Hand: Selected Works by and about the Woman Humanists of Quattrocento Italy*. Binghamton, NY: Medieval and Renaissance Texts and Studies, 1983.

Kinneavy, James. *Greek Rhetorical Origins of Christian Faith*. New York: Oxford UP, 1987.

—. "*Kairos*: A Neglected Concept in Classical Rhetoric." *Rhetoric and Praxis: The Contribution of Classical Rhetoric to Practical Reasoning*. Ed. Jean Moss. Washington, DC: Catholic UP, 1986. 79-105.

Kinneavy, James, and Catherine Eskin. "Kairos in Aristotle's *Rhetoric*." *Written Communication* 11 (1994): 131-42.

Kinney, James. "Tagmemic Rhetoric: A Reconsideration." *College Composition and Communication* 29 (1978): 141-45.

Kirsch, Gesa. *Women Writing in the Academy: Audience, Authority, and Trans-formation.* Carbondale, IL: Southern Illinois UP, 1993.

Kirscht, Judy, Rhonda Levine, and John Reiff. "Evolving Paradigms: WAC and the Rhetoric of Inquiry." *College Composition and Communication* 45 (1994): 369-80.

Kitzhaber, Albert. *Rhetoric in American Colleges, 1850-1900.* Dallas: Southern Methodist UP, 1990.

—. *Themes, Theory, and Therapy.* New York: McGraw-Hill, 1963.

Kneupper, Charles. "Dramatistic Invention: The Pentad as Heuristic Procedure." *Rhetoric Society Quarterly* 9 (1979): 130-36.

—. "Revising the Tagmemic Heuristic: Theoretical and Pedagogical Considerations." *College Composition and Communication* 31 (1980): 160-68.

—."Rhetoric and Probability Theory." *Central States Speech Journal.* 24 (1973): 288-96.

Kneupper, Charles, and Floyd Anderson. "Uniting Wisdom and Eloquence: The Need for Rhetorical Invention." *Quarterly Journal of Speech* 66 (1980): 313-26.

Koestler, Arthur. *The Act of Creation.* New York: Macmillan, 1964.

Kolodny, Annette " Inventing a Feminist Discourse: Margaret Fuller's *Woman in the Nineteenth Century.*" *Reclaiming Rhetorica.* Ed. Andrea Lunsford. Pittsburgh, PA: U of Pittsburgh P, 1995. 137-66.

Kristeva, Julia. *Revolution in Poetic Language.* Trans. Margaret Waller. New York: Columbia UP, 1984.

—. "Word, Dialogue, and the Novel." *The Kristeva Reader.* Ed. Toril Moi. New York: Columbia UP, 1986. 35-61.

La Driére, Craig. "Rhetoric and 'Merely Verbal Art.'" *English Institute Essays.* Ed. D. A. Robertson. New York: Columbia UP, 1949. 123-52.

La Tourneau, Mark. "General and Specific Topics in the De Baptismo of Tertullian." *Rhetorica* 4 (1987): 335-74.

Lacan, Jacques. *Ecrits.* Trans. Alan Sheridan. New York: Norton, 1977.

Lamb, Catherine. "Needed: A Theory of Instruction in the Art of Invention." Conference on College Composition and Communication. Philadelphia, PA. 25 Mar. 1976.

Lamberg, W. "Design and Validation of Instruction in Question-Directed Narrative Writing, Developed through Discrimination Programming." *DAI* 35 (1974): 2839.

Langer, Judith. "The Effects of Available Information on Responses to School Writing Tasks." *Research in the Teaching of English* 18 (1984): 27-44.

—. "Speaking of Knowledge: Conceptions of Understanding in Academic Disciplines." *Writing, Teaching, and the Learning in the Disciplines.* Ed. Anne Herrington and Charles Moran. New York: MLA, 1992. 69-85.

Langer, Judith, and Arthur N. Applebee. *How Writing Shapes Thinking: A Study of Teaching and Learning.* Urbana, IL: NCTE, 1987.

Langston, M. Diane "The Old Paradigm in Computer Aids to Invention: A Critical Review." *Rhetoric Society Quarterly* 16 (1986): 261-84.

Larson, Richard. "Discovery Through Questioning: A Plan for Teaching Rhetorical Invention." *College English* 30 (1968): 126-34.

Larsen, Elizabeth. "Re-Inventing Invention: Alexander Gerard and *An Essay on Genius*." *Rhetorica* 11 (1993): 181-98.

Lauer, Janice M. "Composition Studies: Dappled Discipline." *Rhetoric Review* 3 (1984): 20-29.

—. "Cross-Disciplinarity in Rhetorical Scholarship." *Inventing a Discipline: Rhetoric Scholarship in Honor of Richard E. Young*. Ed. Maureen Daly Goggin. Urbana, IL: NCTE, 2000. 67-79.

—. "Heuristics and Composition." *College Composition and Communication* 21 (1972): 396-404.

—. "Invention in Contemporary Rhetoric: Heuristic Procedures." Diss. University of Michigan, 1967.

—. "Instructional Practices: Toward an Integration." *Focuses* 1 (1988): 3-10.

—. "Issues in Rhetorical Invention." *Essays on Classical Rhetoric and Modern Discourse*. Ed. Robert J. Connors, Lisa S. Ede, and Andrea A. Lunsford. Carbondale, IL: Southern Illinois UP, 1984. 127-39.

—. "A Response to Ann E. Berthoff." *College Composition and Communication* 23 (1972): 208-211.

—. "Rhetorical Invention: The Diaspora." *New Perspectives on Rhetorical Invention*. Ed. Janet Atwill and Janice M. Lauer. Knoxville, TN: U of Tennessee P, 2002. 1-15.

—. "Toward a Meta-Theory of Heuristic Procedures." *College Composition and Communication* 30 (1979): 268-69

—. "Writing as Inquiry: Some Questions for Teachers." *College Composition and Communication* 33 (1982): 89-93.

Lauer, Janice M., Gene Montague, Andrea Lunsford, and Janet Emig. *Four Worlds of Writing* 3rd edition. New York: HarperCollins, 1991.

Lauer, Janice M., et al. *Four Worlds of Writing: Inquiry and Action in Context*. 4th edition. New York: Longman and Pearson Custom Publishing, 2000.

Lazere, Donald. "Invention, Critical Thinking, and the Analysis of Political Rhetoric." *New Perspectives on Rhetorical Invention*. Ed. Janet Atwill and Janice M. Lauer. Knoxville, TN: U of Tennessee P, 2002. 131-47.

—. "Teaching the Political Conflicts: A Rhetorical Schema." *College Composition and Communication* 43 (1992): 194-213.

Le Court, Donna. "WAC as Critical Pedagogy: The Third Stage?" *Journal of Advanced Composition* 16 (1996): 389-405.

LeFevre, Karen Burke. *Invention As a Social Act*. Carbondale, IL: Southern Illinois UP, 1986.

Leff, Michael. "The Forms of Reality in Plato's *Phaedrus*." *Rhetoric Society Quarterly* 11 (1981): 21-23.

—. "Genre and Paradigm in the Second Book of *De Oratore*." *Southern Speech Communication Journal* 51 (1986): 308-25.

—. "The Idea of Rhetoric as Interpretive Practice: A Humanist's Response to Gaonkar." *Rhetorical Hermeneutics: Invention and Interpretation in the Age of Science*. Ed. Alan G. Gross and William M. Keith. Albany, NY: SUNY P, 1997. 89-100.

—. "In Search of Ariadne's Thread: A Review of the Recent Literature on Rhetorical Theory." *Central States Speech Journal* 29 (1978): 73-91.

—. "The Topics of Argumentative Invention in Latin Rhetorical Theory from Cicero to Boethius." *Rhetorica* 1 (1983): 23-44.

L'Eplattenier, Barbara. "Investigating Institutional Power: Women Administrators during the Progressive Era." Diss., Purdue University, 1999.

Lewry, P. Osmund. "Rhetoric at Paris and Oxford in the Mid-Thirteenth Century." *Rhetorica* 1 (1983): 45-64.

Lipscomb, Drema. "Sojourner Truth: A Practical Public Discourse." *Reclaiming Rhetorica*. Andrea Lunsford, ed. Pittsburgh, PA: U of Pittsburgh P, 1995. 227-46.

Liu, Yameng. "Aristotle and the *Stasis* Theory: A Re-Examination." *Rhetoric Society Quarterly* 21 (1991): 53-59.

—. "Invention and Inventiveness: A Postmodern Redaction." *New Perspectives on Rhetorical Invention*. Ed. Janet Atwill and Janice M. Lauer. Knoxville, TN: U of Tennessee P, 2002. 53-63.

Lockwood, Sara E. Husted. *Lessons in English, Adapted to the Study of American Classics: A Textbook for High Schools and Academies*. Boston: Ginn, 1888. *Rhetorical Theory by Women before 1900*. Ed. Jane Donawerth. New York: Rowan and Littlefield, 2002. 223-39.

Logan, Shirley Wilson, ed. *"We Are Coming": The Persuasive Discourse of Nineteenth-Century Black Women*. Carbondale, IL: Southern Illinois UP, 1999.

—. *With Pen and Voice: A Critical Anthology of Nineteenth-Century African-American Women*. Carbondale, IL: Southern Illinois UP, 1995.

Lorch, Jennifer. *Mary Wollstonecraft: The Making of a Radical Feminist*. New York: Berg, 1990.

Lord, Albert B. *The Singer of Tales*. Cambridge, MA: Harvard UP, 1960.

Lonergan, Bernard. *Insight: A Study of Human Understanding*. New York: Philosophical Library, 1957.

Loreau, Max. "Rhetoric as the Logic of the Behavioral Sciences." Trans. Lloyd Watkins and Paul Brandes. *Quarterly Journal of Speech* 51 (1965): 455-63.

Luria, A. R. *The Working Brain*. Trans. Basil Haigh. New York: Basic Books, 1973.

Lunsford, Andrea, ed. *Reclaiming Rhetorica*. Pittsburgh, PA: U of Pittsburgh P, 1995.

Lunsford, Andrea, and Robert Connors. *The St, Martin's Handbook*. 3ʳᵈ ed. New York: St. Martin's, 1996.

Lyne, John. "Bio-Rhetorics: Moralizing and the Life Sciences." *The Rhetorical Turn: Invention and Persuasion in the Conduct of Inquiry*. Ed. Herbert W. Simons. Chicago: U of Chicago P, 1990. 35-57.

Lyon, Arabella. "Rhetoric and Hermeneutics: Division Through the Concept of Invention." *New Perspectives on Rhetorical Invention*. Ed. Janet Atwill and Janice M. Lauer. Knoxville, TN: U of Tennessee P, 2002. 36-52.

Lyotard, Jean-Francois. *The Postmodern Condition: A Report on Knowledge*. Trans. Brain Massumi. Minneapolis: U of Minnesota P, 1984.

Mailloux, Steven. "Rhetorical Hermeneutics." *Critical Inquiry* 11 (1985): 620-41.

—. "Rhetorical Hermeneutics Revisited." *Text and Performance Quarterly* 2 (1991): 233-48.

Maimon, Elaine, Gerald Belcher, Gail Hearn, Barbara Nodine, and Finbarr O'Connor. *Writing in the Arts and Sciences*. Cambridge, MA: Winthrop Press, 1981.

Maimon, Elaine, Barbara Nodine, and Finbarr O'Connor, eds. *Thinking, Reasoning, and Writing*. New York: Longman, 1989.

Marrou, Henri. *A History of Education in Antiquity*. Madison: U of Wisconsin P, 1956.

McComiskey, Bruce. *Gorgias and the New Sophistic Rhetoric*. Carbondale, IL.: Southern Illinois UP, 2002.

—. "Gorgias, *On Non-Existence:* Sextus Empiricus, *Against the Logicians* I.65-87. Translated from the Greek Texts in Hermann Diel's *Die Fragmente der Vorsokratiker*." *Philosophy and Rhetoric* 30 (1997): 45-49.

—. *Teaching Composition as a Social Process*. Logan, Utah: Utah State UP, 2000.

McCloskey, Deirdre. "Big Rhetoric, Little Rhetoric: Gaonkar on the Rhetoric of Science." *Rhetorical Hermeneutics: Invention and Interpretation in the Age of Science*. Ed. Alan Gross and William Keith. Albany, NY: SUNY P, 1997. 101-12.

McGee, Michael. "The 'Ideograph': A Link Between Rhetoric and Ideology." *Quarterly Journal of Speech* 66 (1980): 1-16.

—. "A Materialist Conception of Rhetoric." *Explorations in Rhetoric: Studies in Honor of Douglas Ehninger*. Ed. Michael McGee. Glenville, IL: Scott Foresman, 1982. 23-48.

McKeon, Richard. "The Methods of Rhetoric and Philosophy: Invention and Judgment." *Rhetoric: Essays in Invention and Discovery*. Ed. Mark Backman. Woodbridge, CT: Ox Bow Press, 1987. 56-65.

—. "Rhetoric in the Middle Ages." *The Province of Rhetoric*. Ed. Joseph Schwartz and John Rycenga. New York: Ronald Press, 1965. 172-211.

—. *Rhetoric: Essays in Invention and Discovery*. Ed. Mark Backman. Woodbridge, CT: Ox Bow Press, 1987.

—. The Uses of Rhetoric in a Technological Age: Architectonic Productive Arts." *The Prospect of Rhetoric*. Ed. Lloyd Bitzer and Edwin Black. New York: Prentice-Hall, 1971. 44-77.

McKerrow, Raymie. "Critical Rhetoric: Theory and Praxis." *Communication Monographs* 56 (1989): 91-111.

—. "The Ethical Implications of a Whatelian Rhetoric." *Rhetoric Society Quarterly* 17 (1987): 321-27.

—. "Probable Argument and Proof in Whately's Theory of Rhetoric." *Central States Speech Journal* 26 (1975): 259-66.

McLuhan, Marshall. *The Gutenberg Galaxy: The Making of Typographic Man*. Toronto: U of Toronto P, 1962.

Meador, Prentice. "Skeptic Theory of Perception: A Philosophical Antecedent of Ciceronian Probability." *Quarterly Journal of Speech* 54 (1968): 340-51.

Memering, Dean, and Frank O'Hare. *The Writer's Work: Guide to Effective Composition*. Englewood Cliffs, NJ: Prentice Hall, 1984.

Mendelson, Michael. "The Rhetoric of Embodiment." *Rhetoric Society Quarterly* 28 (1998): 29-50.

Merleau-Ponty, Maurice. *Phenomenology of Perception*. Trans. Colin Smith. New Jersey: Humanities Press, 1986.

Miguel, Marilyn, and Juliana Schiesari, eds. *Refiguring Woman: Perspectives on Gender and the Italian Renaissance*. Ithaca: Cornell UP, 1991.

Miller, Bernard. "Heiddeger and Gorgian *Kairos*." *Visions of Rhetoric*. Ed. Charles Kneupper. Arlington, TX: Rhetoric Society of America, 1987.

Miller, Carolyn. "Aristotle's 'Special Topics' in Rhetorical Practice and Pedagogy." *Rhetoric Society Quarterly* 17 (1987): 61-70

—. "The Aristotelian *Topos*: Hunting for Novelty." *Rereading Aristotle's Rhetoric*. Ed. Alan Gross and Arthur Walzer. Carbondale, IL: Southern Illinois UP, 2000. 130-46.

—. "Classical Rhetoric Without Nostalgia: A Response to Gaonkar." *Rhetorical Hermeneutics: Invention and Interpretation in the Age of Science*. Ed. Alan Gross and William Keith. Albany, NY: SUNY P, 1997. 156-71.

—. "*Kairos* in the Rhetoric of Science." *A Rhetoric of Doing*. Ed. Stephen Witte, Neil Nakadate, and Roger Cherry. Carbondale, IL: Southern Illinois UP, 1992. 310-27.

—. "Invention in Scientific Research in Technical Communication." *Research in Technical Communication: A Bibliographic Sourcebook*. Ed. Michael G. Moran and Debra Journet. Westport, CT: Greenwood, 1985. 117-62.

Miller, Carolyn, and Jack Selzer. "Special Topics of Argument in Engineering Reports." *Writing in Nonacademic Settings*. Ed. Lee Odell and Dixie Goswami. New York: The Guilford Press, 1985. 309-41.

Miller, George, Eugene Galanter, and Karl H. Pribram. *Plans and the Structure of Behavior*. New York: Holt Rinehart & Winston, 1960.

Miller, James. "Rediscovering the Rhetoric of Imagination." *College Composition and Communication* 25 (1974): 360-67.

Miller, Joseph, Michael Prosser, and Thomas Benson. Commentary. "Cassiodorus, '*Institutiones Divinarum et Saecularium Liitterarum, II.2:* 'On Rhetoric.'" *Readings in Medieval Rhetoric*. Ed. Joseph M. Miller, Michael H. Prosser, and Thomas W. Benson. Bloomington, IN: Indiana UP, 1973. 77-78.

Miller, Susan. *Textual Carnivals: The Politics of Composition*. Carbondale, IL: Southern Illinois UP, 1991.

Moriarty, Thomas. "South Africa's Rhetoric of Reconciliation: Changes in ANC and Pretoria Government Rhetoric, 1985-1991." Diss. Purdue University, 1999.

Morris, Charles. *Signs, Language, and Behavior*. Englewood Cliffs, NJ: Prentice-Hall, Inc, 1946.

Moss, Beverly, ed. *Literacy Across Communities*. Cresskill NJ: Hampton Press, 1994.

Moss, Jean Dietz. "The Interplay of Science and Rhetoric in Seventeenth-Century Italy." *Rhetorica* 7 (1989): 23-43.

—. *Rhetoric and Praxis*. Washington, DC: Catholic UP, 1986.

Mosenthal, Peter, Lynne Tamor, and Sean Walmsley, eds. *Research on Writing: Principles and Methods*. New York: Longman, 1983.

Murphy, James, ed. *Rhetoric in the Middle Ages: A History of Rhetorical Theory from Saint Augustine to the Renaissance*. Berkeley, CA: U of California P, 1974.

—. *The Rhetorical Tradition and Modern Writing*. New York: MLA, 1982.

—. "Roman Writing Instruction as Described by Quintilian." *A Short History of Writing Instruction From Ancient Greece to Twentieth-Century America*. Davis, CA: Hermagoras Press, 1990. 19-76.

—, ed. *A Synoptic History of Classical Rhetoric*. Berkeley, CA: U of California P, 1972.

—. *The Three Medieval Arts*. Berkeley: U of California P, 1971.

Murray, Mary. *Artwork of the Mind: An Interdisciplinary Description of Insight and the Search for It in Student Writing*. Cresskill, NJ: Hampton Press, 1995.

Myers, Greg. "The Social Construction of Two Biologists' Proposals." *Written Communication* 2 (1985): 219-45.

Nadeau, Raymond. "Hermogenes' *On Stasis*: A Translation with an Introduction and Notes." *Speech Monographs* (1964): 361-424.

—. "A Renaissance Schoolmaster on Practice." *Speech Monographs* 17 (1950): 171-79.

Nakadate, N., Roger Cherry, and Stephen Witte, eds. *A Rhetoric of Doing.* Carbondale, IL.: Southern Illinois UP, 1992.

Natanson, Maurice, and Henry Johnstone, eds. *Philosophy, Rhetoric, and Argumentation.* University Park, PA: Penn State UP, 1965.

Neel, Jasper. *Plato, Derrida, and Writing.* Carbondale, IL: Southern Illinois UP, 1988.

Nelms, Gerald, and Maureen Goggin. "The Revival of Classical Rhetoric for Modern Composition Studies: A Survey." *Rhetoric Society Quarterly* 23 (1993): 11-26.

Nelson, John, and Allan Megill. ""Rhetoric of Inquiry: Projects and Prospects." *Quarterly Journal of Speech* 72 (1986): 20-37.

Nelson, John. "Political Foundations for the Rhetoric of Inquiry." *The Rhetorical Turn: Invention and Persuasion in the Conduct of Inquiry.* Ed. Herbert W. Simons. Chicago: U of Chicago P, 1990. 258-89.

Nelson, John, Allan Megill, and Donald McCloskey, eds. *The Rhetoric of the Human Sciences.* Madison, WI: U of Wisconsin P, 1987.

Nickerson, Raymond, David Perkins, and Edward Smith. *The Teaching of Thinking.* Hillsdale, NJ: Erlbaum, 1985.

Noddings, Nell. *Caring: A Feminine Approach to Ethics and Moral Education.* Berkeley, CA: U of California P, 1984.

Nietzsche, Friedrich. *On the Genealogy of Morals.* Trans. and ed. Walter Kaufman. New York: Random House, 1967.

Nussbaum, Martha. *The Fragility of Goodness.* Cambridge: Cambridge UP, 1986.

—. "Saving Aristotle's Appearances." *The Fragility of Goodness.* Cambridge: Cambridge UP,1986. 240-63.

Nystrand, Martin, ed. *What Writer's Know: The Language, Process, and Structure of Written Discourse.* New York: Academic Press, 1982. 211-67.

O'Banion, John. "Narration and Argumentation: Quintilian on *Narratio* as the Heart of Rhetorical Thinking." *Rhetorica* 4 (1987): 325-51.

Ochs, Donovan. "Aristotle's Concept of Formal Topics." *Speech Monographs* 36 (1969): 419-25.

—. "Cicero and Philosophic *Inventio.*" *Rhetoric Society Quarterly* 19 (1989): 217-28.

Odell, Lee. "Another Look at Tagmemic Theory: A Response to James Kinney." *College Composition and Communication* 29 (1978): 146-52.

—. "Context-Specific Ways of Knowing and the Evaluation of Writing. " *Writing, Teaching, and Learning in the Disciplines.* Ed. Anne Herrington and Charles Moran. New York: MLA,1992, 86-98.

—. "Discovery Procedures for Contemporary Rhetoric: A Study of the Usefulness of the Tagmemic Model in Teaching Composition." Diss. University of Michigan, 1970.

—."Measuring the Effect of Instruction in Pre-Writing." *Research in the Teaching of English* 8 (1974): 228-40.

—. "Piaget, Problem Solving, and Freshman Composition." *College Composition and Communication* 24 (1973): 36-42.

Olson, Gary. "Diagnosing Problems with Invention." *Journal of Teaching Writing* 4 (1985): 194-202.

Ong, Walter S. J. *Orality and Literacy: The Technologizing of the Word.* London: Methuen, 1982.

—. *The Presence of the Word: Some Prolegomena for Cultural and Religious History.* New Haven, CN: Yale UP, 1967.

—. *Ramus, Method, and the Decay of Dialogue: From the Art of Discourse to the Art of Reason.* Cambridge, MA: Harvard UP, 1958.

—. *Rhetoric, Romance, and Technology: Studies in the Interaction of Expression and Culture.* Ithaca, NY: Cornell UP, 1971

—."Tudor Writings on Rhetoric." *Studies in the Renaissance.* 15 (1968): 39-69.

O'Rourke, Bridget. "Meanings and Practices of Literacy in Urban Settlement Communities: Chicago's Hull House." Diss. Purdue University, 1998.

Overington, Michael. "The Scientific Community as Audience: Toward a Rhetorical Analysis of Science." *Philosophy and Rhetoric* 10 (1977): 143-62.

Overstreet, Harry. *Influencing Human Behavior.* New York: The People's Institute Publishing Co., 1925.

Parnes, Sidney, and Eugene Brunelle. "The Literature of Creativity, II." *The Journal of Creative Behavior* 1 (1967): 191-240.

Parvin, Kathleen. "Toward a Theory for Ethical-Democratic Composition Practice: Transgressing Boundaries of Radical Pedagogy Discourses." Diss. Purdue U, 2000.

Paull, Michael, and Jack Kligerman. *Invention: A Course in Pre-Writing and Composition.* Cambridge, MA: Winthrop Press, 1973.

Peacham, Henry. *The Garden of Eloquence.* London, 1577.

Peadon, Catherine. "Jane Addams and a Social Rhetoric of Democracy." *Oratorical Culture in Nineteenth-Century America.* Ed. Gregory Clark and Michael Halloran. Carbondale, IL: Southern Illinois UP, 1993. 184-207.

—. "Language and Rhetoric in Locke, Condillac, and Vico." Diss., Purdue University, 1989.

Peirce, Charles Sanders. *Complete Published Work Including Selected Secondary Materia*l. Ed. Kenneth Ketner, et al. Greenwich, CT: Johnson, 1977.

—. "What Pragmatism Is." *The Monist* 15 (1905): 161-81.

Penticoff, Richard, and Linda Brodkey. "'Writing about Difference': Hard Cases for Cultural Studies." *Cultural Studies in the English Classroom*. Ed. James Berlin and Michael Vivion. Portsmouth, NH: Boynton/Cook Heinemann, 1992. 123-34.

Perelman, Chaim, and L. Olbrechts-Tyteca. *The New Rhetoric: A Treatise on Argumentation*. Trans. John Wilkinson and Purcell Weaver. South Bend, IN: U of Notre Dame P, 1969.

Perelman, Chaim. *The Realm of Rhetoric*. Trans. William Kluback. South Bend, IN: U of Notre Dame P, 1982.

Perkins, David. *The Mind's Best Work*. Cambridge, MA: Harvard UP, 1981.

Perkins, David, and Gavriel Saloman. "Are Cognitive Skills Context-Bound? *Educational Researcher* 18 (1989): 16-25.

Perl, Sondra. The Composing Processes of Unskilled College Writers." *Research in the Teaching of English* 13 (1979): 317-36.

Perry, William G. *Forms of Intellectual and Ethical Development in the College Years*. New York: Holt, Rinehart, and Winston, 1970.

Peterson, Carla. *"Doers of the Word": African-American Women Speakers and Writers in the North (1830-1880)*. New York: Oxford UP, 1995.

Petragalia, Joseph. "The Constructivist Dialogue in Composition." *Journal of Advanced Composition* 11 (1991): 37-55.

Phelps, Louise. *Composition as a Human Science: Interpretive, Critical, and Rhetorical Perspectives*. New York: Oxford UP, 1988.

—. "Institutional Invention: (How) Is It Possible?" *New Perspectives on Rhetorical Invention*. Ed. Janet Atwill and Janice M. Lauer. Knoxville, TN: U of Tennessee P, 2002. 64-95.

Phelps, Louise, and Janet Emig, eds. *Feminine Principles and Women's Experience in American Composition and Rhetoric*. Pittsburgh, PA: U of Pittsburgh P, 1995.

Piaget, Jean. *The Psychology of Intelligence*. Trans. Malcolm Piercy and D. E. Berlyne. London: Routledge and Paul, 1950.

Pianko, Sharon. "A Description of the Composing Acts of College Freshman Writers." *Research in the Teaching of English* 13 (1979): 5-22.

Pike, Kenneth. *Language in Relation to a Unified Theory of the Structures of Human Behavior*. The Hague: Mouton, 1967.

Plato. *Phaedrus*. Trans. W. C. Hembold and W. G. Rabinowitz. Indianapolis, IN: The Library of Liberal Arts, 1956.

Polanyi, Michael. *Personal Knowledge: Toward a Post-critical Philosophy*. Chicago: U of Chicago P, 1962.

—. *The Tacit Dimension*. Garden City, NY: Doubleday, 1966.

Polya, G. *How to Solve It: A New Aspect of Mathematical Method*. Garden City, NJ: Doubleday Anchor, 1957.

Poovey, Mary. *The Proper Lady and the Woman Writer: Ideology as Style in the Works of Mary Wollstonecraft, Mary Shelley, and Jane Austen*. Chicago: U of Chicago P, 1984.

Porter, James. "Intertextuality and the Discourse Community." *Rhetoric Review* 5 (1986): 34-47.

Poulakos, John. "Terms for Sophistical Rhetoric." *Rethinking the History of Rhetoric*. Ed. T. Poulakos. Boulder, CO: Westview Press, 1993. 53-74.

—. "Toward a Definition of Sophistic Rhetoric." *Philosophy and Rhetoric* 16 (1983): 35-48.

Quandahl, Ellen. "Aristotle's *Rhetoric*: Reinterpreting Invention." *Rhetoric Review* 4 (1986): 128-137.

Quintilian. *Institutio Oratoria*. Trans. H. E. Butler. The Loeb Classical Library. Cambridge, MA: Harvard UP, 1921.

Rabianski, Nancyanne. "An Exploratory Study of Individual Differences in the Use of Freewriting and the Tagmemic Heuristic Procedure, Two Modes of Invention in the Composing Process." Diss. State University of New York at Buffalo, 1979.

Rafoth, Bennet A., and Donald Rubin, eds. *The Social Construction of Written Communication*. Norwood, NJ: Ablex, 1988.

Rainholde, John. *Oxford Lectures on Aristotle's Rhetoric*. Ed. and Trans. Lawrence Green. Newark: U of Delaware P, 1986.

Ramus, Peter. *Arguments in Rhetoric Against Quintilian (1549)* . Trans. Carole Newlands. DeKalb, IL: Northern Illinois UP, 1986.

—. *The Logike of the Moste Excellent Philosopher P. Ramus Martyr*. Trans. Roland Macllmaine. Ed. Catherine Dunne. Northridge, CA: San Fernando Valley State College Renaissance Editions, 1969.

Raymond, James. "Enthymemes, Examples, and Rhetorical Method." *Essays on Classical Rhetoric and Modern Discourse*. Ed. Robert J. Connors, Lisa S. Ede, and Andrea A. Lunsford. Carbondale, IL: Southern Illinois UP, 1984. 140-51.

Redfern, Jenny. "Christine De Pisan and the Treasure of the City of Ladies: A Medieval Rhetorician and Her Rhetoric." *Reclaiming Rhetorica*. Ed. Andrea Lunsford. Pittsburgh, PA: U of Pittsburgh P, 1995. 73-92.

Reid, Paul. "A Spectrum of Persuasive Design." *The Speech Teacher* 13 (1964); 89-95.

Reid, Ronald. "The Boylston Professorship of Rhetoric and Oratory, 1806-1904." *Quarterly Journal of Speech* 45 (1959): 239-57.

Rhetorica ad Herennium. Trans. Harry Caplan. The Loeb Classical Library. Cambridge, MA: Harvard UP, 1954.

Rice, William Craig. *Public Discourse and Academic Inquiry*. New York: Garland Publishers, 1996.

Richards, I. A. *The Philosophy of Rhetoric*. New York: Oxford UP, 1936.

Ricks, Vickie. "'In an Atmosphere of Peril'." *Nineteenth-Century Women Learn to Write.* Ed. Catherine Hobbs. Charlottesville, VA: UP of Virginia, 1995. 59-83.

Rico, Gabriele. *Balancing the Hemispheres: Brain Research and the Teaching of Writing.* Berkeley , CA: U of California, Bay Area Writing Project, 1980.

—. *Writing the Natural Way.* New York Teachers and Writers Collaborative, 1991.

Ricoeur, Paul. *Interpretation Theory: Discourse and the Surplus of Meaning.* Fort Worth: Texas Christian UP, 1976.

Rickert, Thomas. "'Hands Up, You're Free': Composition in a Post-Oedipal World." *Journal of Advanced Composition* 21 (2001): 287-320.

Ritchie, Joy. "Confronting the 'Essential' Problem: Reconnecting Feminist Theory and Pedagogy." *Journal of Advanced Composition* 10 (1990): 249-73.

Robert of Basevorn. *The Form of Preaching. The Three Medieval Arts.* Ed. James Murphy. Berkeley: U of California P, 1971.

Rodrigues, Dawn and Richard Rodrigues. "Computer-Assisted Creative Problem-Solving." *The Computer in Composition Instruction.* Ed. W. Wresch. Urbana, IL. NCTE, 1984. 34-36.

—. "Computer-Assisted Invention: Its Place and Potential." *College Composition and Communication* 35 (1984): 78-87.

Rohman, Gordon. "Pre-Writing: The Stage of Discovery in the Writing Process." *College Composition and Communication* 16 (1965): 106-12.

—. "The Workshop Journal." Unpublished paper. April, 1969.

Rohman, Gordon, and Albert Wlecke. *Pre-Writing: The Construction and Application of a Model for Concept Formation in Writing.* Cooperative Research Project # 2174. Cooperative Research Project of the Office of Education. Washington, DC: US Department of Health, Education, and Welfare, 1964.

Roochnik, David. "Is Rhetoric an Art?" *Rhetorica* 12 (1994): 127-54.

—. *Of Art and Wisdom: Plato's Understanding of Techne.* University Park, PA: Penn State UP, 1996.

Rose, Mike. *Lives On the Boundary: The Struggles and Achievements of America's Under Prepared.* New York: Free Press, 1989.

—. "Rigid Rules, Inflexible Plans, and the Stifling of Language: A Cognitivist Analysis of Writer's Block." *College Composition and Communication* 31 (1980): 389-400.

Rouse, P. Joy. " Margaret Fuller: A Rhetoric of Citizenship in Nineteenth-Century America." *Oratorical Culture in Nineteenth-Century America.* Ed. Gregory Clark and Michael Halloran. Carbondale, IL: Southern Illinois UP, 1993. 110-36.

Royster, Jacqueline Jones. "Perspectives on the Intellectual Tradition of Black Women Writers." *The Right to Literacy*. Ed. Andrea Lunsford, Helene Moglen, and James Slevin. New York: MLA, 1990. 103-12.

—. "To Call a Thing by Its True Name: The Rhetoric of Ida B. Wells." *Reclaiming Rhetorica: Women in the Rhetorical Tradition*. Ed. Andrea Lunsford. Pittsburgh: Pittsburgh UP, 1995. 167-84.

Satterfield, Jay, and Frederick Antczak. "American Pragmatism and the Public Intellectual: Poetry, Prophecy, and the Process of Invention in Democracy." *New Perspectives on Rhetorical Invention*. Ed. Janet Atwill and Janice M. Lauer. Knoxville, TN: U of Tennessee P, 2002. 148-62.

Scardemalia, Marlene, and Carl Bereiter. "Writing." *Cognition and Instruction*. Ed. Ronna F. Dillon and Robert J. Sternburg. Orlando, FL: Academic Press, 1986. 59-81.

Scardemalia, Marlene, Carl Bereiter, and Hillel Goelman. "The Role of Production Factors in Writing Ability." *What Writer's Know: The Language, Process, and Structure of Written Discourse*. Ed. Martin Nystrand. New York: Academic, 1982. 173-210.

Schaub, Mark. "Rhetorical Studies in America: The Place of Averroes and the Medieval Arab Commentators. " *Journal of Comparative Poetics* 16 (1996): 233-54.

Schiappa, Edward. *The Beginnings of Rhetorical Theory in Classical Greece*. Yale UP, 1999.

—. "RHÊTORIKÊ: What's in a Name? Toward a Revised History of Early Greek Rhetorical Theory." *Quarterly Journal of Speech* 78 (1992): 1-15. .

Schleiermacher, Friedrich. *Hermeneutics and Criticism and Other Writings*. Trans. and ed. Andrew Bowie. Cambridge: Cambridge UP, 1998.

Schilb, John. "Cultural Studies, Postmodernism, and Composition." *Contending with Words*. Ed. Patricia Harkin and John Schilb. New York: MLA, 1991. 173-88.

Schwartz, Helen. *Interactive Writing: Composing with a Word Processor*. New York: Holt, Rinehart and Winston, 1985.

—. "Monsters and Mentors: Computer Applications for Humanistic Education." *College English* 44 (1982): 141-52.

—. *ORGANIZE*. Software. Belmont, CA: Wadsworth,

—. *SEEN*: Tutorials for Critical Reading. Software. Iowa City, IA: Conduit, 1989.

—. *PREWRITE*. Software. Princeton, NJ: Author.

Scott, Fred Newton, and Joseph Denney. *The New Composition-Rhetoric, Designed for Use in Secondary Schools*. Boston: Allyn and Bacon, 1911.

Scott, Robert. "Epistemic Rhetoric and Criticism: Where Barry Brummett Goes Wrong." *Quarterly Journal of Speech* 76 (1999): 300-303.

—. "On Viewing Rhetoric as Epistemic." *Central States Speech Journal* 18 (1967): 9-17.

—. "On Viewing Rhetoric as Epistemic: Ten Years Later." *Central States Speech Journal* 27 (1976): 258-66.

—. "Rhetoric is Epistemic: What Difference Does That Make?" *Defining the New Rhetorics*. Ed. Theresa Enos and Stuart Brown. Newbury Park, CA: Sage, 1993. 120-36.

Scribner, Sylvia, and Michael Cole. *The Psychology of Literacy* . Cambridge, MA : Harvard UP, 1981.

Secor, Marie, and Davida Charney. *Constructing Rhetorical Education*. Carbondale, IL: Southern Illinois UP, 1992.

Selfe, Cynthia. "The Electronic Pen: Computers and the Composing Process." *Writing On-line: Using Computers in the Teaching of Writing*. Ed. James Collins and Elizabeth Sommers. Upper Montclair, NJ: Boynton/Cook, 1985.

—. Wordsworth II: Process-Based CAI for College Composition Teachers." *The Computer in Composition Instruction*. Ed. William Wresch. Urbana, IL: NCTE, 1984.174-90.

Selfe, Cynthia, Dawn Rodrigues, and William Oates, eds. *Computers in English and the Language Arts: The Challenge of Teacher Education*. Urbana, IL: NCTE, 1989.

Sherry, Richard. *A Treatise of Schemes and Tropes*. London, 1550.

Shor, Ira, ed. *Freire for the Classroom: A Sourcebook for Liberatory Teaching*. Portsmouth, NH: Boynton/Cook, 1987.

Simmons, Sue Carter. "Radcliffe Responses to Harvard Rhetoric: 'An Absurdly Stiff Way of Thinking'." *Nineteenth-Century Women Learn to Write*. Ed. Catherine Hobbs. UP of Virginia, 1995. 264-92.

Simons, Herbert W. "Are Scientists Rhetors in Disguise? An Analysis of Discursive Processes Within Scientific Communities." *Rhetoric in Transition: Studies in the Nature and Uses of Rhetoric*. Ed. Eugene E. White. University Park, PA: Penn State UP, 1980. 115-30.

—. ed. *The Rhetorical Turn: Invention and Persuasion in the Conduct of Inquiry*. Chicago: U of Chicago P, 1990.

Simpkins, Ann Marie Mann. "The Professional Writing Practices and Dialogic Rhetoric of Two Black Women Publishers: Discourse as Social Action in the Nineteenth Century." Diss. Purdue University, 1999.

Simpson, Jeanne. "Invention Again or How the Skeptic Got into Hot Water." *Journal of Teaching Writing* 4 (1985): 184-92.

Siscar, Gregorio Mayans y. *Rhetórica*. Valencia, 1757.

Sloane, Thomas. *On the Contrary: The Protocol of Traditional Rhetoric*. Washington, DC: The Catholic U of America P, 1997.

—. "Reinventing *Inventio*." *College English* 51 (1989): 461-73.

Smith, Adam. *Lectures on Rhetoric and Belles Lettres Delivered in the University of Glasgow by Adam Smith Reported by a Student in 1762-63*. Ed. John Lothian. Ed. David Potter. Carbondale, IL: Southern Illinois UP, 1971.

Smith, Jeanne. "Native American Composition." *Encyclopedia of English Studies and Language Arts.* Ed. Alan Purves. New York: Scholastic Press, 1994.

Snyder, Jane. *The Woman and the Lyre.* Carbondale, IL.: Southern Illinois UP, 1989.

Spitzer, Michael. "Incorporating Prewriting Software in the Writing Program." *Computers in English and the Language Arts.* Ed. Cynthia Selfe, Dawn Rodrigues, and William Oates. Urbana, IL: NCTE, 1989. 205-12.

Spoel, Philippa. "Re-inventing Rhetorical Epistemology: Donna Haraway's and Nicole Brossard's Embodied Visions." *The Changing Tradition: Women in the History of Rhetoric.* Ed. Christine Sutherland and Rebecca Sutcliffe. Calgary, Alberta: U of Calgary P, 1999. 199-212.

Sprague, Rosamunde, ed. *The Older Sophists: A Complete Translation by Many Hands of the Fragments in Die Fragments Der Vorsokratiker.* Columbia, SC: U South Carolina P, 1973.

Stallard, Charles. "An Analysis of the Writing Behavior of Good Student Writers." *Research in the Teaching of English* 8 (1974): 206-18.

Stanley, Manfred. "The Rhetoric of the Commons: Forum Discourse in Politics and Society." *The Rhetorical Turn: Invention and Persuasion in the Conduct of Inquiry.* Ed. Herbert Simons. Chicago: U of Chicago P, 1990.

Steinmann, Martin, ed. *New Rhetorics.* New York: Scribner's , 1967.

Stewart, Donald. *The Authentic Voice: A Prewriting Approach to Student Writing.* Dubuque, Iowa: W. C. Brown, 1972.

—. "Fred Newton Scott." *Traditions of Inquiry.* Ed. John Brereton. New York: Oxford UP, 1985. 26-49.

—. "The Status of Composition and Rhetoric in American Colleges, 1880-1902: An MLA Perspective." *College English* 47 (1985): 734-46.

Stewart, Donald, and Patricia Stewart. *The Life and Legacy of Fred Newton Scott.* Pittsburgh, PA.: U of Pittsburgh P, 1997.

Strickland, James. "An Annotated Bibliography of Representative Software for Writers." *Computers and Composition* 10 (1992): 25-35.

—. "Prewriting and Computing." *Writing On-line: Using Computers in the Teaching of Writing.* Ed. J. Collins and E. Sommers. Montclair, NJ: Boynton/Cook, 1985.

Stump, Eleonore, ed. *Boethius's De topicis differentiis.* Ithaca, NY: Cornell UP, 1978.

Sullivan, Patricia. "Taking Control of the Page: Electronic Writing and Word Publishing." *Evolving Perspectives in Computers and Composition Studies: Questions for the 1900s.* Ed. Gail Hawisher and Cindy Selfe. Urbana, IL: NCTE, 1991. 21-42.

—. "Visual Markers for Navigating Instructional Texts." *Journal of Technical Writing and Communication* 20 (1990): 255-67.

Sullivan, Patricia, and James E. Porter. *Opening Spaces: Writing Technologies and Critical Research Practices.* Greenwich, CT: Ablex, 1997.

Sutherland, Christine, and Rebecca Sutcliffe, eds. *The Changing Tradition: Women in the History of Rhetoric.* Calgary, Alberta: U of Calgary P, 1999.

Sutherland, Christine. "Mary Astell: Reclaiming Rhetorica in the Seventeenth Century." *Reclaiming Rhetorica.* Ed. Andrea Lunsford. Pittsburgh, PA: U of Pittsburgh P, 1995. 93-116.

Swearingen, C. Jan. " Dialogue and Dialectic: The Logic of Conversation and the Interpretation of Logic." *The Interpretation of Dialogue.* Ed. Tullio Maranhao. Chicago, IL: U of Chicago P, 1990. 47-71.

—. "A Lover's Discourse: Diotima, Logos, and Desire." *Reclaiming Rhetorica.* Ed. Andrea Lunsford. Pittsburgh, PA: U of Pittsburgh P, 1995. 25-52.

—. "Plato." *Encyclopedia of Rhetoric and Composition.* Ed. Theresa Enos. New York: Garland Publishing, 1996. 523-28.

—. "Plato's Feminine: Appropriation, Impersonation, and Metaphorical Polemic." *Rhetoric Society Quarterly* 22 (1992): 109-23.

—. " Plato's Women: Alternative Embodiments of Rhetoric. " *The Changing Tradition: Women in the History of Rhetoric.* Ed. Christine Sutherland and Rebecca Sutcliffe. Calgary, Alberta: U of Calgary P, 1999. 35-46.

—. *Rhetoric and Irony: Western Literacy and Western Lies.* New York: Oxford UP, 1991.

—. "The Rhetor as Eiron: Plato's Defense of Dialogue." *PRE/TEXT* 3 (1982): 289-335.

Tannen, Deborah. *Gender and Discourse.* New York: Oxford UP, 1996.

Tate, Gary, and Edward P. J. Corbett, eds. *Teaching Freshman Composition.* New York: Oxford UP, 1967.

Tebeaux, Elizabeth, and Mary Lay. "The Emergence of the Feminine Voice, 1526-1640: The Earliest Published Books by English Renaissance Women." *Journal of Advanced Composition* 15 (1995): 53-81.

Thiebaux, Marcelle, ed. and trans. *The Writings of Medieval Women: An Anthology.* New York: Garland, 1994.

Thoma, Henry. "Freshman Texts, 1931-1956." *College Composition and Communication* 9 (1957): 35-39.

Thompson, Wayne. "*Stasis* in Aristotle's *Rhetoric*." *Quarterly Journal of Speech* 58 (1972): 134-41.

Tonkovich, Nicole. "Rhetorical Power in the Victorian Parlor: *Godey's Lady Book* and the Gendering of Nineteenth-Century Rhetoric." *Oratorical Culture in Nineteenth-Century America.* Ed. Gregory Clark and Michael Halloran. Carbondale, IL: Southern Illinois UP, 1993. 158-83.

Toulmin, Stephen. *Uses of Argument.* Cambridge: Cambridge UP, 1969.

Travitsky, Betty, ed. *The Paradise of Women: Writings by Englishwomen of the Renaissance*. Westport, CN: Greenwood, 1981.

Trimbur, John. *The Call to Write*. New York: Longman, 1998.

—. "Cultural Studies and Teaching Writing." *Focuses* 1 (1988): 5-20.

Trimmer, Joseph, and James McCrimmon. *Writing with a Purpose*. 9th ed. Boston: Houghton Mifflin Company, 1988.

Underwood, Virginia. "A Survey of Some Rhetorical Heuristics and Their Implications for the Teaching of Composition." Diss. Florida State University, 1980.

Untersteiner, Mario. *The Sophists*. Trans. Kathleen Freeman. Oxford: Alden Press, 1964.

Vatz, Richard. "The Myth of the Rhetorical Situation." *Philosophy of Rhetoric* 6 (1973): 154-61.

Vico, Giambattista. *The New Science of Giambattista Vico*. 1744. Third Edition. Trans. Thomas Bergin and Max Fisch. Ithaca, NY: Cornell UP, 1984.

Villanueva, Victor. *Bootstraps: From an American Academic of Color*. Urbana, IL: NCTE, 1993.

—. "Hispanic/Latino Writing." *Encyclopedia of English Studies and Language Arts*. Ed. Alan Purves. New York: Scholastic Press, 1994.

Vitanza, Victor. "From Heuristic to Aleatory Procedures; Or Toward Writing the Accident." *Inventing a Discipline*. Ed. Maureen Daly Goggin. Urbana, IL: NCTE, 2000. 185-206.

—. "Three Countertheses: Or, A Critical In(ter)vention into Composition Theories and Pedagogies." *Contending with Words*. Ed. Patricia Harkin and John Schilb. New York: MLA, 1991. 139-72.

Vitz, Evelyn. *Medieval Narratives and Modern Narratology*. New York: New York UP, 1989.

von Blum, Ruth, and Michael Cohen. ""WANDAH": Writing-Aid and Author's Helper." *The Computer in Composition Instruction*. Ed. William Wresch. Urbana, IL: NCTE, 1984. 154-73.

Vygotsky, Lev S. *Thought and Language*. Ed. and trans. Eugenia Haufmann and Gertrude Vakar. Cambridge: MIT P, 1962.

Wagner, Betty Jane, S. Zeleman, and A. Malone-Trout. *The Chicago Writing Project Assessment*. Elmhurst, IL: School District 205, 1981.

Wagner, Joanne. "Intelligent Mothers or Restless Disturbers": Women's Rhetorical Styles, 1880-1920." *Reclaiming Rhetorica*. Ed. Andrea Lunsford. Pittsburgh, PA: U of Pittsburgh P, 1995. 185-202.

Wagner, Russell. "Thomas Wilson's *Arte of Rhetorike*." *Speech Monographs* 27 (1960): 1-32.

Walker, Jeffrey. "The Body of Persuasion: A Theory of the Enthymeme." *College English* 56 (1994): 46-65.

Wallas, G. *The Art of Thought*. New York: Harcourt Brace, 1926.

Wang, Haixia. "Chinese Public Discourse: A Rhetorical Analysis of the Newspaper *People's Daily*". Diss. Purdue University, 1993.

—."Invention and the Democratic Spirit in the Teaching of Zhuang ZI." *New Perspectives on Rhetorical Invention*. Ed. Janet Atwill and Janice M. Lauer. Knoxville, TN: U of Tennessee P, 2002. 163-75.

Ward, John. "Women and Latin Rhetoric from Hrotsvit to Hildegard" *The Changing Tradition: Women in the History of Rhetoric*. Ed. Christine Sutherland and Rebecca Sutcliffe. Calgary, Alberta: U of Calgary P, 1999. 121-32.

Warnock, John Phelps, with Harold C. Warnock. *Effective Writing: A Handbook with Stories for Lawyers*. West Lafayette, IN: Parlor Press, 2003.

Warnock, Tilly. *Writing Is Critical Action*. Reading, PA: Addison Wesley Educational Publishers, 1989.

Weaver, Richard. *The Ethics of Rhetoric*. Chicago: Henry Regency Co., 1965.

Welch, Kathleen E. *The Contemporary Reception of Classical Rhetoric: Appropriations of Classical Discourse*. Hillsdale, NJ: Erlbaum, 1990.

Wells, Susan. "Classroom Heuristics and Empiricism." *College English* 39 (1977): 467-77.

Whately, Richard. *Elements of Rhetoric. The Rhetoric of Blair, Campbell, and Whatley with Updated Bibliographies*. Ed. James L. Golden and Edward P. J. Corbett. Carbondale, IL: Southern Illinois UP, 1990.

White, Frederick, and Mary Ann Aschauer. "Toward a Marriage of Two Minds: The Word Processor and Natural Habits of Thought in the 'Discovery' Stage of Composing." *Collected Essays on the Written Word and the Word Processor: From the Delaware Valley Writing Council's Spring Conference, February 25, 1984*. Ed. Thomas Martinez. Villanova, PA: Villanova U 1984. 188-204

Willard, Charity. *Christine de Pizan: Her Life and Works*. New York: Persea Books, 1984.

Williams, Mark, and Theresa Enos. "Vico's Triangular Invention." *New Perspectives on Rhetorical Invention*. Ed. Janet Atwill and Janice M. Lauer. Knoxville, TN: U of Tennessee P, 2002. 192-212.

Williams, Joseph. *The New English*. New York: The Free Press, 1970.

Wilson, Katharina, ed. *Medieval Women Writers*. Athens, Georgia: U of Georgia P, 1984.

Wilson, Lloyd. "The Impact of Methods of Legal Reasoning on the Form and Content of Legal Writing." *Writing in the Arts, Sciences, and Professional Schools*. Ed. Sharon Hamilton. Indianapolis: IUPUI Office of Campus Writing, 2002. 231-44.

Wilson, Thomas. *The Art of Rhetoric (1560)*. Ed. Peter Medine. University Park, PA: Penn State UP, 1994.

Winterbottom, M. *Problems in Quintilian*. London: Institute of Classical Studies, 1970.

—. "Quintilian and the *vir bonus*." *Journal of Roman Studies* 54 (1964): 90-97.

Winterowd, W. Ross. *Composition/Rhetoric: A Synthesis*. Carbondale, IL: Southern Illinois UP, 1986.

—. *The Contemporary Writer: A Practical Rhetoric*. Chicago, IL: Harcourt Brace Jovanovich, 1981.

—. "Dramatism in Themes and Poems." *College English* 45 (1983): 581-88.

—. "Review. *The Prospect of Rhetoric: Report of the National Development Project* by Lloyd Bitzer and Edwin Black. *Philosophy and Rhetoric* 6 (1973): 47-58.

—. *Rhetoric and Writing*. Boston: Allyn and Bacon, 1965.

—. "'Topics' and Levels in the Composing Process." *College English* 34 (1973): 701-9.

Woods, William F. "Nineteenth-Century Psychology and the Teaching of Writing." *College Composition and Communication* 2 (1985): 377-90.

—. "The Reform Tradition in Nineteenth-Century Composition Teaching." *Written Communication* 2 (1985): 377-90.

Worsham, Lynn. "The Question Concerning Invention: Hermeneutics and the Genesis of Writing." *PRE/TEXT* 8 (1987): 197-244.

Wresch, William, ed. *The Computer in Composition Instruction*. Urbana, IL: NCTE, 1984.

—. Writers Helper II. Software. Iowa City, IA: Conduit, 1988.

Wysocki, Anne. "Impossibly Distinct: On Form/Content and Word/Image in Two Pieces of Computer-Based Interactive Multimedia." *Computers and Composition* 18 (2001): 137-62.

Yancey, Kathleen. *Reflection in the Writing Classroom*. Logan, Utah: Utah State UP, 1988.

Yarnoff, Charles. "Contemporary Theories of Invention in the Rhetorical Tradition." *College English* 41 (1980): 552-60.

Young, Richard E. "Arts, Crafts, Gifts, and Knacks." *Reinventing the Rhetorical Tradition*. Ed. Ian Pringle and Aviva Freedman. Conway, AK: L and S Books, 1980. 53-60.

—. "Conceptions of Art and the Teaching of Writing." *The Rhetorical Tradition and Modern Writing*. New York: MLA, 1982. 29-47.

—. "Invention: A Topographical Survey." *Teaching Composition: Ten Bibliographic Essays*. Ed. Gary Tate. Fort Worth, TX: Texas Christian UP, 1976. 1-44.

—. "Paradigms and Problems: Needed Research in Rhetorical Invention." *Research on Composing: Points of Departure*. Ed. Charles Cooper and Lee Odell. Urbana, IL; NCTE, 1978.

—. "Recent Developments in Rhetorical Invention." *Teaching Composition: Twelve Bibliographic Essays.* Ed. Gary Tate. Fort Worth, TX: Texas Christian UP, 1987. 1-38.

Young, Richard, and Alton Becker. "Toward A Modern Theory of Rhetoric." *Harvard Educational Review* 35 (1965): 450-68. Rpt. W. Ross Winterowd. *Contemporary Rhetoric: A Conceptual Background with Readings.* New York: Harcourt Brace Jovanovich, 1975. 123-43.

Young, Richard, Alton Becker, and Kenneth Pike. *Rhetoric, Discovery, and Change.* New York: Harcourt, Brace, Jovanovich, 1970.

Young, Richard, and Frank Koen. "The Tagmemic Discovery Procedure: An Evaluation of Its Uses in the Teaching of Rhetoric." Washington, DC: National Endowment for the Humanities, 1973.

Young, Richard E., and Yameng Liu, eds. *Landmark Essays on Rhetorical Invention in Writing.* Davis, CA: Hermagoras Press, 1994.

Zhao, Heping. "*Wen Sin Diao Long*: An Early Chinese Rhetoric of Written Discourse." Diss. Purdue University, 1990.

Zimmerman, Donald and Dawn Rodrigues. *Research and Writing in the Disciplines.* Fort Worth, TX: Harcourt, Brace, Jovanovich, 1992.

Index

A

down the scale · 4th & 3rd finger

_A, E, B♭_

Carolina Hills

CPSIA information can be obtained at www.ICGtesting.com
Printed in the USA
LVOW11s0741270614

391991LV00002B/634/P